Young Adult Resources Today

Young Adult Resources Today

Connecting Teens with Books, Music, Games, Movies, and More

Don Latham
Melissa Gross

ROWMAN & LITTLEFIELD
Lanham • Boulder • New York • Toronto • Plymouth, UK

Published by Rowman & Littlefield
4501 Forbes Boulevard, Suite 200, Lanham, Maryland 20706
www.rowman.com

10 Thornbury Road, Plymouth PL6 7PP, United Kingdom

British Library Cataloguing in Publication Information Available

Library of Congress Cataloging-in-Publication Data

Latham, Don, 1959–
Young adult resources today : connecting teens with books, music, games, movies, and more / Don Latham, Melissa Gross.
pages cm
Includes bibliographical references and index.
ISBN 978-0-8108-9311-5 (cloth : alk. paper)—ISBN 978-0-8108-8799-2 (ebook)
1. Young adults' libraries–Activity programs. 2. Young adults–Books and reading. 3. Libraries–Special collections–Young adult literature. 4. Mass media and youth–Activity programs 5. Libraries and teenagers–Activity programs I. Gross, Melissa. II. Title.
Z718.5.L37 2014
027.62'6–dc23
2014003037

Printed in the United States of America

Contents

Spotlights!

Acknowledgments

We would like to thank a number of people without whose guidance and support this book would not have been possible. Our editor Charles Harmon has provided a firm guiding hand, thoughtful advice, and encouragement throughout the process. Several doctoral students assisted with research and offered helpful insights: Ji Hei Kang (nonfiction), Robert Stephens (poetry), and Jonathan Hollister (graphic novels, manga, and manhwa).

Our many students over the years, especially those in Information Needs of Young Adults, have inspired us and taught us much about young adults and their information needs and interests.

Finally, we would like to express our deepest thanks to Scott and Josh, who through their continual love and support help us to be serious about our work without taking ourselves too seriously.

Preface

This book was born from our love of young adult resources and our passionate belief that connecting young adults with these resources can make an important difference in their lives. Through our experiences teaching courses on young adults and young adult resources, we discovered that textbooks in this area tend to focus on young adult literature, library services for young adults, or the information behavior of young adults. We wanted a book that would examine young adult resources and services through the lens of young adult development and information behavior. The purpose of this book, then, is to offer just such an approach, integrating research, theory, and practice related to understanding and promoting young adult resources.

The primary audience for this book consists of library and information studies instructors and their students in young adult courses, but we feel that practicing youth services librarians in public libraries and school librarians in secondary schools will find the book useful as well. Other possible audiences include library administrators, secondary school teachers, and faculty and students in schools of education.

We have attempted to provide a broad overview of the range of resources available to young adults, from fiction and nonfiction to poetry and lyrics, from graphic novels and movies to games and social media tools. In discussing young adult literature, we have employed a genre framework. Certainly, there are numerous ways of thinking about literature, but a genre framework seems especially useful, as it provides librarians with an understanding of the wide range of the literature types available for meeting young adults' informational and recreational needs. Such an understanding is important when a librarian is engaging in collection development, readers' advisory, or program development. In addition, we have tried to complement our definitions of resource types with specific examples of each and tried to balance classic titles with more contemporary ones. That said, we freely acknowledge that the examples included here represent our favorites, and we hope that instructors and students will add their favorites to their resource toolkits.

Young Adult Resources Today: Connecting Teens with Books, Music, Games, Movies, and More is divided into nine chapters. Chapter 1 serves as the introduction and includes brief histories of young adult resources and young adult services. Chapter 2 discusses young adult development, focusing on the socially constructed nature of young adulthood, the process of moving from childhood to adulthood, and the psychological aspects of young adult development. Chapter 3 introduces models and research related to the information behavior of young adults, as well as the importance of multiple literacies for young adults. Chapter 4 focuses on young adults' technology use and examines social media, gaming, and privacy, identity, and safety issues. Chapter 5 looks at fiction and fan fiction. The chapter presents an overview of the various genres popular with young adults, including fiction that they create themselves. Chapter 6 discusses nonfiction and the different types of nonfiction read by young adults, while chapter 7 looks at poetry, music, and lyrics. Chapter 8 considers special forms and formats, including graphic novels, picture books for young adults, movies, and magazines and zines. Chapter 9, the final chapter, brings it all together with a discussion of formal and informal learning environments, issues related to information and technology access, planning and evaluating services for young adults, and collaborating with other information professionals to better serve young adults.

Each chapter has a bulleted list of main topics at the beginning, a brief summary toward the end, a list of implications for practice, and some questions to think about and discuss. In addition, chapters 2 through 9 include "Spotlight!" sections that highlight and discuss a particular kind of service or activity for young adults. Finally, appendixes are included that provide a list of young adult book awards, a bibliography of recommended young adult books, and a bibliography of professional resources for working with young adults. Of course, no book, this one included, should be considered as the "last word" on the topic but rather as a conversation starter intended to open up a world of exciting possibilities for research, theory, and practice related to understanding and promoting young adult resources.

Chapter One

Introduction

This chapter discusses the following topics:

- Young adults in the 21st century
- Key terms and definitions
- A brief history of young adult resources
- A brief history of young adult services
- Implications for practice
- Questions to think about and discuss

YOUNG ADULTS IN THE 21ST CENTURY

Today's young adults are as diverse as the society in which they live. They reflect a number of different racial and ethnic identities, varying levels of access to and sophistication with technology, and a wide range of preferences for informational and recreational materials. They come from different socioeconomic backgrounds, and they may be receiving their education through public school, private school, or homeschooling. Anyone working with young adults today is likely to encounter immigrant teens; LGBTQ teens (lesbian, gay, bisexual, transgender, questioning); and differently abled teens. Some teens are living on the margins because of poverty, homelessness, incarceration, substance abuse, and physical and/or sexual abuse. At the same time, today's teens are living in a world that is shrinking and in a society that is becoming more global due to a variety of political, economic, and technological factors. It is a challenging and extremely exciting time to be an information professional serving young adults.

The purpose of this book is to further an understanding of the young adult resources that are available and the information services that can be provided to help young adults access these resources, whether for information or recreation or both.

KEY TERMS AND DEFINITIONS

Several key concepts inform the ideas in this book, and it's important that we define these terms at the outset. Perhaps the most important is the term that identifies the main focus of the book—"young adult." The Young Adult Library Services Association (YALSA) defines young adults as people ranging from 12 to 18 years of age, and that is the definition that we use in this book. These are generally middle and high school students. There are several related terms that we should define as well, for they can help us understand more clearly the concept of young adult. The term "children," for example, is defined by the Association for Library Service to Children as including those from birth through age 14 years. "Tweens" are defined as those 9 to 12 years old. Clearly, both definitions overlap with the definition of "young adult." At the upper end of the young adult age range are "older young adults," ages 18 to 24 years. This is a group that psychologist Jeffrey Arnett calls "emerging adults,"[1] and it's an age range that YALSA has recently become more interested in. This book focuses on young people 12 to 18 years old, but what we say about resources and services can also apply to older children, to tweens, and to emerging adults.

Another important concept is information behavior, which Marcia Bates defines as "the many ways in which human beings interact with information, in particular, the ways in which people seek and utilize information."[2] "Information seeking" generally refers to the process by which people look for information to accomplish a specific purpose (even if it's just to satisfy curiosity). Recreational reading, another aspect of information behavior, refers to the reading that people choose to do for pleasure. However, information seeking is never just about information, just as recreational reading is never just about recreation. Information behavior can be motivated by multiple purposes, and individuals may experience central and collateral benefits and challenges in any given information encounter. That's why is it always important to consider context when looking at the information behavior of any given person.

Resources consist of anything that provides potentially useful information and/or recreational opportunities. Today's digital world offers myriad resources, from print and electronic materials to movies, music, and people, and information providers need to be aware of the various resources available to meet the diverse needs of their users. Information services typically involve services for individual users, as well as programs for groups of users. Individual services can include reference services (helping people locate information to address a particular need), homework help (providing one-on-one assistance in helping students complete homework assignments), and readers' advisory (helping people identify recreational reading material). Programming can include exhibits of materials, book talks, discussion groups, movie screenings, author visits, poetry slams, creative writing or drawing workshops, and instructional sessions.

Another term that often comes up in relation to young people, especially when preparing them for adulthood, is "literacies." No longer used to denote only reading and writing (although these skills are just as important as ever), the term is now more typically seen in its plural form, suggesting the constellation of skill sets needed for success in the 21st century. Such skill sets include information literacy, media literacy, information and communication technology literacy, visual literacy, scientific literacy, health literacy, financial literacy, and global literacy, to name just a few. Sometimes the term "multiple literacies" is used to refer to these diverse and complex skills; sometimes "multimodal literacies" is used, suggesting the various modes of communication with which people must be fluent in today's information-rich world. Not surprising, a number of standards have been developed to describe and set benchmarks for these different skills sets. Some of the more widely known and influential standards are the *Framework for 21st Century Learning*, developed by the Partnership for 21st Century Skills (http://www.p21.org/); the *Standards for the 21st Century Learner*, developed by the American Association of School Librarians (http://www.ala.org/aasl/standards-guidelines/learning-standards); the *Information Literacy Competency Standards for Higher Education*, developed by the Association of College and Research Libraries (http://www.ala.org/acrl/standards/information-literacycompetency); and the *Common Core State Standards*, developed by the National Governors Association Center for Best Practices and the Council of Chief State School Officers (http://www.corestandards.org/). These standards are discussed in more detail in chapter 3. At their heart, all these standards focus on the importance of critical thinking, regardless of the communication mode that one is using to access, use, and/or create information.

A BRIEF HISTORY OF YOUNG ADULT RESOURCES

As we will see in chapter 2, the phenomenon that we call "adolescence" or "young adulthood" is a concept that dates only as far back as the early 20th century. Naturally, there were no books written and published specifically for young adults before the concept of "young adult" was actually invented. Nevertheless, the age group that we now call "young adults" were readers, at least many of them were, but what they read were books intended for a "general audience." Books such as Jonathan Swift's *Gulliver's Travels*, Dan-

iel Defoe's *Robinson Crusoe*, Louisa May Alcott's *Little Women*, Mark
Twain's *The Adventures of Tom Sawyer* and *Adventures of Huckleberry
Finn*, Robert Louis Stevenson's *Treasure Island* and *Kidnapped*, Jules
Verne's *Twenty Thousand Leagues under the Sea*, Kate Douglas Wiggin's
Rebecca of Sunnybrook Farm, and Lucy Maud Montgomery's *Anne of Green
Gables* were widely read, and many of these continue to be popular today.[3]
Beginning in the mid-19th century, the two most popular kinds of books
were domestic novels and dime novels.[4] Domestic novels focused on morality and social conservatism, were read primarily by women (and girls), and
were exemplified by books such as Susan Warner's *The Wide, Wide World*
and August Jane Evans Wilson's *St. Elmo*. Dime novels, in contrast, focused
more on adventure and "thrills and chills than tears"[5] and were read primarily by men (and boys). Such books included Westerns, Horatio Alger Jr.'s
rags-to-riches stories, and Thomas Bailey Aldrich's *The Story of a Bad Boy*.

In the early part of the 20th century, mystery series books became popular, spurred by the offerings of the (Edward) Stratemeyer Syndicate: Nancy
Drew, the Hardy Boys, Tom Swift, and the Bobbsey Twins. The late 1930s
and the 1940s saw the advent of the comic book and the introduction of such
superheroes as Superman, Batman, and Wonder Woman. A number of books
with teen appeal were published, including Maureen Daly's *Seventeenth
Summer*,[6] Betty Smith's *A Tree Grows in Brooklyn*,[7] and J. D. Salinger's *The
Catcher in the Rye*.[8]

Most literary scholars date the beginnings of the young adult novel to
either the early 1940s, with the publication of Maureen Daly's *Seventeenth
Summer*,[9] which tells the story of a summer romance, or to the late 1960s,[10]
with the publication of S. E. Hinton's *The Outsiders*.[11] Hinton's novel, about
rival gangs in Tulsa, Oklahoma, is generally acknowledged as the first of
what came to be called "problem novels." The name comes the fact that these
novels tended to focus on a particular social issue, or "problem," and sometimes on several problems within a single book. Other early examples, along
with their particular issues, include Robert Lipsyte's *The Contender*[12] (gangs
and drug addiction), John Donovan's *I'll Get There, It Better Be Worth the
Trip*[13] (homosexuality), Paul Zindel's *The Pigman*[14] (betrayal and death),
Norma Klein's *Mom, the Wolfman, and Me*[15] (single motherhood), Robert
Cormier's *The Chocolate War*[16] (school bullying), and Judy Blume's *Are
You There God? It's Me, Margaret*[17] (religious doubt) and *Forever*[18] (teenage sex). Many of these books generated controversy because they dealt with
difficult issues that some adults felt were inappropriate for a young adult
audience. A more serious criticism, though, had to do with the low quality of
many of the problem novels. While the examples listed here are still well
regarded, many other books of this ilk sacrificed character and plot development for melodrama and didacticism. For this reason, these books soon fell
out of favor with librarians, teachers, parents, and young adults themselves.

The 1980s and 1990s, as Michael Cart notes,[19] were characterized by the rising popularity of series books, particularly in the romance genre (think Francine Pascal's *Sweet Valley High* series) and horror genre (think R. L. Stine's *Goosebumps* series). This period also saw an increase in the number of multicultural authors publishing books about multicultural young adults. African American authors such as Mildred Taylor and Walter Dean Myers, Asian American authors such as Laurence Yep, and Latino/Latina American authors such as Sandra Cisneros and Gary Soto published books that reflected the diversity of American culture and gave voice to those who previously had been greatly underrepresented in young adult literature. A third phenomenon of the 1980s, one that Cart does not specifically mention, was the increase in the number of graphic novels being published. Though many of these books, such as Alan Moore and Dave Gibbon's *Watchmen*[20] and Art Spiegelman's *Maus I,*[21] were intended for adults, young adults read them— especially older young adults. Moreover, the recognition that these books received helped pave the way for more young adult–focused graphic novels in the decades to come. In the 1990s, graphic novels in general and manga (Japanese graphic novels) in particular grew in popularity.

Overall, though, the 1990s witnessed a downturn in the number of books being published for young adults, due to a number of factors. Budget cuts that had been enacted in the 1980s were still being felt by libraries in the 1990s.[22] Publishers knew that school and public libraries had less money to spend on books, especially fiction for young adults. The middle school movement, grouping students into sixth, seventh, and eighth-grade schools, led to publishers focusing more on books for tweens.[23] In addition, there were actually fewer young adults during this period. The baby boomers' children were no longer teenagers, and their children's children were not yet teenagers.[24] While children's publishing thrived during this time, young adult publishing languished. Yet another factor may have been the Internet, which by the late 1990s was available in more and more homes. Publishers have long had to compete with a variety of things that command young adults' attention; the Internet was yet one more enticement for teens to do something other than read a book.

But there is another side to the growing use of the Internet, one that is beneficial to both young adults and publishers in the long run. As Marc Aronson notes, the Internet offers ways for young adults to share information about books and even to publish their own works.[25] As we discuss in chapter 5, the phenomenon of fan fiction—in which fans of a particular book or series create their own stories based on the characters—has been greatly facilitated by the Internet and social media in particular. In addition, the Internet has had an influence on a number of books published from the 1990s on. In *Radical Change: Books for Youth in a Digital Age*, Eliza Dresang surveys books for young people (children and young adults) published mostly during the 1990s and describes three basic kinds of "radical" (i.e., fundamental) change that she observed in these works: changing forms and formats, changing perspectives, and changing boundaries.[26] "Changing forms and formats" describes visual and structural changes in books, as well as interactive elements and multiple layers of meaning. "Changing perspectives" refers to the use of multiple perspectives and the perspectives of people previously marginalized, including the perspectives of young people themselves. And "changing boundaries" reflects the inclusion of subjects previously forbidden, portrayals of characters in new ways, and unresolved endings. The increasing prevalence of these changes, Dresang argues, is due largely to the effects of the digital age fostered by the Internet: connectivity, interactivity, and access. Indeed, a number of young adult books published since Dresang's book first appeared in 1999 have demonstrated one or more types of radical change.

Published just a year later, Roberta Seelinger Trites's *Disturbing the Universe: Power and Repression in Adolescent Literature* analyzed the important cultural work accomplished by many young adult books.[27] Trites argued that young adult literature is less about coming-of-age stories and identity development and more about socializing young adults as they move toward adulthood: "to depicting how potentially out-of-control adolescents can learn to exist within institutional structures."[28] Drawing on the work of a number of postmodern theorists—including Judith Butler, Michel Foucault, Marilyn French, and Jacques Lacan—Trites examined the power relations evident in much young adult literature, focusing on certain common motifs: institutions (school, government, church), authority, sex, and death. Appearing at the end of the millennium, Trites's book not only provided an alternative way of thinking about the cultural role of young adult literature but also helped further elevate its status as an object of serious academic inquiry.

The first decade of the 21st century has been marked by the emergence of blockbuster series books, such as *Harry Potter*, *Twilight*, and the *Hunger Games*.[29] Graphic novels have continued to grow in popularity, with more being produced specifically for young adults. Poetry has enjoyed a renaissance, and verse novels—narratives written as a series of poems—have proliferated. Multicultural literature has become more prevalent and more multicultural, featuring not just characters of racial and ethnic diversity but also LGBTQ characters and differently abled characters as well. The establishment of the Michael L. Printz Award in 2000 to recognize outstanding books for young adults has brought visibility to young adult literature and encouraged the publication of high-quality books.

In the last decade or so, people have become more aware of books with "crossover" appeal. As has long been the case, a number of books intended for adults have become popular with young adults as well, and since 1998 this phenomenon has been recognized through the Alex Awards, which are given annually to books written for an adult audience but considered to have special appeal for young adults. Crossover reading works the other way as well, as a number of recent books intended for young adults have become popular with adult readers too. Dystopian books—that is, novels that depict totalitarian societies—are currently being widely read by both young adults and adults.

In the last 20 years or so, nonfiction works have received increasing attention. In 2010, YALSA implemented the Excellence in Nonfiction for Young Adults Award, recognizing the best nonfiction books published during the previous year. Through its work, nonfiction writers such as Jim Murphy, Russell Freedman, Elizabeth Partridge, Susan Campbell Bartoletti, Phillip Hoose, and Marc Aronson have demonstrated both the informational and the artistic potential of the genre. With the recently adopted *Common Core State Standards*, emphasizing the importance of nonfiction reading in the upper grades, it seems likely that the number of high-quality works of nonfiction published each year will only continue to increase.

The last couple of decades have also seen a proliferation of formats. Libraries have long been quick to adapt to changing formats and the changing needs and desires of their patrons. Libraries that once collected movies on VHS now collect them on DVD and Blu-ray. Vinyl records have given way to CDs, and cassette tapes—once, *the* format for audio books—are now extinct. Print books are still popular, but e-books are popular as well, and more and more serials are available online. Libraries are increasingly making materials available online, especially e-books and audio books, but not all publishers and vendors have been cooperative in developing pricing models that allow libraries to do this. Proliferating formats offer enormous challenges but also exciting opportunities for librarians, especially those who work with young adults.

A BRIEF HISTORY OF YOUNG ADULT SERVICES

Just as resources for young adults have a history, so do library services. The first library for youth was opened (in Brooklyn) as early as 1823; however, it would be nearly a century later before the first public library (in Kansas City) would offer dedicated services for young people, and it wasn't until 1994 that a public library (in Los Angeles) opened a space within the library using teen-friendly design features.[30] The first professional resource devoted specifically to young adult services was E. Leyland's *Public Libraries and the Adolescent*, published in 1937. Influential young adult librarian Margaret A. Edwards's landmark book *The Fair Garden and the Swarm of Beasts: The Library and the Young Adult*[31] appeared in 1969. The American Library Association also began devoting attention to the topic of young adult services in the first part of the 20th century. The Young People's Reading Roundtable was formed in 1930 as part of the Children's Library Association; then in 1947, the roundtable was granted status as a separate section. The Young Adult Services Division was established in 1957 and in 1992 was renamed the Young Adult Library Services Association.[32]

Generally speaking, it seems that collections for young adults preceded services for young adults, which in turn preceded dedicated spaces for young adults in public libraries. School libraries, of course, were a different matter. In 1920, the National Education Association, along with the North Central Association of Colleges and Schools, issued a report on how to organize and equip libraries in secondary schools. Five years previous, the School Libraries Section of the American Library Association had held its first meeting. This section was renamed the American Association of School Librarians in 1944, and it became a separate division in its own right in 1951.[33]

As libraries began providing services to young adults, these services tended to mirror the objectives of the library as a cultural institution. In the 1930s and 1940s, public libraries, according to Virginia Walter and Elaine Meyers, saw their mission as threefold: to promote reading, to support education, and to encourage civic engagement for the improvement of society.[34] No doubt, these were the objectives of school libraries as well, although supporting education was obviously first and foremost. Various services and programs were developed in each of these areas, many of which continue today. To promote reading, for example, librarians used readers' advisory and book talks.[35] Both of these continue to be staples of young adult services in most libraries. To support education, librarians conducted outreach to schools and provided reference assistance to both formal students and independent learners. Now called "homework help," these services, which languished from the 1960s through the late 1990s, are now experiencing a resurgence.[36] And to support civic engagement, librarians offered lectures by guest speakers, panel discussions, films, music performances, and exhibits.[37] Although many libraries still sponsor these kinds of activities, it might be argued that they are now offered more in the service of the first two objectives—promoting reading and supporting education.

Over the last couple of decades, the YALSA has implemented a number of initiatives designed to foster various literacies and to promote library use. As previously mentioned, YALSA has established several awards and booklists, including lists voted on by teens, to recognize outstanding books and other materials for young adults and to promote these books to teens, parents, and teachers. In addition, in 1998 Teen Read Week was instituted as a way of encouraging both recreational and informational reading among teens.[38] And in 2007, Teen Tech Week was instituted[39] for the purpose of bridging "the gap between in-school and out-of-school time, helping teens learn through digital media so they can achieve more academically and develop the digital and media literacy skills they will need in order to be informed, productive citizens."[40]

In addition to a proliferation of services for teens, the increasing number of professional books on the topic published in the past two decades attests to the growing emphasis that libraries are giving to this user group. The first edition of Patrick Jones's *Connecting Young Adults and Libraries: A How-to-Do-It Manual for Librarians* was published in 1992.[41] Three subsequent editions have appeared, with Michele Gorman and Tricia Suellentrop taking over the primary authorial duties in the fourth edition.[42] This excellent resource discusses everything from readers' advisory and book talking to homework help, movie screenings, and summer reading programs. It also emphasizes the importance of marketing and evaluating services, and it encourages librarians to get young adults and other partners in the community involved in the process.

Other professional books published within the last decade have focused on the diversity and complexity of young adults. Jennifer Burke Pierce's *Sex, Brains, and Video Games: A Librarian's Guide to Teens in the Twenty-first Century*,[43] for example, looks at the issues and opportunities that arise from our greater understanding of adolescent brain development, the exponential growth of technology, and the increasing diversity of our society in general and young adults in particular. Heather Booth, in *Serving Teens through Readers' Advisory*,[44] offers strategies for talking with young adults about their reading needs and interests and for helping connect them with the right resources. Sheila B. Anderson, in *Extreme Teens: Library Services to Non-traditional Young Adults*,[45] advocates for providing an array of information services to homeless teens, incarcerated teens, immigrant teens, and LGBTQ teens. The last group, LGBTQ teens, is the exclusive focus of Hillias J. Martin Jr. and James R. Murdock's *Serving Lesbian, Gay, Bisexual, Transgender, and Questioning Teens: A How-to-Do-It Manual for Librarians*.[46] And urban teens are the focus of *Urban Teens in the Library: Research and Practice*, edited by Denise Agosto and Sandra Hughes-Hassell.[47] The essays in this volume look at a variety of issues related to serving urban teens, from their recreational reading preferences to their health information needs, from their participation in online social networking to their need for a reimagined space within the library.

Many mid- to large-size libraries now offer not only specific services for young adults but also spaces where they can congregate to access information, share ideas, and collaborate on projects. Some of these spaces qualify as "makerspaces," places equipped with technology so that young people can create their own information products in various media. A noteworthy example of such a space is Chicago Public Library's YOUMedia, established in 2009 "to enable teens to be more than just consumers of digital media, but to be creators as well."[48] Its philosophy statement reflects a commitment to promoting new literacies, along with education and civic engagement: "The goal of YOUmedia's physical and online spaces is to support young people in participating with digital media . . . so that, in time, there is a substantial increase in the number of youth in Chicago who use online resources and new media as tools to engage in inquiry about their neighborhoods, the city, and the world."[49] It is important to acknowledge that rural libraries, because of their small size and limited budgets, are often unable to provide separate spaces for teens. Nevertheless, many of them can and do provide young adults with access to collections and technology, as well as librarians trained to serve a range of user groups, including young adults.

SUMMARY

Today's young adults reflect the diversity of our society at large, and information professionals who work with young adults have many opportunities at their disposal. While generations of young adults have been readers, it was not until the late 1960s that a literature written specifically for young adults appeared. Since then, with the exception of a decline during the 1990s, the genre has flourished. By the same token, information services for young adults have flourished as well, with many libraries now offering not just collections specifically for young adults and librarians dedicated to serving them but also particular spaces—real and virtual—where young adults can work, read, create, and interact. This book is intended to orient its readers to the world of 21st-century young adults and the resources and services that can instill in young adults a lifelong passion for reading and learning.

IMPLICATIONS FOR PRACTICE

- Information professionals can provide more effective resources and services by understanding the great diversity of the young adults they serve.
- Resource collections for young adults should include adult works, "classics" of young adult literature, and contemporary works for young adult readers, as well as a variety of formats.
- Information professionals should be prepared to offer services to young adults on a one-on-one basis and develop programs that can be offered to groups of young adults.

QUESTIONS TO THINK ABOUT AND DISCUSS

1. Do you recall reading a book when you were a young adult that made a significant impression on you? What was the book, and why was it so important to you?

2. What can libraries do to facilitate the social aspect of reading among young adults (e.g., sharing opinions and recommendations, reading together)?
3. What can be done to make the library a friendly place for the diverse group of young adults that it serves?
4. How can libraries without staff and/or space devoted to young adults still provide effective services to this user group?

NOTES

1. Jeffrey Arnett, *Emerging Adulthood: The Winding Road from the Late Teens through the Twenties* (New York: Oxford University Press, 2004).

2. Marcia J. Bates, "Information Behavior," 2010, http://pages.gseis.ucla.edu/faculty/bates/articles/information-behavior.html.

3. Carl M. Tomlinson and Carol Lynch-Brown, *Essentials of Young Adult Literature*, 2nd ed. (Boston: Pearson, 2010).

4. Kenneth L. Donelson and Alleen Pace Nilsen, *Literature for Today's Young Adults*, 7th ed. (Boston: Pearson, 2005).

5. Donelson and Nilsen, *Literature for Today's Young Adults*, 54.

6. Maureen Daly, *Seventeenth Summer* (New York: Dodd, Mead, 1942).

7. Betty Smith, *A Tree Grows in Brooklyn* (New York: Harper & Brothers, 1943).

8. J. D. Salinger, *The Catcher in the Rye* (New York: Little, Brown, 1951).

9. Maureen Daly, *Seventeenth Summer* (New York: Dodd, Mead, 1962).

10. Caroline Hunt, "Young Adult Literature Evades the Theorists," *Children's Literature Association Quarterly* 21, no. 1 (1996): 4–11.

11. S. E. Hinton, *The Outsiders* (New York: Viking, 1967).

12. Robert Lipsyte, *The Contender* (New York: Harper & Row, 1967).

13. John Donovan, *I'll Get There, It Better Be Worth the Trip* (New York: Harper & Row, 1969).

14. Paul Zindel, *The Pigman* (New York: Harper Trophy, 1968).

15. Norma Klein, *Mom, the Wolfman and Me* (New York: Knopf, 1972).

16. Robert Cormier, *The Chocolate War* (New York: Knopf, 1974).

17. Judy Blume, *Are You There God? It's Me, Margaret* (New York: Yearling, 1970).

18. Judy Blume, *Forever* (Scarsdale, NY: Bradbury, 1975).

19. Michael Cart, *Young Adult Literature: From Romance to Realism* (Chicago: American Library Association, 2010).

20. Alan Moore, *Watchmen*, illus. Dave Gibbons (New York: DC Comics, 1987).

21. Art Spiegelman, *Maus I: A Survivor's Tale—My Father Bleeds History* (New York: Pantheon Books, 1986).

22. Marc Aronson, "Coming of Age: One Editor's View of How Young Adult Publishing Developed in America," *Publishers Weekly* (February 11, 2002), 82–86.

23. Cart, *Young Adult Literature*, 2010.

24. Aronson, 2002.

25. Aronson, "Coming of Age," 2002.

26. Eliza T. Dresang, *Radical Change: Books for Youth in a Digital Age* (New York: H. W. Wilson, 1999).

27. Roberta Seelinger Trites, *Disturbing the Universe: Power and Repression in Adolescent Literature* (Iowa City: University of Iowa Press, 2000).

28. Trites, *Disturbing the Universe*, 7.

29. J. K. Rowling's Harry Potter series, Stephenie Meyer's Twilight series, and Suzanne Collins's the Hunger Games series are discussed in more detail in chapter 5.

30. Anthony Bernier, Mary K. Chelton, Christine A. Jenkins, and Jennifer Burek Pierce, comp., "Two Hundred Years of Young Adult Library Services," *Voice of Youth Advocates* 28,

no. 2 (2005): 106–11. This chronology of milestones in youth services draws on numerous sources. Much of what appears in the young adult services section of this chapter comes from this timeline.

31. Margaret A. Edwards, *The Fair Garden and the Swarm of Beasts: The Library and the Young Adult*, centennial ed. (Chicago: American Library Association, 2002).

32. Bernier et al., "Two Hundred Years."

33. Bernier et al., "Two Hundred Years."

34. Virginia A. Walter and Elaine Meyers, *Teens and Libraries: Getting It Right* (Chicago: American Library Association, 2003), 3.

35. Walter and Meyers, *Teens and Libraries*, 9–10.

36. Walter and Meyers, *Teens and Libraries*, 12–13.

37. Walter and Meyers, *Teens and Libraries*, 15.

38. Walter and Meyers, *Teens and Libraries*, 21.

39. Michele Gorman and Tricia Suellentrop, *Connecting Young Adults and Libraries: A How-to-Do-It Manual for Librarians*, 4th ed. (New York: Neal-Schuman, 2009), 44.

40. Young Adult Library Services Association, "Teen Tech Week," 2013, http://teentech-week.ning.com/.

41. Patrick Jones, *Connecting Young Adults and Libraries: A How-to-Do-It Manual for Librarians* (New York: Neal-Schuman, 1992).

42. Gorman and Suellentrop, *Connecting Young Adults and Libraries*.

43. Jennifer Burek Pierce, *Sex, Brains, and Video Games: A Librarian's Guide to Teens in the Twenty-first Century* (Chicago: American Library Association, 2008).

44. Heather Booth, *Serving Teens through Readers' Advisory* (Chicago: American Library Association, 2007).

45. Sheila B. Anderson, *Extreme Teens: Library Services to Nontraditional Young Adults* (Westport, CT: Libraries Unlimited, 2005).

46. Hillias J. Martin Jr. and James R. Murdock, *Serving Lesbian, Gay, Bisexual, Transgender, and Questioning Teens: A How-to-Do-It Manual for Librarians* (New York: Neal-Schuman, 2007).

47. Denise E. Agosto and Sandra Hughes-Hassell, eds., *Urban Teens in the Library: Research and Practice* (Chicago: American Library Association, 2010).

48. Chicago Public Library, "YOUMedia," 2013, http://youmediachicago.org/10-philosophy/pages/56-philosophy.

49. Chicago Public Library, "YOUMedia."

Chapter Two

Young Adult Development

This chapter covers several aspects of young adulthood:

- Socially constructed nature of young adulthood
- Dimensions of development (physical, cognitive, emotional, social, moral)
- Positive psychology and learned optimism
- Spotlight! Young adult advisory boards
- Implications for practice
- Questions to think about and discuss

Young adulthood is a time of dynamic change, similar to the first years of life, in which a baby demonstrates an impressive rate of growth—physically, cognitively, emotionally, and socially. Young adults also experience rapid growth in all these areas as they move toward the self-sufficiency required in adulthood. Understanding young adults and having a knowledge of the materials developed for them is central to supporting their information needs, helping them achieve information literacy skills, and fostering their desire to be lifelong learners is all aspects of their lives. Knowledge of young adulthood will inform the development and provision of information services and improve the information professional's ability to effectively interact with and integrate young adults into information-providing environments, whether physical or virtual.

As noted in chapter 1, there is no "official" definition of young adulthood, and an individual's experience of this time of life depends on the culture and historical time in which one is growing up, as well as factors such as relative affluence, access to educational opportunities, geographical location, and personal characteristics. Because individuals vary in terms of their rates of development, life circumstances, and personal characteristics, it is a good idea to avoid making assumptions about them based on knowledge of the group. It is also important to get to know the young adults with whom you work as individual people. Understanding what is known about young adulthood will, however, aid in recognizing the issues that young adults face and the information needs and behaviors that they exhibit. It will also help information professionals to connect with the wide range of young adults they serve.

SOCIALLY CONSTRUCTED NATURE OF YOUNG ADULTHOOD

Young adulthood has not always been recognized as a special stage of development. In earlier times, it was not unusual for a young person to take on adult responsibilities at an age at which today, in the United States, she or he would be entering middle school. Society's opinion of whether a young person belongs at home, at school, in the workforce, or in the military depends on the economic and political conditions. For example, if jobs are scarce, keeping young people in school may be favored. Likewise, the need for national defense may make an adult out of what in otherwise peaceful times would be considered a child. The idea that young adulthood is a distinct stage of human development was first proposed by psychologist G. Stanley Hall in his 1904 book *Adolescence: Its Psychology and Its Relations to Physiology, Anthropology, Sociology, Sex, Crime, Religion, and Education.*[1] Hall famously described adolescence as a period of life characterized by Sturm und Drang (storm and stress), and he consolidated in two massive volumes all that was known about adolescence at that time. Interestingly, many of his observations about adolescence reflect understandings that are still held today.[2] Among these are a view that young adults are in a phase of physical development, that peer relationships become extremely important to them, that they are influenced by media, and that they may experience depressed mood, sensation seeking, and an increased propensity for crime.

Over the history of the United States, increased mechanization of labor, urbanization, higher levels of industrialization, the institution of child labor laws, and the expansion of educational opportunities have all contributed to a lengthening of the period of development leading to adulthood. Up until the 20th century, young people were treated like adults.[3] They had responsibility to their families and contributed to family incomes through their work on farms and in factories. As mechanization increased, the need for a large labor force shrank: as a result, changes in law made it illegal for young people to work; the period of dependence on parents lengthened; and the expectation that young adults belonged in school grew.[4] The period of offspring's dependence on their parents has continued to lengthen in response to the increasing complexity of work in the information age. A new developmental phase called "emerging adulthood" has begun to be popularized by Arnette.[5] Emerging adulthood is a phase between young adulthood and adulthood, and it is characterized by the trend that many young people today are marrying and becoming parents later in life and remaining self-focused in exploring what they want in life in terms of love and work. This new phase of development also reflects the increasing need for advanced education to become a fully participating member of society today.

YOUNG ADULT DEVELOPMENT: MOVING FROM CHILDHOOD TO ADULTHOOD

Young adulthood is a transition between childhood and adulthood where developmental changes and life experience combine to inform individual perceptions of the self in terms of identity and the possibilities that the individual has for contributing to society as well as for personal satisfaction in life. Young adults are working toward a stable sense of identity and the ability to develop positive relationships, gain independence, and be self-directed, as well as a level of emotional maturity that allows them to handle and integrate life experiences.

While in our society the life sequence of emerging adulthood may be increasingly extending the period of development that prepares for adulthood, it must be remembered that an extended period of development is not afforded to all young adults. Many will be full participants in society, will have responsibility for children of their own, and will be facing the burdens of adulthood soon after or even during their young adult years.

Physical Development

Physical development, particularly in terms of sexual maturity, is one of the key facets of development that many people associate with young adulthood. During this time, young people experience many physical changes, including growth spurts, weight gain, changes in skin and smell, and the development of secondary sex characteristics. Puberty is a stage of development that takes several years to complete. However, the onset of puberty varies widely, and it is one of many indicators suggesting that the span of normal development is wide. It has become increasingly common for girls to begin breast development as early as 7 years of age and menstruation as early as 10 years of age. Therefore, it is important to recognize that the onset of puberty does not always line up with general ideas about when young adulthood begins.

The normal physical changes expected during adolescence bring with them many information needs. Research has shown that children who are prepared for the onset of puberty handle the transition better than children who do not know what to expect.[6] Likewise, research has demonstrated that young people who receive comprehensive sex education, which includes information about contraceptives, sexually transmitted diseases, and disease prevention, are more likely to delay having sexual intercourse, have fewer sexual partners, and use contraception when sexually active.[7] A recent study by the Guttmacher Institute found that educating young adults about contraception correlated with a decrease in risky sexual behavior.[8]

The national Youth Risk Behavior Survey, performed every 2 years by the Centers for Disease Control and Prevention, collects descriptive data from a representative sample of young people, grades 9 through 12, in the United States. These data indicate that 47 percent of students reported having had sex, 33.7 percent were currently sexually active, and 12.9 percent did not use any method to prevent pregnancy the last time they had sex. Furthermore, 15.3 percent report that they have had four or more sexual partners.[9]

Other data indicate that 21 percent of new HIV cases reported in 2011 were in people 13 to 24 years old and that about half of reported sexually transmitted infections were in young people 15 to 24 years old.[10] While the pregnancy rate among young adults in the United States has declined since it peaked in 1990, there are still roughly 750,000 pregnancies each year among young women in the 15- to 19-year age range.[11] Young adult women are less likely to receive prenatal care, and their babies are more likely to be low weight. These young women often do not complete high school (or a GED) before the age of 22 and are very unlikely to attain a college degree before the age of 30.[12]

Clearly, young adults have a need for information about reproduction and reproductive health, sexual identity, and sexually transmitted diseases. But they also need information related to general wellness that includes, but is not limited to, information about body image, nutrition, and exercise. Young adults who mature on the early or late side of normal may have additional concerns related to fitting in socially, which may include a sense of isolation, depression, high-risk behaviors, and being the target of bullying.[13]

An aspect of physical development that has come to light with the advent of magnetic resonance imaging techniques is the understanding that brain development continues into the young adult years. It has long been recognized that brain development is at its most dynamic in very young children, and it is believed that the majority of brain development has taken place by the age of 6. Brain development proceeds through a process of overproduction of neurons (brain cells) and synapses (connections between brain cells), followed by a period in which the number of synapses declines as connections that are used strengthen and those that are not used disappear. While our understanding of adolescent neurodevelopment is evolving, it has been learned that significant changes take place in the brain during this period of life. For example, Jay N. Giedd, of the National Institute of Mental Health, has learned that the brain experiences another period of growth before the onset of puberty in the area in charge of executive functions (the prefrontal cortex), followed by another period during which the number of synapses is again reduced. This area of the brain is important for planning, memory, mood regulation, and organizing. [14]

Since the brain gets rid of synapses that are weak and retains those that are strengthened through use, this may suggest that the connections available to the adult brain will be those retained during adolescence as determined by the activities and interests in which individuals are engaged. [15] Said another way, young adults may be setting themselves up, at least in part, for certain kinds of abilities in adulthood by the pathways and connections they make through the experiences they have and the activities they participate in. This may mean that how young adults spend their time is critical to the kinds of connections in their brains that will be retained into adulthood. So the choice to practice an instrument, to dance or paint, or to read or otherwise understand the world better versus watching television, for example, may have long-term effects. [16]

Because it is not completely known which aspects of brain development are associated with genetics versus environment, it may be too soon to use recent findings about brain development to inform policy issues or how education is delivered. However, there is some evidence that brain development during this time may at least partially explain why learning a new language is harder after puberty, why there can be an increase in risk taking behavior during young adulthood, or even why tolerance for alcohol may be higher during this time of life. [17]

Cognitive Development

The ability to think is another form of development that continues into young adulthood. Jean Piaget and Eric Erickson are two theorists whose work has strongly influenced our understanding of cognitive development, providing foundational ideas about the sequence of development over the life span.

Jean Piaget's classic model of cognitive development describes growth in the ability to think as a series of four stages, which begins at birth and may be completed as early as 11 years of age. [18] The formal operational stage is the fourth and last stage, and it is characterized by the ability to think in abstract terms. Piaget describes this ability in several ways, pointing to achievements such as the ability to think about thinking, to move from the actual to the possible, to bring together data and ideas, and to think logically and hypothetically.

Before reaching this stage, thinkers (ages, 7–11) are described as being in the concrete operational stage, in which they have some ability to reason in a logical fashion but are limited in this regard to only that which they have experienced. Within this limitation, they can perform various kinds of mental operations, such as classifying objects, ordering them, and placing them in hierarchical relationships. They can make inferences about objects and processes with which they are familiar, and they can understand the conservation of volume and mass. The familiar example is a child's ability to understand that a specified volume of liquid does not change when it is poured into a different size or shape of container.

While the phases of development that Piaget outlines are generally accepted, research has since shown that cognitive development is not as strictly tied to age as Piaget conceptualized it. It is understood now that while it is possible for an 11-year-old to enter the formal operational stage, other 11-year-olds will not. And while improvements in cognition will continue through young adulthood, it is not uncommon for abstract thinking to become fully attained sometime in the twenties. It has also been demonstrated that some people never reach the formal operational stage of development.[19] For these reasons, it is important not to assume on the basis of age or other indicators of maturity that individuals are abstract thinkers.

Another approach to understanding cognitive development during young adulthood is offered by Eric Erikson, who describes development over the life course as a series of "crises" that individuals are confronted with.[20] His model of psychosocial stages includes eight successive crises, five of which occur before the onset of puberty. Erickson says that from the onset of puberty to age 18, the main crisis that young people are dealing with is identity versus role confusion. During this stage, young people become increasingly aware that adulthood is imminent and that they will need to find their senses of identity and independence to move forward in life. This means that the question "Who am I?" is the primary focus of this stage of development. Aspects of identity associated with this question include ideas about goals, vocation, sexual orientation, gender roles, and other life issues. This is a time in which peer relationships become central and in which young people try on different identities and roles in establishing a sense of self-identity. This kind of experimentation is important during this phase of life. Young adults who develop strong personal identities have a healthy level of self-confidence, are comfortable in a variety of relationships, and will be ready to find their places in the world.

Emotional Development

The idea that there is only one kind of intelligence was disrupted by Gardner in the early 1980s when he introduced his theory of multiple intelligences, which expanded the view of intelligence from a single trait to a set of skills that demonstrate the various ways that humans process information. The original set of intelligences that he identified included musical, bodily–kinesthetic, logical–mathematical, linguistic, spatial, interpersonal, and intrapersonal.[21] These are skills that all humans possess, although individuals have unique profiles in terms of the combination of abilities that they have developed.

The theory of multiple intelligences brought with it new questions for researchers and educators. In the early 1990s, Goleman, informed by Gardner's work, described emotional intelligence, which takes the idea of intelligence in a new direction by emphasizing the role of feeling as an intelligence or mind, as opposed to intelligences that have to do with rational thought. Goleman sees emotional intelligence as an ability that can be developed in individuals across five domains: knowing one's emotions (the ability to recognize feelings as they erupt), managing emotions in an appropriate way (e.g., self-soothe, shake off moods), using emotion in service to personal goals (a reason to pay attention, delay gratification, etc.), recognizing emotions in others (empathy), and managing emotions in others (interpersonal skill).[22]

The development of these skills has been demonstrated to have many benefits. People who have a high level of emotional intelligence tend to be popular, to become leaders, and to have good interpersonal relationships. Emotional intelligence also affects levels of interpersonal conflict, depression, resilience, eating disorders, substance abuse, and other health issues. Emotional development is tied to other kinds of development, and the changes that come with puberty also bring on the need for the development of new emotional and social skills. Young people who have been developing emotional intelligence over the course of their lives have some protection from life stressors, such as peer and academic pressures, and an increased ability to build close friendships and deal with life crises when they happen.[23] The good news is that emotional intelligence skills can be learned (even in adulthood). The ability to recognize emotional intelligence skills in one's self and others and to find ways to promote them is an aspect of development that is important to understand when interacting with young adults.

Social Development

Another type of development in young adulthood related to identity, independence, and intimacy has to do with relationships with others. As young people become less dependent on parents and family, which have been central influences, they begin the normal process of separating themselves from parents to find their places in the world. At the same time, relationships with peers increase in importance. Over the course of young adulthood, a typical pattern is for young people to become part of a group of same-gender friends, then develop a group of mixed-gender friends, then form dyads, close

friends, and romantic relationships that mainly happen in one-on-one config-
urations.[24] In this process of socialization, young adults deal with issues of
acceptance around issues of conformity, achievement, participation in
groups, physical attractiveness, and reputation. [25]

Peer groups provide young adults a view of what the world looks like
outside their own families, as well as opportunities to develop friendship
skills and intimate relationships with others. Just as a good foundation in the
family is associated with healthier outcomes, young adults who establish
positive relationships with peers tend to do well in school and have more
self-esteem. Likewise, just as there can be developmental problems associated with poor parenting, negative peer relationships and social isolation in
young adulthood are associated with a range of problems, including depression, bullying, anxiety, and lower self-esteem. [26]

Parents are still important to young adults. Studies have shown that attachment to family is positively correlated with lower levels of smoking,
alcohol, and drug use; later first sexual intercourse; and lower rates of attempted suicide. [27] Family love is the first kind of love that individuals experience, and it sets the stage for intimate relationships with others later in life.
Friendships and the experience of romantic love are normal developments in
establishing intimate relationships with others. Romantic relationships differ
in that they are related to the development of sexual maturity. With sexual
maturity comes a desire for a new kind of closeness that in the right circumstances will develop in a context of mutual respect, honest communication,
and affection.

Generally speaking, first romantic relationships often occur within the
context of the peer group. Group dating later gives way to pairing, in which
couples spend time by themselves. First relationships tend not to last very
long, and for some young people, the length of the relationship may be an
indicator of whether to become sexually active. A 2006–2008 survey of teens
in the United States indicated that only 13 percent of 15-year-olds have had
sex but that, by age 19, 70 percent have had intercourse at least once. [28]

Adults can play a role in the lives of young adults. Although peer relationships are important to youth, young adults are interested in what the adults in
their lives have to say and look to them as models for how to be in the world.
Young people need guidance in cultivating and navigating social and romantic relationships. It is important to understand what a healthy relationship is
and to develop emotional and communication skills. In addition to sexuality
education, young adults also have relationship-based questions about how to
decide whether or not to have sex, how to say no, how to talk about sex, how
to explore alternatives to sex, how to know if this is love, and so forth.

Young adults also need information about how to deal with the darker
side of relationships. The Centers for Disease Control and Prevention reports
that dating violence is a public health problem that needs to be taken serious-

ly. Survey findings indicate that 22.4 percent of women and 15.0 percent of men experienced some form of partner violence between the ages of 11 and 17.[29] Studies of youth indicate that 15 to 40 percent feel that they have perpetrated violence toward a dating partner.[30] The violence of concern in these studies includes physical, emotional, and sexual violence that takes place both in person and in electronic venues. The effects of dating violence on health are many and may include depression, underachievement, drug and alcohol use, and other unhealthy behaviors. Once established, partner violence is a behavior that can continue to affect relationships into adulthood. Early intervention and prevention strategies are important. This is a place where adult help and community initiatives can make a difference in individual lives by promoting respectful, nonviolent relationships.

Breakups will happen in both friendships and romantic relationships, and there is a need to work through feelings of sadness and grief when relationships change or end. Emotional support can be critical at such times, as breakups can be the cause of depression, suicide, and murder.[31] Grief can also affect performance at school and general health. Adults can help by respecting feelings and encouraging self-care. Self-expression and understanding of the process of grief can help rebuild the confidence needed to move ahead.

Moral Development

Moral development has to do with perceptions of right and wrong behavior and the values that a person holds in life. There are many ways that morals are learned, and as with other kinds of development, it starts within the context of the family but is also influenced by school life, friends, important adult role models, the community, and the world at large as perceived through various media. Two major theories of moral development that are relevant to young adults are Kohlberg's stages of moral development[32] and Gilligan's[33] stages of the ethics of care. Interestingly, both models have at their roots Jean Piaget's work with children.

Kohlberg studied children and adolescents using a method in which he presented fictional situations and asked his respondents to discuss the behavior in the story and to share their reasoning concerning whether the characters in the story did the right thing or not. Kohlberg then categorized and arranged the data into stages. The resulting model is composed of three levels, each of which comprises two stages. In this model, individuals develop along a set path (i.e., the first level must be completed before an individual can advance to the second level), but individuals can remember and continue to understand the logic and moral arguments of previous stages.[34] It should also be remembered that this model is concerned with moral thought, not actions.

Level 1 of Kohlberg's model is called *preconventional morality*, and it describes an orientation in which morality is experienced as that imposed by external authority. In the first stage of this level—obedience and punishment orientation—moral thinking relies on established rules and the consequences that go with breaking them. In the second stage—individualism and exchange—individuals still use rules as a guide for moral behavior, but they have begun to understand that different authorities have different rules. Despite this recognition, the focus on the consequences of behavior continues to be the threat of punishment. An individual has a choice about what to do, but part of that choice involves weighing outcomes in terms of consequences, if caught. Kohlberg associates this level with children from birth to about age 9.

Level 2 is called *conventional morality*, and here the conception of moral behavior is based less on personal outcomes and more on community standards. Stages 3 and 4 are nested in this level. At stage 3, morality is evaluated on the basis of personal traits and the motives and the extent to which the community would agree that the actions of the individual are correct. This need for general agréement is extended in stage 4—maintaining the social order—in the attitude that what individuals do must be guided by what serves society. The law is to be obeyed, not to avoid personal consequences, but to preserve social order. Kohlberg associates level 2 with young people approximately between the ages of 9 and 20.

At level 3—postconventional morality—people begin to see beyond the way things are, and they think about what is right and fair in a more complex way. Stages 5 and 6 occur at this level. A person at stage 5—social contract and individual rights—expects a person's basic rights to be protected, considers whether society is functioning in a good and fair way, and expects a democratic process for changing the rules if doing so will improve how society functions. At stage 6—universal principles—an individual moves beyond the idea that a democratic change process is always enough, since a majority can ignore the welfare of a minority group. At this level, the focus is on principles of justice that apply to everyone. Issues of impartiality, personal dignity, and equal respect become important concerns in determining the right action. Kohlberg does not expect individuals under the age of 20 to be at this stage of development and notes that some people may never develop this far.

Just as Kohlberg's model is informed by Piaget, Gilligan's stages of the ethic of care[35] were developed in reaction to Kohlberg's model. The subjects of Kohlberg's studies were mainly male. In contrast to Kohlberg's findings, in her interviews with women, Gilligan discovered that women's moral concerns tend to be centered on the question of what is the caring thing to do, rather than on what the rules say. Furthermore, women tended to score lower than men using Kohlberg's stages. Gilligan did not accept the explanation that women are morally inferior to men; rather, she asserted that women have a different moral orientation that is also important to understand. Gilligan developed her own stage model to reflect what she saw happening with women. In contrast to the stage models proposed by Piaget and Kohlberg, in Gilligan's model, women move from one stage to the other based on a developing sense of self rather in response to cognitive growth.

There are three stages in Gilligan's model, and movement from one stage to the next signals a transition in a person's sense of self. There are no ages associated with the stages and no expectation that an individual has to transition out of one stage into another.

The first stage is the preconventional stage, and people at this stage of development focus on their survival. To transition to the next stage of development, the individual must begin to understand that a self-only perspective is selfish and begin to recognize that she or he has some responsibility for other people. Stage 2 is the conventional stage, and here sacrifice of the self in service of others becomes the measure of goodness. The typical example of a person at this level of moral development is the mother or wife who sublimates her needs for those of her family. Just as a person can live one's whole life from a self-centered perspective, it is also possible for a person to get stuck in a service-to-others role, which may not be good for him or her personally. To get to stage 3 of Gilligan's model, an individual must make the transition from only using service to others as a measure of goodness to the realization that both the self and others are important and that caring must take both the self and others into account. At the postconventional stage, individuals seek to balance the needs of the self and others and to do no harm to either.

Both Kohlberg's model and Gilligan's have important things to say about how moral thinking develops. They represent different dimensions of moral thinking, provide different ways of assessing morality, and provide different but not necessarily incompatible views of how individuals develop (or do not develop) as they find their places in the world.

POSITIVE PSYCHOLOGY, LEARNED OPTIMISM, AND RESILIENCE

While research in psychology covers an array of topics, until about 1990 it focused to a large extent on issues of understanding and treating illness, rather than understanding and promoting health. Thus, it is no surprise that the first descriptions of adolescence focused on the Strum und Drang[36] and the difficulties of dealing with young adults. A new research focus called *positive psychology*, however, continues to gain ground in demonstrating that mental health and resilience in the face of difficulty can be promoted and taught. Learning to be optimistic has been demonstrated as a factor that lessens the occurrence of depression, increases achievement, and results in better health. Learned optimism has been demonstrated to be helpful in school, the workplace, and the military, as well as in the areas of parenting and cognitive behavioral therapy.

Seligman's[37] research began with an interest in learned helplessness, a condition where people have lost a sense of connection between what they do and the outcomes that they experience in life. People in this state are more likely to be depressed and to react negatively to adverse life events. In his work, Seligman came to understand that some people are resilient to the conditions that result in learned helplessness and that this difference could be explained as explanatory style.

People who are optimistic see adverse conditions as temporary rather than permanent, specific to the current situation rather than a condition pervasive in life as a whole, and do not blame themselves when negative events happen. While it is natural for individuals to feel sad and depressed in the face of negative experiences, people who have an optimistic explanatory style are more resilient and bounce back from negative experiences more quickly. In contrast, people with pessimistic explanatory styles have a more difficult time overcoming depression and are more prone to longer depressed periods.

Learning-optimism techniques use Seligman's ABCDE model as a framework. This model extends Ellis's ABC model, which isolates a chain of events for examination: *ABC* stands for *adversity, belief, consequence*. Adversity is the experience that a person is confronted with; belief is the way that a person thinks about the adversity; and consequence describes what the person does or thinks as a result of his or her belief. For example, adversity might be a situation where a classmate doesn't return your friendly "hello" in the hall. Belief might be "She doesn't like me." The consequence in this scenario might be that you pick a fight with her.

In learning to be optimistic, it is important to begin to understand personal beliefs and consequences. This is achieved in a journal—by keeping track of personal experiences and the beliefs and consequences associated with them. The *D* in Seligman's model stands for *disputation*, a process of counteracting negative beliefs with alternative explanations. In the hallway example, you might consider that your classmate is dealing with some bad news that you don't know about. You might decide to overlook the incident, remembering the fight that you had with your mother before school. The idea is that by challenging the negative thoughts, you can change them and develop a more optimistic and positive pattern of thoughts and behaviors. If you are successful with disputation, you will reach a stage of energization (E), in which you can enjoy your accomplishment in overcoming your pessimistic outlook.

Working through these stages using the ABCDE techniques can help young adults cope with daily problems as well as significant adverse life events if and when they are faced with them. Seligman offers specific techniques to help adults teach children (and themselves) to adopt an optimistic way of thinking.[38] If practiced, the techniques become second nature. Adults who are optimistic or who learn to be will also experience improved outcomes and will provide better role models for the young people with whom they work.

Research and thinking about young adults has moved away from a focus on how to handle issues with young adults to one that focuses on how to promote healthy development. Theory is increasingly moving away from stage models and other ways of thinking about development, including relational models that take into account both the individual and the context in which development takes place. This has resulted in changes in governmental policy about how programs and services should be constructed to best help youth. There has been a shift from a focus on individuals and their problems to a focus on how to promote positive youth development for all young people, troubled or not.[39] The approaches to positive youth development that result from this kind of thinking tend to be community based and recognize that adult mentorship and community support are powerful tools in raising youth who have a sense of competence based on attainments in skill, knowledge, and expertise; who understand that they have something useful to contribute to society; who feel like they belong to a community; and who believe that they have some autonomy in their lives.[40] Catalano et al.[41] note that "the positive youth development construct of competence, covers five areas of youth functioning including social, emotional, cognitive, behavioral, and moral competencies."

The number of competencies that youth may develop is variously described by different writers. For example, Benson[42] presents a framework of developmental assets that includes 40 elements culled from the research literature. In contrast, the "five C's of positive youth development, competence, confidence, connection (to family, peers, community), character, and caring compassion" are a good way to summarize what many of these programs are trying to achieve.[43]

Positive psychology and the "positive youth development" approach demonstrate that young people benefit from engagement with adults and that this can be accomplished in a variety of ways, including mentoring and volunteer activities that help young people attain skills, achieve a sense of belonging, and develop a healthy sense of identity. Information services for youth and the development of information competence both have a role to play in the healthy development of young adults.

SPOTLIGHT!

Young Adult Advisory Boards

One of the best ways to ensure a vibrant life for young adult services is to involve young adults in all aspects of the programs and services targeted to this user group. Young adult advisory boards,[a] also referred to as teen advisory boards, will help you understand how to best serve this population and will be a great help in all aspects of planning, designing, marketing, delivering, and evaluating library services. Likewise, they will help young adults better understand what the library is and how it works, as well as the nature of the relationship between the library and its users.

   Young adult advisory boards are consistent with the objectives of positive youth development (discussed in this chapter) in which young people develop a positive sense of community through engagement with adults, which helps to develop skills, a sense of belonging, and a healthy sense of identity.[b] Young adult advisory boards are also consistent with service learning programs in schools, which seek to enrich learning and strengthen the development of civic responsibility through meaningful community service experiences.[c]

Setting up a young adult advisory board:

- Make sure that you have administrative approval and support before setting up a young adult advisory board.
- Funding for the board may be provided by the library, through grants, or in fund-raising activities performed by the board (e.g., car washes, bake sales).
- Members of the young adult advisory board are typically volunteers. However, they should commit to service for a set period (e.g., 1 year) and should understand that they will represent their peers.
- The target size of the board will depend on the size of the library and the local community. In a public library setting, one approach is to seek representation from each middle school and high school that the library serves. In the school library, representation from each grade may be important. Also consider whether you need members who have specific skills and what kind of training the library can provide to board members.

- There should be a designated person from the library (librarian or other staff) who has primary responsibility for the young adult advisory board, although other librarians and staff may be involved in special projects or help with complex plans.

Working with a young adult advisory board:

- Plan a regular meeting schedule. Meetings may be used for informal discussion, brainstorming, planning, working, and feedback sessions. Topics and tasks must be meaningful to the board members and the library. Be ready to listen!
- Make sure that ideas, suggestions, and decisions that come from the board are actualized in a timely manner.
- Keep in contact with board members. Notice if someone is missing, and follow up to see how she or he is doing. Be available if members want to talk.
- Be aware of the academic calendar, and don't schedule meetings or programs that conflict with school activities.
- Support the social aspects of board membership. Make sure that there are refreshments and time to hang out before and after business is conducted.
- Remember to say thank you and to let board members know how important their participation is to the library. Providing small rewards or special treats periodically for a job well done is always a good idea.

Notes:

a. Diane P. Tuccillo, *Library Teen Advisory Groups* (Lanham, MD: VOYA Books, 2005).

b. National Clearinghouse on Families and Youth, *Putting Positive Youth Development into Practice: A Resource Guide* (Washington, DC: Family and Youth Services Bureau, 2007).

c. National Service-Learning Clearinghouse, *What Is Service Learning?* 2013. http://www.servicelearning.org/what-is-service-learning.

SUMMARY

Young adults have a lot to accomplish in moving toward adulthood. They experience several types of development and may develop faster in some areas than in others. The normal range for all types of development is broad, and the dimensions of development progress at their own pace. Some levels of development may not be completed until adulthood, and some may never be reached at all. This means that it is not unusual for a young adult to be advanced in one area and behind in another. This can cause all kinds of discontinuities and inconsistencies that are difficult for young people and the adults around them. These differences in development can affect the relationships between young people and the degree to which they are accepted or feel that they fit in. Advanced abilities in some areas may raise the expectations that adults have about what young adults should be able to do, what are reasonable expectations for their behavior, or how much they should be able to achieve. These assumptions may be wrong, even though they seem reasonable on the basis of young adults' appearance and behavior. Although young adults are at risk in many ways, positive psychology offers them and the adults around them strategies for promoting health and resilience. Although young adults are focused on peer relationships, parents and other adults continue to be important sources of information and guidance and can do much to promote healthy development and resilience in young people.

IMPLICATIONS FOR PRACTICE

- Services for young adults need to take into account the wide range of abilities and developmental levels. Remember that an individual may be advanced in one area of development and behind in another. Be careful about assumptions and expectations based on one aspect of development (e.g., physical maturity, evidence of abstract thought, social development).
- Adults are important influences. Be a good role model while being approachable.
- Some information skills can be derived from developmental sequence. For example, young people need to be prepared for puberty, and they need information about sexuality.
- Reserve judgment. Be open and objective. The information needs of young adults encompass topics that may be uncomfortable to share or hear. Nonetheless, they are important and can be life changing. Remember: it is your professional role to provide developmentally appropriate information. However, it is also important to remain within the scope of your professional training. Referral to community resources and social agencies is a valid part of your work. The more you know about available services in the community, the better able you will be to respond to the wide range of potential information needs that young adults may express.

QUESTIONS TO THINK ABOUT AND DISCUSS

1. What can information professionals do to ensure that young adults have access to information about reproduction, sexuality, and related topics?
2. Given that some of the information that young adults need may be considered controversial and that some parents and other adults may protest the provision of this information to young people, how can information professionals negotiate this potentially tricky terrain?
3. How can understanding of developmental issues be used to inform collection development and other information services?
4. How might maturity in one area (e.g., physical or cognitive) lead an adult to overestimate a young adult's ability? Likewise, how might immaturity in one or more areas (e.g., social, emotional) lead to an underestimation of ability?
5. How might learned optimism help a young adult deal with developmental issues?
6. How might competence with information be an aid to healthy youth development?
7. What can information professionals do to engage young people in ways that promote skill building, a sense of belonging, and a sense of control over some aspect of their lives?

NOTES

1. G. Stanley Hall, *Adolescence: Its Psychology and Its Relations to Physiology, Anthropology, Sociology, Sex, Crime, Religion, and Education*, 2 vols. (New York: Appleton, 1904).

2. Jeffrey J. Arnett, "G. Stanley Hall's Adolescence: Brilliance and Nonsense," *History of Psychology* 9, no. 3 (2006): 186–97.

3. Miriam Braverman, *Youth, Society, and the Public Library* (Chicago: American Library Association, 1979).

4. Braverman, *Youth, Society*.

5. Jeffrey J. Arnett, *Emerging Adulthood: The Winding Road from the Late Teens through the Twenties* (New York: Oxford University Press, 2004).

6. American Psychological Association, "Developing Adolescents: A Reference for Professionals," http://www.apa.org/pi/cyf/develop.pdf.

7. Centers for Disease Control and Prevention, Division of Adolescent and School Health, "About US: Bringing High-Quality HIV and STD Prevention to Youth in Schools," April 2, 2013, http://www.cdc.gov/healthyyouth/about/hivstd_prevention.htm; National Guidelines Task Force, *Guidelines for Comprehensive Sexuality Education: Kindergarten–12th Grade*, 3rd ed. (Manhattan, NY: Sexuality Information and Education Council of the United States, 2004), http://www2.gsu.edu/~wwwche/Sex%20ed%20class/guidelines.pdf.

8. Jennifer Frost, Laura Duberstein Lindberg, and Lawrence B. Finer, "Young Adults' Contraceptive Knowledge, Norms and Attitudes: Associations with Risk of Unintended Pregnancy," *Perspectives on Sexual and Reproductive Health* 44, no. 2 (2012): 107–16.

9. Centers for Disease Control and Prevention, "Trends in the Prevalence of Sexual Behaviors and HIV Testing National YRBS: 1991–2011," June 20, 2013, http://www.cdc.gov/healthyyouth/yrbs/pdf/us_sexual_trend_yrbs.pdf.

10. Guttmacher Institute, "In Brief: Facts on American Teens' Sexual and Reproductive Health, June, 2013," December 22, 2013, http://www.guttmacher.org/pubs/FB-ATSRH.html.

11. Guttmacher Institute, "In Brief."

12. Guttmacher Institute, "In Brief."

13. American Psychological Association, "Developing Adolescents."

14. Jay N. Giedd, "The Teen Brain: Insights from Neuroimaging," *Journal of Adolescent Health* 42 (2008): 335–43.

15. Linda Spear, "Adolescent Neurodevelopment," *Journal of Adolescent Health* 52 (2013): S7–S13.

16. Sara Spink, "Adolescent Brains Are a Work in Progress: Here's Why," June 20, 2013, http://www.pbs.org/wgbh/pages/frontline/shows/teenbrain/work/adolescent.html.

17. Giedd, "The Teen Brain"; Spear, "Adolescent Neurodevelopment."

18. Jean Piaget and Barbel Inhelder, *The Psychology of the Child* (New York: Basic Books, 1969).

19. F. Phillip Rice and Kim Gale Dolgin, *The Adolescent: Development, Relationships, and Culture*, 12th ed. (New York: Pearson, 2008).

20. Eric H. Erickson, *Childhood and Society*, 2nd ed. (New York: W. W. Norton, 1963).

21. Howard Gardner, *Multiple Intelligences: New Horizons* (New York: Basic Books, 2006).

22. Daniel Goleman, *Emotional Intelligence* (New York: Bantam Books, 1995).

23. Goleman, *Emotional Intelligence.*

24. American Psychological Association, "Developing Adolescents."

25. Rice and Dolgin, *The Adolescent.*

26. Rice and Dolgin, *The Adolescent.*

27. Rice and Dolgin, *The Adolescent.*

28. Guttmacher Institute. "In Brief."

29. Centers for Disease Control and Prevention, "Teen Dating Violence," August 22, 2012, http://www.cdc.gov/ViolencePrevention/intimatepartnerviolence/teen_dating_violence.html.

30. Centers for Disease Control and Prevention, "Teen Dating Violence."

31. American Psychological Association, "Developing Adolescents"; Rice and Dolgin, *The Adolescent.*

32. Lawrence Kohlberg, *The Psychology of Moral Development: The Nature and Validity of Moral Stages* (San Francisco: Harper & Row, 1987).

33. Carol Gilligan, *In a Different Voice* (Cambridge, MA: Harvard University, 1982).

34. William C. Crain, *Theories of Development: Concepts and Applications* (Englewood Cliffs, NJ: Prentice-Hall, 1985).

35. Crain, *Theories of Development.*

36. Hall, *Adolescence.*

37. Martin Seligman, *Learned Optimism; How to Change Your Mind and Your Life* (New York: Vintage Books, 2006).

38. Martin Seligman, *The Optimistic Child* (New York: Houghton Mifflin, 1995).

39. Richard Catalano, M. Lisa Berglund, Jean A. Ryan, Heather S. Lonczak, and J. David Hawkins, "Positive Youth Development in the United States: Research Findings on Evaluations of Positive Youth Development Programs," *Annals of the American Academy of Political and Social Science* 591, no. 98 (2004): 98–123.

40. National Clearinghouse on Families and Youth, "Putting Positive Youth Development into Practice: A Resource Guide," 2007, http://ncfy.acf.hhs.gov/publications/positive-youth-development-practice.

41. Catalano et al., "Positive Youth Development."

42. Peter L. Benson, "Developmental Assets and Asset-Building Community: Conceptual and Empirical Foundations," in *Developmental Assets and Asset-Building Communities: Implications for Research, Policy, and Practice,* ed. Richard M. Lerner and Peter L. Benson (New York: Kluwer Academic/Plenum, 2003), 19–43.

43. Richard M. Lerner, "Developmental Assets and Asset-Building Communities: A View of the Issues," in *Developmental Assets and Asset-Building Communities*, 3–18; National Clearinghouse on Families and Youth, "Putting Positive Youth."

Chapter Three

Young Adult Information-Seeking Behavior

This chapter covers the following:

- Models of young adult information-seeking behavior
- Research on young adult information-seeking behavior
- Spotlight! Book discussion groups
- Multiple literacies and young adults
- Implications for practice
- Questions to think about and discuss

Young adult information-seeking behavior is an area of research that has a short history and presents a variety of excellent questions for research and practice that are only beginning to be answered. At first, researchers and professionals interested in young adults had to rely on understandings based on what was known about adult information-seeking behavior. Over the last 20 years, this has begun to change. This chapter explores models of information-seeking behavior and related research that have informed young adult-oriented research and practice, as well as current conceptions of the literacies seen as providing a foundation for effective information behaviors.

MODELS OF YOUNG ADULT INFORMATION-SEEKING
BEHAVIOR

Models in the social sciences provide a way of thinking about human behavior that seeks to inform understanding of processes and events.[1] Well-conceived models reveal implications that make prediction possible and facilitate the ability to influence outcomes. Many models of information-seeking behavior have been developed in the field of library and information science.[2] However, most models based on the actual or desired information behaviors of young adults have been process models related to the completion of research projects or meant to detail information literacy skills. Four models are discussed here that have been important for conceptualizing young adult information behavior: the imposed query, the information search process, everyday-life information seeking, and the everyday-life information needs of urban teenagers.

Model 1: The Imposed Query

One useful way of thinking about information needs is illustrated by the imposed query model.[3] This model, developed by Gross, is the result of observation of youth in a public library setting, and it is informed by Taylor's process of question formulation,[4] which describes the development of questions; by Belkin's anomalous state of knowledge,[5] which outlines the difficulties of asking about something that is not known or understood; and by Dervin's sense-making theory,[6] which describes information seeking as related to context and as a process in which individuals construct meaning.

The imposed query model has been tested and verified in studies of a variety of user groups, including children, young adults, and adults. The imposed query differentiates between self-generated questions (i.e., created and transacted by the same person for his or her own uses) and imposed queries (i.e., created by one person who gives the question to one or more people to transact). Understanding the type of question that a user is attempting to address has many implications for how well the question is transacted with an intermediary (information professional or system; see Table 3.1).

Imposed queries are questions being transacted for someone else—that is, the person seeking information or resources to address a inquirer's question may not be able to offer specifics about what the imposer is looking for. Research on reference services in the public library revealed 14 categories of imposers.[7] The majority of imposed queries were being transacted at the

Table 3.1. Comparison of the Context of Information Need by Type

Self-Generated Information Seeking	Imposed Information Seeking
Questions come from	Questions come from
• Developmental tasks	• Teachers
• Leisure/recreation	• Employers
• Life experience	• Family members
• Curiosity/interests/hobbies	• Peers (friends, classmates)

adult reference desk for, in order of magnitude, employers, instructors, spouses, and children. Typical imposers for young adults include teachers, employers, family (parents, siblings), and peers (friends, classmates).

In information-providing contexts, the successful resolution to an imposed query depends on how well understanding of the question was transferred from the imposer to the agent who is tasked with finding a response. The quality of the transfer, in turn, can depend on several factors, including the personal characteristics and skills of the imposer and agent, the relationship between the imposer and the agent, the characteristics of the information intermediary (whether a person or a system), and the resources available.

As the subject of an imposed query is developed by the imposer, it may or may not be of any relevance to the agent, which can also impede successful resolution of the question as well as affect the agent's attitude toward the work involved in responding to the query. Questions imposed by others often have parameters associated with them, such as due dates, required resource types, and the extent to which an agent may need to apply his or her own intellectual or creative skills in responding to the question.

Self-generated questions spring from the life context of the user, and information professionals can expect the user to answer questions about what kind of information or resources are needed and to know whether his or her need has been met or not. Self-generated questions spring from the individual's personal characteristics and life context. For young adults, these questions may arise from developmental tasks (e.g., "Am I still growing?"), leisure or recreational needs (e.g., pleasure reading), problems or issues of concern (e.g., parents' divorce, what to do this summer), or their own curiosity, interests, or hobbies (e.g., vegetarian cooking, improving basketball skills).

Model 2: The Information Search Process

The majority of models developed around youth information seeking focus on the process of responding to school assignments or building information literacy skills. These models began to appear in the 1980s as the approach then called *bibliographic instruction* moved away from teaching specific library skills and toward teaching a user-centered process that contextualized the use of library skills in relationship to problem solving and critical thinking.[8] Several such process models were developed and popularized. However, Kuhlthau's information-seeking process (ISP) model[9] stands out from the rest in several respects. One of the strengths of the ISP is that the model is theory based, using Kelly's personal construct theory, and has been extensively tested in school, public, and academic libraries and with users representing a variety of age levels.[10] The ISP model was first developed and tested in the context of the school library with secondary school students, and it is unique in that it provides a full explication of the cognitive and affective states that students experience as they go through the process of responding to a research assignment for class. The ISP can be used to understand the point of view of a student's experience in taking on the role of agent for an imposed query.

Using the ISP model, students are made aware that there are six stages that they can expect to go through in responding to a research assignment: initiation, selection, exploration, formulation, collection, and presentation.[11] Each stage has both cognitive and affective experiences associated with it that students can expect to experience and that fluctuate depending on the student's relative sense of success achieved at each step and one's use of time in working toward a due date. A graphic presentation of the ISP model is available on Kuhlthau's website (http://comminfo.rutgers.edu/~kuhlthau/ information_search_process.htm).

Research is described as a process of constructing meaning and learning that exist for the life of the assignment. In general, students engaged in the research process can expect to move cognitively from a sense of ambiguity to one of specificity and affectively from a feeling of uncertainty toward a sense of confidence. In terms of actions, students move from a search focused on finding relevant information to searches focused on pertinent information as understanding and interest in the topic grow.

From the students' point of view, the process is also influenced by the nature of the specific task, the time available, one's personal interest in the project, and the kind of information available. One of the implications of the model is that a sense of uncertainty, even anxiety, is to be expected in the early stages of the process. Students can learn to see anxiety as a normal response to uncertainty, and they can come to understand that, sometimes, finding needed information can increase uncertainty rather than alleviate it. For information intermediaries, the student's experience of uncertainty indicates the need for guidance, assistance, or other support and thus signals an opportune moment for helping the student achieve the task that she or he is not prepared to do alone.[12]

Model 3: Everyday-Life Information Seeking

The everyday-life information-seeking model was developed by Savolainen to fill a gap in the literature related to information seeking that takes place outside the context of the workday world and to explicate the social and psychological factors that help to shape it.[13] This makes it a suitable lens for considering self-generated information seeking. Interestingly, the everyday-life information-seeking model, though not developed with young adults in mind, has been widely used in studies of youth information-seeking behavior, and it provided the framework for one of the few models developed to explicate an empirical model of urban teens' everyday-life information needs.[14]

Discussion of Savolainen's everyday-life information-seeking model begins with the concept "way of life," which has to do with how people organize everyday activities not related to their work obligations.[15] People make personal choices about how to manage their free time, and they tend to develop habits or regular routines. To manage their personal lives, individuals must make certain choices, such as how much time they will spend on work and nonwork activities, what their priorities are concerning the purchase of various products and services, and what hobbies or interests they will pursue. The choices that an individual makes in these three areas reveal how his or her life is structured. An individual can manage and maintain these aspects of life only to the extent that he or she has achieved "mastery of life." Another way to think about this is that once a preferred way of life is achieved, how can it be protected and maintained? Mastery of life involves being able to solve problems that threaten the achieved equilibrium in ways that are consistent with a person's values and beliefs. Seeking information to solve problems is an important aspect of mastery of life.

Mastery of life is described by Savolainen as learned through the process of socialization and thus may reflect social class and culture. When things are going well, managing day-to-day activities may not take much effort. However, when problems erupt, active management strategies such as information seeking may be needed to regain the previous sense of comfort, predictability, and personal meaning previously experienced. Savolainen categorizes four approaches to mastery of life that people may adopt depending on their tendency to approach problem solving from a cognitive versus affective standpoint, as well as the extent to which they approach problem solving from an optimistic versus pessimistic expectation.

> *Optimistic-cognitive mastery of life:* The individual engages in problem solving as a cognitive activity and believes that an optimal solution can be achieved through analysis and use of multiple information sources and channels.
>
> *Pessimistic-cognitive mastery of life:* The individual perceives the use of analysis and multiple resources as central to problem solving; however, he or she also recognizes that an optimal solution may not be possible.
>
> *Defensive-affective mastery of life:* The individual believes that a solution to the problem can be found, but his or her affective state may affect his or her ability to actively engage in a systematic search for information. Feelings about the situation may lead to behaviors such as information avoidance and wishful thinking.

Pessimistic-affective mastery of life: The individual does not seek information for problem solving, out of a belief that there is nothing one can do to affect outcomes.

Model 4: The Everyday-Life Information Needs of Urban Teenagers

As is clear from its name, Agosto and Hughes-Hassell's empirical model of the everyday-life information needs of urban teenagers takes the construct of everyday-life information seeking as a starting point for thinking about the specific information needs of urban teens.[16] Agosto and Hughes-Hassell chose to study urban teens, as this group has not been given much attention in the literature. Urban—or inner city—teens have special circumstances in that they live in high-density areas of low socioeconomic status and may lack strong role models. As such, libraries are in a good position to provide the information they need.[17] Qualitative methods were used to gather the data to support building the model, and 27 teens (14–17 years old) participated in the study.

The conclusion was that everyday-life information seeking for these teens centered on issues related to achieving adulthood to better understand themselves and the world. The researchers conceptualized urban teen everyday-life information-seeking behavior as supporting development of the social self, the emotional self, the reflective self, the physical self, the creative self, the cognitive self, and the sexual self, and they related these to a typography of 28 topics that the teens identified as areas of information need that they experience.[18] The resulting model provides guidance for information professionals working with teens, as well as direction for further research.

RESEARCH ON YOUNG ADULT INFORMATION-SEEKING BEHAVIOR

Young adult information-seeking behavior is a growing area of research interest. However, many gaps remain in this literature,[19] and research findings are limited by small sample sizes, few replications, and rare follow-up studies.[20] Findings in existing research reports are often difficult to tease out, as the definitions of young adults used by various researchers are not always made explicit and do not always agree. For example, Bilal[21] refers to middle school age youth as "children," which may lead some readers interested in young adults to overlook her important work. Furthermore, the participants in research focused on youth sometimes represent a range of ages that can include children and young adults or even children, young adults, and adults in the same study. This can make it difficult to tease out which findings apply to which developmental level. Studies are also limited in that much of what is known relates to the context of school and information-seeking behavior related to school assignments (i.e., imposed queries). Less is known about information-seeking behavior related to everyday-life needs (i.e., self-generated queries).

YALSA recently updated its research agenda and identified four priority areas, including research questions for each, where gaps in the research need to be filled: impact of library services, reading and resources, information-seeking behavior and needs, and informal and formal learning environments.[22] *YALSA's National Research Agenda on Libraries, Teens, and Young Adults 2012–2016* also contains a bibliography of works related to each area of focus.

Information Needs

There are several dimensions to understanding the information needs of young adults. For example, some information needs can be extrapolated from understandings of development, as outlined in chapter 2. Other information needs are determined by adults for young adults and may be expressed through school curricula and by parents and other adults interested in the welfare of youth. One of the characteristics of a need is that an individual can have a need without knowing that the need exists.[23] Thus, adults such as parents, teachers, coaches, ministers, and health professionals are considered to have some responsibility in identifying the information needs of young people and to assist youth in developing knowledge and skills needed for healthy development. [24]

In contrast to these approaches, research in the field of information-seeking behavior tends to be most interested in how specific user groups articulate their own relationship with information, including what kind of information they need, how they prefer to go about finding it, and what they do with the information they find.

One example related to imposed information-seeking behavior is Bowler's work,[25] which examines the metacognitive knowledge that students employ. Using Kulhthau's ISP as a framework, Bowler identified 13 categories of metacognitive knowledge that assist students as they work through the ISP:[26]

Balancing: making choices
Building a base: gaining foundational knowledge
Changing course: knowing when to change strategies
Communicating: asking for help, talking the problem out
Connecting: relating new knowledge to known knowledge
Knowing that you don't know: self-knowledge
Knowing strengths and weaknesses: self-assessment
Parallel thinking: thinking about more than one thing at a time
Pulling back and reflecting: getting some distance from a problem

Scaffolding: finding cognitive support
Understanding curiosity: role of interest in completing assignments
Understanding memory: keeping track of information
Understanding time and effort: time management

All these characteristics of metacognitive knowledge provide insight into how students successfully manage imposed queries. Understanding curiosity, however, is of special interest. Bowler found that the experience of curiosity was both pleasurable and painful for students.[27] In imposed information seeking, curiosity can help motivate students and keep them engaged in the completion of the assignment. The downside, however, when information seeking is imposed is that curiosity needs to be managed in terms of curiosity about content and curiosity about the ISP to stay on task. Students in Bowler's study needed to manage their curiosity and associated emotions of pleasure, pain, and frustration related to feelings of personal interest—emotions to which they could not fully attend—to meet the specifications and deadlines associated with the assignment. Curiosity needs to be maintained as a source of engagement with the task but also curtailed in the later stages of the ISP to bring the process to a successful conclusion in terms of meeting the teacher's expectations for the assignment. The tension that Bowler describes may be evidence of the situation where an imposed task starts to take on characteristics of a self-generated query as the student's interest is engaged. However, because of its imposed nature, the question must be responded to in the context of the assignment, and aspects of the topic that become personally interesting may need to be suppressed (at least for the time being) in favor of meeting teacher expectations and achieving a desired grade.

Posten-Anderson and Edwards[28] interviewed 28 girls (13 and 14 years old) about their information needs and found that their concerns centered on relationships, education, and work (which did not include homework or understanding course content). Furthermore, the types of information that they sought included facts, interpretations, and understandings. Of these, information needs for facts were the most easily satisfied. Questions were much harder to satisfy when they related to understanding or required interpretation, judgments, opinions, assessments of personal skills, or the development of strategies for dealing with personal situations. The girls perceived that the information needed for education and work was more available than the information needed for relationship concerns. In addition, the girls did not perceive the school library as being able to help them with their relationship concerns. A main information source was talking to other people.

Shenton and Dixon,[29] studying youth aged 3 to 18 years, constructed 12 categories of information needs that include both content and affective needs: "advice, spontaneous 'life situation' information, personal information, affective support, empathetic understanding, support for skill development, school-related subject information, interest-driven information, self-development information, preparatory information, reinterpretations/supplementations, and verification information."

Myers, Fisher, and Marcoux[30] studied the information needs of tweens (9–13 years old), with a special focus on the use of people as information sources. The tweens who participated in this study revealed information needs that mainly reflected short-term needs, including "school work, social events and relationships, sports and hobbies, consumer information, fashion and popular culture, neighborhood information, and stuff."[31] In addition, tweens indicated a need for information on staying safe and related issues, such as bullying, dangerous strangers, and dealing with drug and alcohol users. Tweens also revealed their need in interpersonal relationships to exchange "secret" information and the related need for maintaining privacy and establishing trust in relationships. These young people were also skeptical about the ability of formal resources to meet their personal information needs.

Latrobe and Havener[32] studied the school and personal information needs of high school honor students. They determined that for these students, school-related information needs were not only the most prevalent reason that they sought information but also the "most pressing" information needs. Other categories of information sought by these students included general information, future plans, relationships, current lifestyles, and health. An additional interesting finding in this study was students' conscious decision at times not to seek information, even though they believed that the information they needed was available. Students also reported figuring situations out on their own, without consulting information sources. In situations perceived as personal and subjective, the relevance of information sources was perceived to be low. Other reasons for not pursuing an information need were lack of available time, low priority, procrastination, and denial.[33]

Resource Preferences

The major resource types used by young adults for both imposed and self-generated information needs include other people, the Internet, and books. Young adults' use of social media, virtual worlds, and games is discussed in chapter 4.

People. One of the most consistent findings of research on information-seeking behavior is that people prefer other people as information sources.[34] People go to people first out of ease or convenience, in recognition of special expertise, and because they expect others to understand their personal context or situation regarding their information need. A preference for people is also demonstrated in the literature on young adult information-seeking behavior.[35]

In response to the understanding that peers are an important information source for young adults, Koo[36] investigated the information-seeking behaviors of newly arrived Korean immigrant youth, who had yet to establish relationships with peers in their new context. Although she designed her research using everyday-life information seeking as a framework, these socially isolated young adults primarily described information needs related to doing well in school, which was the main reason why they relocated to the United States. They articulated their information needs as improving English skills to facilitate school-related activities; social skills to facilitate friendships, fit in with peers, and acclimate to American culture; and study skills to ensure success in competitive academic environments in both the United States and Korea. These students also preferred people when they sought information. Rather than seeking information from peers, however, they demonstrated a heavy reliance on parents (especially mothers), teachers, and figuring things out on their own. Although this study focuses on immigrant youth, it is worth considering the impact on information-seeking behavior when thinking about other subgroups of young people who may feel socially isolated, such as youth who are being bullied or who are critically ill.

Internet. Young adults are also heavy users of the Internet. The most recent Pew Research Center report, *Teens and Technology 2013*, indicates that since 2006, young adults consistently demonstrate a higher use of the Internet than what is seen in adults 18 years and older.[37] Furthermore, young adults have been quick to adopt mobile technology. Today, almost all young adults, 12 to 17 years old, have cell phones, and the Pew report found that 37 percent of teens owned smartphones in 2012. Overall, three quarters of teens access the Internet using mobile devices. However, young adults from lower-income and lower-education homes continue to be less likely than more advantaged young people to access the Internet but "are just as likely and in some cases more likely than those living in higher income and more highly educated households to use their cell phone as a primary point of access."[38]

Similar to studies of information needs, library and information science studies of the use of electronic resources by young adults have been primarily interested in the context of school. These studies have uniformly found that most students like using the Internet, but they also indicate that students are not very skilled in using it to find information.[39] Vansickle[40] investigated whether differences in academic track (technical, college preparatory, and honors) affected students' ability to search the web. By self-rating their ability, participants reported that they taught themselves to use the Internet or they learned from friends. They all believed that they had "adequate" search skills, and there was no statistically significant difference in search knowledge by academic track.[41]

Recent research findings continue to question the extent to which young people are being taught to find, evaluate, and use information via formal instruction in school. Surveys of first-year college students reveal that students are very confident about their information skills and tend to be satisfied with the information they find, even though their information literacy skills are poor. When asked where they learned to find information, they credit a variety of sources (classroom teacher, school and public librarians, parents), but the majority of them report a perception of being "self-taught."[42]

Bilal's study of seventh graders' use of search engines for imposed and self-generated information seeking revealed difficulties in finding information due to a lack of skill in using search engines.[43] The participants were more successful in completing imposed assignments requiring the retrieval of factual information than they were in those requiring the construction of an answer from more than one resource. Bilal also investigated self-generated information seeking and found that students performed better on self-generated tasks and experienced a higher level of satisfaction with their search results.

Williams points out the need to recognize student development of reading, technology, and other literacies outside the classroom.[44] Many students have identities as readers and writers in the online environment that could inform classroom work as well as provide scaffolding for students with less access to or knowledge of technology.

Books. In addition to their interest in online reading and writing, young adults continue to read books in both print-based and electronic formats.[45] The use of books is often required in school assignments but is also a means for meeting self-generated needs for information and recreation. Research going back to the 1940s demonstrates that young people spend a limited amount of time reading for recreational purposes,[46] and research has shown that recreational reading declines with age, with 12 years old being a point at which time spent reading for pleasure drops significantly.[47] Gross found in her study of elementary schoolchildren that the use of books for imposed queries rose with grade level and was accompanied by a fall in book use for self-generated queries such that by sixth grade, the majority of book use was for school assignments.[48]

A number of national surveys have resulted in concern about the amount of time that young people spend reading.[49] As Moyer has noted, the definition of reading in these studies is fairly restricted, given the proliferation of media and the variety of reports that demonstrate young adult interest and participation in communication technologies.[50] Nonetheless, a 2009 National Endowment for the Arts study demonstrated an increase in reading, and more recent studies continue to support this finding.[51]

The 2010 Kaiser Family Foundation report on media use among 8- to 18-year-olds found that survey participants reported reading for pleasure an average of 38 minutes per day (down from 43 minutes in 2004).[52] Some other interesting findings about reading from this report are that reading for pleasure decreases with age (perhaps due to increases in school work), that heavy readers (an hour or more per day) earn better grades in school, that young people are less likely to use other media while reading for pleasure, and time spent on screen (computer or television) does not appear to be replacing time spent with print media.

A 2012 Pew report found that among 16- to 29-year-olds, 83 percent had read a book in the last year.[53] Young people read for school (or work), pleasure, and current events and to learn about topics of interest. E-books were more popular with 18- to 24-year-olds than among high school students, but young readers were more likely to read e-books on computers or on their cell phones than on dedicated e-book readers.

Due to the proliferation of communication technologies, it is increasingly important to integrate print and electronic sources into discussions about young adult reading and writing. Isolating the use of print from other formats (e.g., e-books, blogs, wikipages) does not give a full picture of young adult engagement with reading. Some works, especially reference works such as dictionaries and encyclopedias, are actually easier to use in electronic format. Why would using them online not count as reading? Full-text articles from magazines, newspapers, and academic journals are easier to access online, and they provide the same content. Novels, short stories, and poetry are increasingly accessible online. For example, Cory Doctorow made his novel *Little Brother* available for free download, in addition to distributing print copies available in bookstores.[54] Likewise, publishers have begun marketing books by posting chapters on their websites before full publication, offering short works online as "extras," and allowing for previews of content before purchase.[55] An impressive array of young adult literature is available online in full text for free. One place to begin locating these works is the Gizmo Freeware site.[56]

Sales reports indicate a rise in the purchase of young adult books in e-book format.[57] While an increasing amount of content from professional authors is available in nonprint formats, there are many websites where young adults can publish their own writing as well as read works published by their peers. As noted in the 2009 *JWT Trendletter*, reading is changing, and "the book isn't dying, it is evolving."[58] Williams described the impact of young adult immersion in literacy practices outside of school: "Computer technology has resulted in a generation as deeply and consistently immersed in writing as any in years."[59]

One of the customary observations made about young adults today is that generations born after 1980 (or thereabouts) have grown up in a world in which digital information and a proliferation of electronic media are commonplace. Sometimes termed *digital natives, millennials,* or *generation Y,* these young people are generally believed to be at home in the digital world and find technology easy to navigate.[60] There is increasing evidence, however, that this characterization does not apply across the board. Not all young people have an aptitude for technology, and comfort with technology is not necessarily an indicator of sophisticated use of technology or information literacy skills.[61]

Keep in mind: adults developed the media that youth are using, and beliefs about the effects of technology on younger generations are adult ideas minimally informed by young people themselves.[62] Herring proposes that the Internet generation is a transitional generation influenced by adult perceptions of young people's use of media and the extent to which young people embrace, resist, or subvert adult constructions made about them. Herring suggests that a "true" Internet generation will consist of those born at a time when digital technologies are completely taken for granted: "Babies born starting in the year 2050—the grandchildren and great-grandchildren of today's 'Internet Generation'—will enter a world in which digital technologies will have been an integral part of life for all . . . and in which the only reliable memories of pre-Internet life will be found in archives and historical accounts."[63]

Another issue to think about is how youth are "changed" by technology. Throughout the history of the development of formats for the communication, recording, and storage of information from writing on rocks forward, there has been analog conversation related to how new media will change culture, how culture changes media, and how the two mutually determine the forms, adoption, and use of technologies. Studies of youth show that they are less likely to feel that their use of technology defines who they are. Youth "understand that technology is not a solution to their problems. . . . It just helps people who know what they are looking for, find it."[64]

The first of those born after 1980 (millennials) are now in college and the workforce. Young adults—people currently between the ages of 12 and 18—increasingly represent a new generational divide, those born in the early 21st century, and they are being dubbed *generation Z* or the *iGeneration*. Generation Z is currently being typified by the prevalence of mobile technology. Research on these young people reveals that they have a strong attachment to their mobile phones and a preference for interacting online over communicating in person and they value the ability to be online over material goods and activities, such as going to the movies, to a restaurant, or to a sporting event.[65] It is likely that much of their reading, writing, and other literacies will be developed using electronic formats. Will this increasing emergence in technology change them? Will they change the nature of future technologies? Or will new technological developments result from the interaction between people and technology?

SPOTLIGHT!

Book Discussion Groups

Book discussion groups, where readers get together to talk about books, can take many forms and can include an array of book types. Book discussion groups can meet face-to-face or have virtual meetings. They can be used with assigned or recreational reading, and they can be adult supervised or self-directed. Book discussion groups can be organized around a specific genre or format or cover a variety of book types following the interests of the members. In thinking about books to propose for a book discussion group, remember that it is possible to incorporate numerous genres and formats. Don't forget about nonfiction!

Why start a young adult book discussion group?
   Book discussion groups

* Promote reading and provide social support for learning.
* Support the attainment of 21st-century literacies.
* Facilitate critical thinking and deeper understanding of texts.
* Give participants a venue in which to express their feeling, voice their opinions, and talk about ideas.
* Offer young adults a chance to practice leadership skills.

Tips:

* Start by involving the young adult advisory group in plans to develop the book discussion group. Initial members may be sought among young people who frequent the library. Find out what kind of discussion group would be attractive to them.
* The book discussion group can be a good way to bring young people into the library through outreach to other organizations in the community that are interested in young people.
* Book discussion groups do best when they set up guidelines for participation ahead of time and when they make sure that all members agree on how the group will function. Consider: How often will the group meet? Where will the group meet? How will books be chosen? Who will moderate the group? How will members communicate between meetings?
* A first item of business should be for members to give the discussion group a name. This helps build a sense of community.

- Book discussion group reading requires multiple copies of a single title. Reading choices will take some planning, whether you are considering using interlibrary loan or starting a collection especially for book club use in your library.
- If you can, provide food. Food promotes conversation.
- Consider a blog or wiki as one way to keep track of books that the group has read (or wants to read) and member book reviews.
- Make sure that there is time for members to socialize as well as discuss books.
- Recognize that groups take time to stabilize and that it is natural for membership to change over time.
- Let members take charge as much as possible. Members can help publicize the discussion group, develop discussion questions, and take turns leading the meetings. Adult supervised book discussion groups will be more meaningful for members if they feel ownership for the group.

MULTIPLE LITERACIES AND YOUNG ADULTS

As noted here, the proliferation of technologies, the information explosion, and the increasing complexity of our society have expanded the way that we think about literacy beyond the attainment of basic abilities in reading, writing, and arithmetic. Today, the potential for success is enhanced for people who have information literacy skills, information and communications technology skills, and media skills. In addition, there is a need for competence in content areas such as science, technology, engineering, and math, as well as other literacies, such as health, finance, and civics.

Unfortunately, available data suggest that a majority of young adults do not have the information literacy skills they need by the time that they complete high school.[66] This means that many are entering higher education or the workforce less prepared for their futures than what is optimal for them as individuals and society as a whole. There are similar concerns for other literacies as well. For example, there is a widespread popular belief that young people who have been raised in the digital age have a natural level of comfort and ability with technology. This belief is beginning to be debunked by research. Studies that measure information literacy skills, for example, demonstrate that not all young people have an affinity for technology and that comfort with technology does not necessarily correlate with skill level. Likewise, there is a well-documented concern with young adults' level of achievement in content areas such as science, technology, engineering, and math that are needed to fuel the future economy.[67]

The need to ensure that young adults attain a variety of literacies has led to the development of standards in education and librarianship that provide frameworks defining the knowledge and skills that young adults (and adults) need to maximize their future success. Three standards that relate directly to the concerns of information professionals are the *Framework for 21st Century Learning*, the American Association of School Librarians' *Standards for the 21st Century Learner*, and the *Common Core State Standards Initiative*.

Framework for 21st Century Learning

The *Framework for 21st Century Learning* is the product of the Partnership for 21st Century Skills, founded in 2002.[68] The partnership brought together a variety of stakeholders—such as the U.S. Department of Education, AOL Time Warner, Apple Computer, Cisco Systems, Dell Computer, Microsoft, the National Education Association, and others—to start a nationwide conversation about what kind of skills young people need. This work resulted in the development of the *Framework for 21st Century Learning*, which has now been formally adopted by 18 states. The framework focuses on building educational environments that support student outcomes in four areas, as well as the systems necessary to achieve desired student outcomes. Support systems include standards and assessments, curriculum and instruction, professional development, and learning environments. Student outcomes are categorized into four areas of focus: core subjects (the three *R*'s) and 21st-century themes, life and career skills, learning and innovation skills (the four *C*'s), and information media and technology skills.

Core subjects and 21st-century themes. Core subjects, or the three *R*'s, represent content areas and 21st-century themes that are identified as essential for everyone. Core subjects go beyond traditional reading, writing, and arithmetic to include all the core content areas identified in the No Child Left Behind Act of 2001. Core subject areas are English, reading or language arts, world languages, arts, mathematics, economics, science, geography, history, and government and civics. The 21st-century themes are content areas that are incorporated into learning to elevate knowledge in the core areas. Themes include global awareness; financial, economic, business, and entrepreneurial literacy; civic literacy; health literacy; and environmental literacy.

Life and career skills. This category of student outcomes is meant to provide students with the attributes needed to successfully navigate complex life and work environments. Abilities identified as needed in this area include flexibility and adaptability, initiative and self-direction, social and cross-cultural skills, productivity and accountability, and leadership and responsibility.

Learning and innovation skills. Creativity, critical thinking, communication, and collaboration are the four *C*'s defined as central to learning and being an innovator. Similar to life and career skills, the four *C*'s are seen as essential for life in an increasingly complex society and as critical for future success.

Information media and technology skills. This skill set recognizes that our society is and continues to be media rich and that individuals need to know how to access information, keep up with technological advancements, and collaborate and make original contributions using technological tools. The three key skills areas defined for student outcomes in this category are information literacy, media literacy, and information and communications technology literacy.

Standards for the 21st Century Learner

The American Association of School Librarians' document *Standards for the 21st Century Learner* focuses on teaching information literacy skills in schools, recognizing that information literacy has become a multidimensional concept involving basic literacies, such as the ability to read, as well as visual, technological, and other literacies.[69] These various literacies are reflected in defined skills, dispositions, responsibility, and self-assessment, identified as needed for individuals to learn independently or as members of a learning community.

The standards outline four areas of ability essential to learning for which skills, dispositions, responsibilities, and the ability of students to self-assess should be taught and evaluated. The first area of ability, "Inquire, think critically, and gain knowledge," harnesses curiosity to fuel the development of questions, the desire to consider the efficacy of information, and the ability to connect new learning to other knowledge previously gained.

The second area of ability, "Draw conclusions, make informed decisions, apply knowledge to new situations, and create information," focuses on information use. This area emphasizes that information gained can not only address current questions and product development but can also be applied to other situations and be used to fuel later investigations.

The third area of ability, "Share knowledge and participate ethically and productively as members of our democratic society," asserts the idea that individuals have a role to play in the creation of information, that it is important to connect learning to real world contexts, and that being a part of a community of learners requires various communication and technology skills. The ethical use of information and the use of information to promote democratic ideals are emphasized here.

The fourth area of ability, "Pursue personal and aesthetic growth," recognizes the personal dimension of information literacy and that lifelong learning for self-generated information needs is as essential to success as being able to be effective in imposed information-seeking contexts. It includes dispositions such as reading for pleasure as well as organizing information to facilitate responding to personal information needs.

Common Core State Standards Initiative

The major goal of the *Common Core State Standards Initiative* is to "provide a consistent, clear understanding of what students are expected to learn, so teachers and parents know what they need to do to help them."[70] The standards apply across K–12 grade levels and pertain to the subject areas of mathematics and English language arts, which includes standards for history, social studies, science, and technical subjects. Specific standards are provided for each grade level for each subject area. These standards describe what a student should learn and what teachers are responsible for teaching at a fine level of detail. The standards are meant to "define college and career readiness" and "lay out a vision of what it means to be a literate person in the twenty-first century."[71]

The *Common Core* has been adopted by the majority of states. Both the *Framework for 21st Century Learning* and the *Standards for the 21st Century Learner* have been cross-referenced to the *Common Core State Standards,* making it plain how these various standards overlap and support one another. The Partnership for 21st Century Skills provides access to the "P21 Common Core Toolkit" on its website,[72] and the American Association of School Librarians provides a "crosswalk" of the *Common Core State Standards* and the *Standards for the 21st Century Learner* on their website.[73]

SUMMARY

Young adults have a wide variety of information needs that span both imposed and self-generated contexts. Information needs can spring from the process of maturation, personal experience and interests, education and work, and may be identified by young adults themselves or the adults in their lives. Other people are the preferred source for information, followed closely by the Internet, but young adults also use print sources. As the number and variety of electronic media proliferate and modern society becomes more complex, it has become necessary to develop a variety of literacies. Standards such as the *Framework for 21st Century Learning*, the American Association of School Librarians' *Standards for the 21st Century Learner*, and the *Common Core State Standards Initiative* provide guidance to the support of lifelong learning and the types of knowledge and skills that students will need when they enter the workforce.

IMPLICATIONS FOR PRACTICE

- Models are one way to articulate facets of information seeking that are important and to promote discussion about personal experience and improved ways to facilitate information-seeking behavior.
- Information professionals should recognize that information seeking for self-generated questions is a different process, with different parameters and goals, than the process called for in an imposed query.
- Young adults' information needs related to school work are increasingly dictated by frameworks defined and imposed by government, professional associations, and other constituents.
- Assumptions that young adults are naturally good with technology, can easily find information, and have other related competencies are faulty. It is better to assume a lack of proficiency until skills are demonstrated.

QUESTIONS TO THINK ABOUT AND DISCUSS

1. How does understanding how young adults look for information inform professional practice?
2. What are some indicators of uncertainty that would indicate that students need assistance in their information search process?
3. What is the value of understanding information needs from the point of view of young adults?
4. What relationship do you think young adults have with technology? Consider discussing this question with young people.
5. How do the various standards for teaching and learning information, media, and technology literacies inform or possibly limit the role of information professionals who work with young adults?
6. Should literacies be taught to young adults, or should information professionals respond to the "natural" information behaviors that young people exhibit? Explain your thinking.

NOTES

1. Charles A. Lave and James G. March, *An Introduction to Models in the Social Sciences* (New York: University Press of America, 1993).
2. Donald Case, ed., *Looking for Information: A Survey of Research on Information Seeking, Needs, and Behavior*, 3rd ed. (Bradford, England: Emerald Group, 2012).
3. Melissa Gross, *Studying Children's Questions: Imposed and Self-Generated Information Seeking at School* (Lanham, MD: Scarecrow Press, 2006).
4. Robert S. Taylor, "The Process of Asking Questions," *American Documentation* 13, no. 4 (1962): 391–96.
5. Nicholas J. Belkin, "Anomalous States of Knowledge as a Basis for Information Retrieval," *Canadian Journal of Information Science* 5 (1980): 133–43.

6. Brenda Dervin and Patricia Dewdney, "Neutral Questioning: A New Approach to the Reference Interview," *Reference Quarterly* 25, no. 4 (1986): 506–13.

7. Melissa Gross and Matthew L. Saxton, "Who Wants to Know? Imposed Queries in the Public Library," *Public Libraries* 40 (2001): 170–76.

8. Nancy Pickering Thomas, Sherry R. Crow, and Lori L. Franklin, *Information Literacy and Information Skill Instruction: Applying Research to Practice in the 21st Century School Library* (Santa Barbara, CA: Libraries Unlimited, 2011).

9. Carol C. Kuhlthau, *Seeking Meaning: A Process Approach to Library and Information Services*, 2nd ed. (Westport, CT: Libraries Unlimited, 2004).

10. Carol C. Kuhlthau, "Kuhlthau's Information Search Process," in *Theories of Information Behavior*, ed. Karen Fisher, Sanda Erdelez, and Lynne E. F. Mckechnie (Medford, NJ: Information Today, 2005), 230–34.

11. Kuhlthau, *Seeking Meaning*, 82.

12. Kuhlthau, "Kuhlthau's Information Search Process."

13. Reijo Savaolainen, "Everyday Life Information Seeking," in *Theories of Information Behavior*, 143–48.

14. Denise Agosto and Sandra Hughes-Hassell, "Toward a Model of the Everyday Life Information Needs of Urban Teenagers, Part 1: Theoretical Model," *Journal of the American Society of Information Science and Technology* 57, no. 10 (2006): 1394–403; Denise Agosto and Sandra Hughes-Hassell, "Toward a Model of the Everyday Life Information Needs of Urban Teenagers, Part 2: Empirical Model," *Journal of the American Society of Information Science and Technology* 57, no. 11 (2006): 1418–426.

15. Reijo Savaolainen, "Everyday Life Information Seeking: Approaching Information Seeking in the Context of 'Way of Life,'" *Library and Information Science Research* 17 (1995): 259–94.

16. Agosto and Hughes-Hassell, "Toward a Model."

17. Agosto and Hughes-Hassell, "Toward a Model."

18. Agosto and Hughes-Hassell, "Toward a Model."

19. Denise Agosto, "Young Adults' Information Behavior: What We Know So Far and Where We Need to Go from Here," *Journal of Research on Libraries and Young Adults* (2011), http://www.yalsa.ala.org/jrlya/.

20. Melissa Gross, "Youth Information Needs and Behaviors," in *Encyclopedia of Library and Information Sciences*, 3rd ed., ed. Marcia Bates and Mary Niles Maack (New York: Taylor & Francis Group, 2010).

21. Dania Bilal, "Children's Use of the Yahooligans! Web Search Engine: I. Cognitive, Physical, and Affective Behaviors on Fact-Based Search Tasks," *Journal of the American Society for Information Science* 51, no. 7 (2000): 646–65; Dania Bilal, "Children's Use of the Yahooligans! Web Search Engine: II. Cognitive and Physical Behaviors on Research Tasks," *Journal of the American Society for Information Science and Technology* 52, no. 2 (2001): 118–36; Dania Bilal, "Children's Use of the Yahooligans! Web Search Engine: III. Cognitive and Physical Behaviors on Fully Self-Generated Search Tasks," *Journal of the American Society for Information Science and Technology* 53, no. 13 (2002): 1170–183.

22. Young Adult Library Services Association, *YALSA's National Research Agenda on Libraries, Teens, and Young Adults 2012–2016* (Chicago: American Library Association, 2011), http://www.ala.org/yalsa/guidelines/research/researchagenda.

23. Andrew Green, "What Do We Mean by User Needs?" *British Journal of Academic Librarianship* 5, no. 2 (1990): 65–78.

24. Virginia A. Walter, "The Information Needs of Children," *Advances in Librarianship* 18 (1994): 112–15.

25. Leanne Bowler, "A Taxonomy of Adolescent Metacognitive Knowledge during the Information Search Process," *Library and Information Science Research* 32, no. 1 (2010): 27–42; Leanne Bowler, "The Self-Regulation of Curiosity and Interest during the Information Search Process of Adolescent Students," *Journal of the American Society for Information Science and Technology* 61, no. 7 (2010): 1332–44.

26. Bowler, "A Taxonomy."

27. Bowler, "The Self-Regulation of Curiosity."

28. Barbara Posten-Anderson and Susan Edwards, "The Role of Information in Helping Adolescent Girls with Their Life Concerns," *School Library Media Quarterly* 22 (1993): 25–30.

29. Andrew K. Shenton and Pat Dixson, "Youngster's Use of Other People as an Information Seeking Method," *Journal of Librarianship and Information Science* 35, no. 4 (2003): 22.

30. Eric M. Myers, Karen E. Fisher, and Elizabeth Marcoux, "Studying the Everyday Information Behavior of Tweens: Notes from the Field," *Library and Information Science Research* 29, no. 3 (2007): 310–31.

31. Myers et al., "Studying the Everyday Information," 13.

32. Kathy Howard Latrobe and W. Michael Havener, "Information-Seeking Behavior of High School Honors Students: An Exploratory Study," *Journal of Youth Services in Libraries* 10 (1997): 188–200.

33. Latrobe and Havener, "Information-Seeking Behavior," 191.

34. Roma Harris and Patricia Dewdney, *Barriers to Information: How Formal Help Systems Fail Battered Women* (Westport, CT: Greenwood, 1994).

35. Denise Agosto and Sandra Hughes-Hassell, "People Places and Questions: In Investigation of the Everyday Life Information Seeking Behaviors of Urban Young Adults," *Library and Information Science Research* 27, no. 2 (2005): 141–63; Latrobe and Havener, "Information-Seeking Behavior"; Myers et al., "Studying the Everyday Information"; Posten-Anderson and Edwards, "The Role of Information"; Shenton and Dixson, "Youngster's Use of Other People."

36. Joung Hwa Koo, "Recent South Korean Immigrant Adolescents' Everyday Life Information Seeking When Isolated from Peers: A Pilot Study," *Journal of Research on Libraries and Young Adult* 3 (2012), http://www.yalsa.ala.org/jrlya/; Joung Hwa Koo, "Adolescents' Information Behavior When Isolated from Peer Groups: Lessons from New Immigrant Adolescents' Everyday Life Information Seeking," PhD diss., The Florida State University, 2013, http://www.lib.fsu.edu/find/etds.html.

37. Mary Madden, Amanda Lenhart, Maeve Duggan, Sandra Cortesi, and Urs Gasser, *Teens and Technology* (Washington, DC: Pew Research Center, 2013).

38. Madden et al., *Teens and Technology*, 2.

39. Raya Fidel, Rachel K. Davies, Mary H. Douglass, Jenny Holder, Carla J. Hopkins, Elisabeth J. Kushner, Bryan K. Miyagishima, and Christina D. Toney, "A Visit to the Information Mall: Web Searching Behavior of High School Students," *Journal of the American Society for Information Science* 50, no. 1 (1999): 24–37; Heidi Julien and Susan Barker, "How High-School Students Find and Evaluate Scientific Information: A Basis for Information Literacy Skills Development," *Library & Information Science Research* 31, no. 1 (2009): 12–17; Andrew Large, Jamshid Beheshti, and Haidar Moukdad, "Information Seeking on the Web: Navigational Skills of Grade-Six Primary School Students," in *Proceedings of the 62nd ASIS Annual Meeting*, Washington, DC, October 31–November 4, 1999; Raven McCrory Wallace, Jeff Kupperman, Joseph Krajcik, and Elliot Soloway, "Science on the Web: Students Online in a Sixth-Grade Classroom," *Journal of Learning Sciences* 9, no. 1 (2000): 75–104.

40. Sharon Vansickle, "Tenth Graders' Search Knowledge and Use of the Web," *Knowledge Quest* 30, no. 4 (2002): 33–37.

41. Vansickle, "Tenth Graders' Search," 36.

42. Melissa Gross and Don Latham, "What's Skill Got to Do with It? Information Literacy Skills and Self-Views of Ability among First Year College Students," *Journal of the American Society for Information Science & Technology* 63, no. 3 (2012): 574–83; Don Latham and Melissa Gross, "Broken Links: Undergraduates Look Back on Their Experiences with Information Literacy in K–12 Education," *School Library Media Research* 11 (2008), http://www.ala.org/ala/mgrps/divs/aasl/aaslpubsandjournals/slmrb/slmrcontents/volume11/latham-gross.cfm.

43. Bilal, "Children's Use of the Yahooligans! I–III."

44. Bronwyn T. Williams, "Leading Double Lives: Literacy and Technology in and out of School," *Journal of Adolescent & Adult Literacy* 48, no. 8 (2005): 702–6.

45. Kathryn Zickuhr, Lee Rainie, Kristen Purcell, Mary Madden, and Joanna Brenner, *Younger Americans' Reading and Library Habits* (Washington, DC: Pew Research Center's Internet & American Life Project, 2012).

46. Linda Teran Strommen and Barbara Fowles Mates, "Learning to Love Reading: Interviews with Older Children and Teens," *Journal of Adolescent & Adult Literacy* 48, no. 3 (2004): 188–200.

47. Gross, *Studying Children's Questions*; Vivian Howard, "The Importance of Pleasure Reading in the Lives of Young Teens: Self-Identification, Self-Construction, and Self-Awareness," *Journal of Librarianship and Information Science* 43 (2011): 46–55; Strommen and Mates, "Learning to Love Reading."

48. Gross, *Studying Children's Questions*.

49. National Endowment for the Arts, *Reading at Risk: A Survey of Literary Reading in America*, Research Division Report 46 (Washington, DC: National Endowment for the Arts, 2004); National Endowment for the Arts, *To Read or Not to Read: A Question of National Consequence*, Research Division Report 47 (Washington, DC: National Endowment for the Arts, 2007).

50. Jessica E. Moyer, "Teens Today Don't Read Books Anymore: A Study of Difference in Interest and Comprehension Based on Reading Modalities. Part 1: Introduction and Methodology," *Journal of Research on Libraries and Young Adults* 1, no. 1 (2010), http://www.yalsa.ala.org/jrlya.

51. National Endowment for the Arts, *Reading on the Rise* (Washington, DC: National Endowment for the Arts, 2009).

52. Victoria J. Rideout, Ulla G. Foehr, and Donald F. Roberts, *Generation M2: Media in the Lives of 8- to 18-Year-Olds* (Menlo Park, CA: Henry J. Kaiser Family Foundation, 2010), http://kaiserfamilyfoundation.files.wordpress.com/2013/01/8010.pdf.

53. Zickuhr et al., *Younger Americans' Reading*.

54. Cory Doctorow, *Little Brother* (New York: Tor Teen, 2008), http://craphound.com/littlebrother/download/.

55. Karen Springen, "Are Teens Raised to Download iTunes? Are Kids Going Online to Get Novels, Too?" *Publishers Weekly* (February 20, 2012): 20–23.

56. mr6n8, "Free eBooks Online for Teens and Young Adults," April 14, 2013, http://www.techsupportalert.com/free-books-teen-young-adult.

57. Springen, "Are Teens Raised to Download iTunes?"

58. Will Palley, *Gen Z: Digital in Their DNA* (April 12, 2012), 3, http://www.jwtintelligence.com/2012/04/april-trend-report-examines-digital-world-gen/#axzz2UmYtsLEV.

59. Williams, "Leading Double Lives," 703.

60. Pew Research Center, "Millennials: Confident. Connected. Open to Change," February 24, 2010, http://www.pewsocialtrends.org/2010/02/24/millennials-confident-connected-open-to-change/; Marc Prensky, "Digital Natives, Digital Immigrants," 2001, http://www.marcprensky.com/writing/prensky%20-%20digital%20natives,%20digital%20immigrants%20-%20part1.pdf.

61. Bowler, "The Self-Regulation of Curiosity"; Jin-Soo Chung and Delia Newman, "High School Students' Information Seeking and Use for Class Projects," *Journal of the American Society for Information Science & Technology* 58, no. 10 (2007): 1503–17; Eric M. Myers, Karen E. Fisher, and Elizabeth Marcoux, "Making Sense of an Information World: The Everyday Life Information Behavior of Preteens," *Library Quarterly* 79, no. 3 (2009): 301–41.

62. Susan C. Herring, "Questioning the Generational Divide: Technological Exoticism and Adult Constructions of Online Youth Identity," in *Youth, Identity, and Digital Media*, ed. David Buckingham (Cambridge, MA: MIT Press, 2008), 71–92.

63. Herring, "Questioning the Generational Divide," 83.

64. Herring, "Questioning the Generational Divide," 79.

65. Palley, *Gen Z*.

66. Educational Testing Service, *ICT Literacy Assessment: Preliminary Findings* (Princeton, NJ: Educational Testing Service, 2006), http://www.ets.org/Media/Products/ICT_Literacy/pdf/2006_Preliminary_Findings.pdf ; Melissa Gross and Don Latham, "Attaining Information

Literacy: An Investigation of the Relationship between Skill Level, Self-Estimates of Skill, and Library Anxiety," *Library & Information Science Research* 29, no. 3 (2007): 332–53; Peter D. Hart Research Associates / Public Opinion Strategies, *Rising to the Challenge: Are High School Graduates Prepared for College and Work? A Study of Recent High School Graduates, College Instructors, and Employers* (Washington, DC: Peter D. Hart Research Associates / Public Opinion Strategies, 2005), http://www.achieve.org/node/548; Jorden K. Smith, Lisa M. Given, Heidi Julien, Dana Ouellette, and Kathleen Delong, "Information Literacy Proficiency: Assessing the Gap in High School Students' Readiness for Undergraduate Academic Work," *Library and Information Science Research* 35, no. 2 (2013): 88–96.

67. U.S. Department of Education. *Improving Science, Technology, Engineering, and Mathematics (STEM) Education* (Washington, DC: U.S. Department of Education, 2012), http://www2.ed.gov/about/overview/budget/budget13/crosscuttingissues/stemed.pdf.

68. Partnership for 21st Century Skills, "Overview," http://www.p21.org/overview.

69. American Association of School Librarians, *Standards for the 21st Century Learner* (Chicago: American Library Association, 2007), http://www.ala.org/aasl/guidelinesandstandards/learningstandards/standards.

70. *Common Core State Standards Initiative*, "Implementing the Common Core State Standards," 2012, http://www.corestandards.org/.

71. *Common Core State Standards Initiative*, "Implementing the Common Core," 2012, para. 6.

72. Partnership for 21st Century Skills, "Tools and Resources," http://www.p21.org/index.php?option=com_content&view=article&id=1005&Itemid=236.

73. American Association of School Librarians, "Crosswalk of the *Common Core* and the *Standards for the 21st Century Learner*," http://www.ala.org/aasl/guidelinesandstandards/commoncorecrosswalk.

Chapter Four

Social Media and Games

This chapter covers young adults' use of social media and games, provides representative examples of currently popular media, and discusses issues of safety, privacy, and the development of identity online. Topics covered in this chapter include

- Social networking sites
- Multiuser virtual environments
- Games
- Spotlight! Gaming in the library
- Privacy, identity, and safety
- Spotlight! Internet safety
- Implications for practice
- Questions to think about and discuss

YOUNG ADULTS' USE OF SOCIAL MEDIA AND GAMES

It is commonly accepted knowledge that young adults are heavy users of technology for communication, content download, and recreation. Research shows that young adults are adapting readily to the use of mobile devices and that teens are increasingly using these devices to access the Internet.[1] There is a variety of applications available on mobile devices, many of which are free.

Young adults use numerous technologies for a myriad of activities. They are heavy users of texting and social media sites.[2] Yet, while teens use telephones, e-mail, and Twitter, they do not engage with these media at the level of frequency that they use texting and social networking sites (SNSs).[3] In addition to using the Internet for self-generated information needs, most young adults report using it to complete research assignments for school.[4] A recent Kaiser Family Foundation study reports that among 8- to 18-year-olds, video gaming is increasing and "the increase has been in cell phone and handheld playing rather than console playing."[5]

While these findings are useful for understanding young adult preferences for media and how they use it, they do not address what relationships young people have with the media and how they experience its use. Ito et al. undertook a three-year ethnographic study of young people's use of digital media in their everyday lives.[6] The researchers looked at how the social aspect of media use relates to engagement with media, interests, and the development of expertise. The report categorizes media use by young people in three ways: hanging out, messing around, and geeking out. Young people may engage in any and all of these relationships with media and may engage in more than one at a time.

"Hanging out" is about the desire to be with friends and how friendship interactions are extended by the use of media. Young adults want to get together with friends, and digital media allows them to do this when they cannot be physically together; it also allows them to socialize while they are completing other tasks (doing homework, engaging in hobbies, watching television, etc.). Digital communication—the sharing of content such as websites, video, music, pictures, and text—is the way that friendships are developed and maintained, and it provides content for social interactions. The use of media is also integrated into time that young people spend together offline in terms of shared media use when they are physically together (e.g., playing games, sharing music), as well as in terms of content used in social exchanges (e.g., talking about music they listened to, content they posted or reacted to).

"Messing around" describes a relationship with media as a source for finding information. It involves the use of search engines and other online information sources, and it tends to involve serendipity, experimentation, and play to locate content—rather than the kind of formalized searching associated with imposed queries, such as school assignments, or goal-directed self-generated information searching to complete a task, such as looking for cheat codes for games. Searching Google, browsing Wikipedia, and jumping links from site to site often reflects general open searching that does not have a defined goal in mind. This process is often used to gain knowledge in a new area of interest, attain technical (or other) skills, or develop competence in a game, utilizing tutorials, blogs, online forums, and videos. Messing around is also conceptualized as "experimentation" or "play," and it describes self-directed learning practices that young adults use to develop the expertise needed to participate in discussion and activities without needing to expose their novice status.

"Geeking out" describes an intense involvement, interest, and specialized knowledge that may be associated with technology. Deep interest and involvement in books (fandom) or with sports are considered examples of geeking out. It does not have to be strictly related to an interest in technology. Geeking out, however, does express a level of knowledge and skill that facilitates the navigation of sophisticated electronic content and makes possible participation in communities that share a high level of expertise in specific content areas. The ability to find as well as produce information is a hallmark of geeking out that is required to excel at complicated online games.

Ito et al. also point out that these genres of interaction with technology are dependent on access to computers, connectivity, and the ability to be autonomous when using technology. This kind of autonomy is fostered by personal ownership of technology. For young adults, access to the Internet is increasingly facilitated by ownership of smartphones and mobile devices such as iPods and mp3 players.[7] Furthermore, the digital divide appears to be closing on more than one front. In addition to access to mobile devices, most young adults today have access to a computer at home and at school.[8]

SOCIAL NETWORKING SITES

An SNS is an online service designed to facilitate social interaction. SNSs require users to register with the sites, and they allow users to establish personal profiles within the system, set up a social network, and connect with others around shared interests.[9] While these services do allow people to make connections with strangers, they are often used to maintain relationships with people that individuals are already connected with in some way offline.

SNSs are a common feature in the life of young adults.[10] They are the fastest-growing area of online activity, and 73 percent of 13- to 17-year-olds have an account on an SNS.[11]

Preference for specific SNS sites has changed over time and will likely continue to change in the future. While early on, MySpace (https://myspace.com/) was the most popular service, use of Facebook (https://www.facebook.com/) has since become more prevalent.[12] Current trends indicate that Tumblr is growing in popularity,[13] as is the phone app Instagram (owned by Facebook), which may be drawing users away from Facebook.

Tumblr (https://www.tumblr.com/), founded in 2007, is a subscription service that combines blogging with social media features. Users can share content that they have developed or are interested in, and they can connect to people that are interested in the same content. From a social media perspective, the focus is on common interests rather than relationships with friends and family. Examples of the types of content that can be shared in Tumblr are text, images, sound files, and animations, uploaded from the user's desktop, browser, phone, or e-mail. Users can follow others with similar interests and comment freely without worrying about word limits. Users can also have fun designing their pages to develop their own unique looks.

Instagram (http://instagram.com/#) supports sharing photographs and interfaces with Facebook, Twitter, Tumblr, Flickr, Foursquare, and e-mail. It allows users to edit their photos by providing a variety of filters that can make photos look more professional; users can also add effects to images to make them more interesting. This service is currently available only on iPhone and Android.

Other SNSs that are growing in popularity among young adults include Viddy, Pheed, Path, and Snapchat.[14] Viddy (http://www.viddy.com/) is an app that allows users to create videos complete with music and effects and to upload and publish them directly to Facebook, YouTube, Tumblr, and Twitter from a mobile device. Users can also choose to share with other Viddy users or limit access to the video to specified people via e-mail or text. Like other SNSs, it allows users to follow one another as well as search content within Viddy and access popular and new videos posted to the service.

Pheed (https://www.pheed.com/) is another SNS app that allows users to create and share a variety of content, such as text, photos, video, and audio. Pheed is unique in that it also incorporates fee-based services that allow users to subscribe to channels where live broadcasts are aired. Users can also host their own live events and charge for viewing.

Path (https://path.com/) is an SNS that is meant to be more intimate than Facebook, allowing users to share whatever is currently happening in their lives with friends and family. Path supports private one-on-one and small group messaging and chat features. Users share what they are doing, listening to, and thinking, and they can send "stickers" for a small fee. Content has the feel of a personal journal, and it can be published directly to Facebook, Foursquare, Tumblr, and Twitter from this platform when wider distribution of a moment is desired. Path also allows users to import content from these other SNSs directly into Path.

Some other sites that are less used by young adults but with which several SNSs interface include Twitter, Flickr, and Foursquare. Twitter (https://twitter.com/) is a service that allows users to share information, opinions, and comments in short "tweets" of 140 characters or less. Flickr (http://www.flickr.com/) is a site that supports sharing photos, and Foursquare (https://foursquare.com/) allows users to discover and save information about things to see and do in just about any geographical location, as well as recommendations and reviews provided by other Foursquare users.

Book Related Social Media and Apps

Several SNSs discussed here allow for sharing, discussing, and rating book titles. For example, a number of libraries, publishers, and young adults interested in books and reading have Facebook sites that seek to provide a community for young adult readers.

In addition to the SNSs discussed so far, there are SNSs and apps created expressly for people interested in books and reading. These sites are useful places to find book recommendations, discuss books with others, and learn more about favorite books and authors. Though not all of these sites are specifically for young adults, many include content of interest to young adults.

Goodreads (http://www.goodreads.com/) is a free site that was purchased by Amazon.com in 2013.[15] Goodreads provides a place where members can fill their "bookshelves" with books, post and read book reviews, find out what friends are reading, play trivia games, and engage in book discussions. It includes a book recommendation search engine and the ability to browse books by category and view the titles that proved most popular in the annual Goodreads Choice Awards (there are categories for best young adult fiction and best young adult fantasy and science fiction).

YALSA's Teen Book Finder (http://www.ala.org/yalsa/products/teen-bookfinder) is an app that works with iPod Touch, iPad, and iPhone devices. The app makes available the last three years of YALSA award lists and other lists. It allows users to search by title, author, genre, award, or booklist. Three titles are featured on the homepage and refreshed every day. In addition, this app allows users to find a book at a local library, build their own booklists, and share books on Twitter and Facebook.

There are also apps that provide interactive book experiences. For example, Versu (http://www.versu.com/) is a free iPad app that offers readers a chance to become the characters in a story. This app offers several story titles, and users decide which character in a story they want to be, providing their own dialogue, actions, reactions, and goals. Other characters in the story react, and the plot and ending of the story reflect the choices that the app user makes. Future versions of this app promise to allow users to make up their own characters, if they wish, and insert them into the story.

Beware Madame La Guillotine (http://timetravelertours.com/beware-mme-la-guillotine/) allows readers to interact with history—specifically, with a young stalker and murderess (Charlotte Corday) in Paris during the French Revolution. Readers can use the app to tour hot spots of Paris related to history, participate in games and activities related to the content, or just enjoy the story and pictures.

High School Bites (https://itunes.apple.com/us/app/high-school-bites/id441353691?mt=8) is a game app based on *The Chronicles of Vladimir Tod*, in which the protagonist, Vlad, faces all the typical developmental challenges of young adulthood with the added complications that come from having a vampire father and human mother. Oh, and a vampire slayer is out to get him![16] The game app is similar to the Pac-Man game of old except that it involves running down the school hallways to avoid vampire slayers while collecting blood bags and blood-filled peanut butter and jelly sandwiches to earn points. Available for iPhone, iPad, and iPod Touch.

MULTIUSER VIRTUAL ENVIRONMENTS

Another way that teens socialize and build online identities and communities is in multiuser virtual environments (MUVEs). Users of virtual worlds construct avatars that represent themselves in these environments. While some MUVEs are games, others are worlds that have been created where the users themselves construct the space and determine what happens in the environment. Users can visit MUVEs to hang out and socialize with friends; to attend live performances, poetry slams, and other gatherings; to play games; or to just explore the space. MUVEs may duplicate real-world settings (current or historical) or present a fantasy world. Some MUVEs allow users to construct their own space within the MUVE. There is also software that allows users to build their own social websites, such as Ning (https://www.ning.com/what-is-ning/). Users build their own "look" and identities in virtual environments, and they can use them to represent themselves as they are in life, in ways that they hope to be, or they can try on different identities to discover what possible identities are like.

Perhaps the most well-known virtual environment is Second Life (http://secondlife.com/whatis/?lang=en-US). It is a three-dimensional world populated by avatars, where users can purchase land, build their own environments, hold and attend events, make art, take pictures, create videos, and more. From 2005 to 2010, Teen Second Life was a "teen only" destination where 13- to 17-year-olds could meet in a private space where adults were admitted only under certain circumstances.[17] Teen Second Life closed in 2010, and the age for participation in Second Life was lowered to 16, but areas of Second Life that contain mature content continue to limit access to users 18 and older. Younger users, 13 to 15 years old, are given access only to portions of Second Life hosted by educational and nonprofit organizations of which they are members, and they are not allowed to make purchases from the Second Life Marketplace.

Another example of a MUVE used by young people is Habbo Hotel (https://www.habbo.com). To join Habbo, users must be 13 or older. Typical of virtual worlds, users create avatars and decorate their own rooms in the hotel. Habbo Hotel is a place to meet people and hang out, chat, date, create and play games, and join in competitions. Citizens can also get involved in the community in a number of ways, such as getting on committees to plan events and celebrations. Habbo is a free site but also has goods that can be purchased with real-world dollars. The currency used in Habbo is called Habbo credits, and these allow users to buy virtual furniture, clothes, and gifts for use in the Habbo Hotel world.

Whyville (http://www.whyville.net/smmk/nice), originally created in 1999, is a virtual world designed for teens and preteens. It currently has more than 5 million users,[18] who are citizens of Whyville, which has its own newspaper, government structure, and points of interest. Whyville has a "clam"-based economy, and users can earn clams by playing educational games and engaging in educational activities. Content on Whyville is created by a variety of well-known sources, such as the Getty and NASA, and it covers a variety of interests, including art, math, science, civics, and economics. The Whyville site encourages teachers to register and to incorporate Whyville in their teaching plans.

GAMES

Playing electronic games is a popular activity, especially for younger teens.[19] Among the types of devices that young adults have at home, 86 percent report owning a video game player (e.g., Wii, Xbox), and 68 percent own a handheld game player (e.g., Gameboy, PSP).[20] Of course, games can also be played via computer and mobile devices. In the Ito et al. study,[21] they found that 90 percent of respondents play electronic games and 24 percent play games every day. They also found that game playing is often a young person's first experience with a computer and that games are typically introduced in childhood. Gaming is a major form of entertainment for both genders and for all ages and socioeconomic levels.

Games can be a place to "hang out," "mess around," or "geek out." They can fill the need to waste time, get away from regular life, spend time with friends and family, or become deeply immersed in a game reality that involves other players. However, interest in many virtual reality games is concerned mainly with the game itself; socializing is secondary.[22] Games can provide social opportunities to build technical expertise in a natural, fun way. Skills are developed as part of playing the game and interacting with others, and they can be augmented through information seeking related to game play.[23] Increasingly, the value of using a games approach to education and training is being acknowledged and adopted in schools, business, and lifelong learning contexts. Games whose main purpose is not recreational are sometimes referred to as "serious games."

One way to think about recreational games is to categorize them by those that people can play on their own, those that facilitate social interaction, and those where social interactions are built around the games themselves.[24] Of course, games that can be played in solitude can also be played and shared in social situations, but the social situation is not required for play in this category of games.

Some games are specific to game players, computers, or mobile devices. Others are available through a variety of electronic media. Games are so pervasive that many computers and mobile devices come preloaded with games. First-person shooter games are a genre of video gaming in which the player takes on the point of view of a character in the game. These games, as the name implies, often involve shooting and a relationship to the game that is a personal perspective on the action.

Massively multiplayer online role-playing games (MMORPGs) are another genre of multiplayer video games. MMORPGs take place in virtual worlds that are persistent, which means that the play is continuous, involving whatever players are there. The game does not stop when a player leaves, and it is understood that he or she will need to catch up on activities and events that happened in his or her absence. MMORPG worlds are complex landscapes that have highly developed cultures, economies, and histories. Players take on characters, or roles, that they become when in the virtual world, and they interact with other characters developed by other people for play. Avatars developed for play in an MMORPG can be projections of players' actual identities or identities that the players wish to try on, or the avatar may be considered no more than a piece needed to play the game and, as such, have less significance to the player.[25]

Some examples of popular games that can be played in solitude or in the presence of others include Angry Birds, Plants vs. Zombies, Halo, DOOM, and Grand Theft Auto. In Angry Birds (http://www.rovio.com/en/our-work/games/view/1/angry-birds), players take on the cause of the birds against the egg-stealing pigs. These birds are angry! Players help the birds out by using them as projectiles in giant slingshots. There are a number of spin-offs of this popular title, which is available on a variety of platforms.

In Plants vs. Zombies (http://www.popcap.com/), players must defend against zombies, and their only line of defense is to hurl plants. What a way to protect your brain from being eaten! Different plants have different effects on the zombies. This game started as a PC/Mac game and is available on a variety of platforms.

Halo (http://www.halowaypoint.com/en-us/) is a first-person shooter science fiction game of interstellar war originally developed for the Xbox that allows for multiplayer matches. Many spin-off games, as well as novels, graphic novels, and videos based on the game's narrative, have been produced   and   continue   to   be   released   (http://halo.wikia.com/wiki/

Main_PageMain_Page). In 2011 Titan Books published *Halo: The Art of Building Worlds,*[26] which brings together the history and art of this longtime popular game, and it is just one example of how participating in video games may actually encourage the reading of print books.

DOOM (http://www.doomworld.com/) is also a first-person shooter game, but this one is based in the horror genre, as the point of the game is to fight off invading demons. Aside from its popularity, DOOM stands out in that its code was made generally available in 1997. The game has since been modified in endless ways by hackers, coders, and game players, and continued modification is encouraged.

Grand Theft Auto (http://www.rockstargames.com/grandtheftauto/) is another video game that has been wildly popular and expanded into a game series. It is available across a variety of platforms. Grand Theft Auto is a single-player game that, depending on the version, allows the player to fight crime in any of a variety of sites modeled after the real world and involves a lot of fast driving.

Some games that lend themselves well to social play, where the focus is on spending time with friends or family, include apps such as Temple Run and Words with Friends. In Temple Run (http://www.imangistudios.com/), players try to escape from the temple with a stolen idol while being chased by a variety of creatures and avoiding obstacles and traps of various types. To earn points and power while running, the player must collect coins and grab "power-ups" and "upgrades." The game ends when the player dies, however long that takes. Multiple characters can be played in the game, and friends can compete for the high score. Like other popular games, there are a series of Temple Run games. Temple Run can be played on mobile devices and online.

Words with Friends (http://www.wordswithfriends.com/) is a word game that can be played on a mobile device or on Facebook. The game is very similar to the board game Scrabble in that it involves forming words horizontally or vertically using letter tiles and starting from a place on the "board." There is a built-in dictionary of acceptable words, and the game ends when a player runs out of tiles.

Unlike the games described here, which provide entertainment and facilitate socializing, MMORPGs are games that draw people who have a high interest in the game for its own sake. There is a social component because other people are playing at the same time, but players are mainly there to play and be immersed in the environment. Having said that, research shows that 80 percent of players play with friends, family, or romantic partners and that friendships and even marriages result from play.[27]

These games are very complex and require knowledge, skills, and practice. This is a context where specialized knowledge is built, and players gain social status based on gaming ability. Players spend an average of 22 hours a week in play, and 60 percent of participants in a study of MMORPGs reported playing for 10 hours at a time.[28]

There are several types of social groups that develop around play. For example, there may be certain tasks within a game that cannot be accomplished by a single player but rather require coordination among players. In this case, members need to find a group to accomplish the task. There are also long-term groups referred to as *guilds* or *clans* that form to work on developing a skill, bringing novice players along, or achieving other goals related to playing the game.

Yee argues that MMORPGs offer young adults an environment in which they can safely experiment with identity as well as develop social skills and leadership skills that are transferable to their everyday lives.[29] Leadership training is another skill embedded in play that can be developed in the context of the game. Gee argues that video games are a "technology built around identities. . . . They operate with—that is, they build into their designs and encourage—good principles of learning, principles that are better than those in many of our skill-and-drill, back-to-basics, test-them-until-they-drop schools."[30] While there have been research studies that describe ties between violent games and negative affect and behavior, recent critiques of these studies question the validity of the measures used and the internal validity of the designs, pointing to the need to consider the influence of contextual variables (e.g., family environment, symptoms of depression) on outcomes.[31] Today, there are many adults who have grown up playing video games of various types, and their continued popularity and integration into learning environments suggest that games are here to stay. Other research is emerging that demonstrates increases in problem-solving skills and grades associated with video games that require the development of strategies to win,[32] and findings are beginning to challenge the idea that video games promote aggressiveness in players.[33]

Another facet of MMORPGs is that the development of expertise and knowledge can involve information seeking that takes place outside the game in addition to knowledge that may be acquired in clans or other social groups developed around the game. Cheats, cheat codes, fan sites, modifications, hacks, game guides, and so on, can all be useful to players seeking to advance in the game.

Some examples of popular MMORPGs are World of Warcraft and Star Wars. World of Warcraft (http://www.worldofwarcraft.com/) takes place in a fantasy realm that contains imaginary creatures, quests, and magic. This persistent virtual world has millions of players and is broken up into realms to support the number of people who want to play. Players develop a main character that they want to be, but they can also develop alternate characters that can be active in the game. This allows players to experience different roles in the game. It is possible for players to play on their own, but as a player advances in the game, social interaction becomes increasingly necessary to continue advancing in the game, as each player typically has a set of characteristics or skills and will benefit from alliances with others. There is a wide range of novels, short stories, manga, and e-books based on the World of Warcraft universe. World of Warcraft offers a free level of play but above that requires a subscription.

Star Wars: The Old Republic (http://www.swtor.com/) is a relatively new MMORPG set in the *Star Wars* story but in a time before the popular motion pictures take place. Players pick sides (Galactic Republic or Sith Empire) and take one of many familiar roles from the story, such as Jedi knight or Sith warrior. Books have been published describing how the game was created,[34] and it has been the subject of Internet comics and novels since before its release. Star Wars has a free play option, but full access to the game requires a subscription.

SPOTLIGHT!

Gaming in the Library

Libraries have a long history of collecting and circulating games as well as developing programs that focus on games.[a] Studies show that game clubs have the potential to engage students in learning, improve academic skills, and promote information literacy.[b] Games promote competition and cooperation as well as friendships based on common interests and a sense of community.[c]

Promoting games in the library can attract young users, increase use of the library as a social space, and help the library achieve its mission, goals, and objectives, whether to support recreation or learning. Game programs can increase young adult participation in other library programs, such as book clubs, volunteer programs, and summer reading programs.[d]

Learning to design games can help students develop not only technical skills but also problem-solving, communication, collaboration, and other literacy skills.[e] Libraries are increasingly supporting "maker spaces" where users can create their own games.[f]

Tips:

- Think about the space available in the library for gaming. Find a location that can accommodate a large group and the noise that peo-

ple and games will generate and that has good lighting and a sufficient number of power outlets. The space should also be comfortable
and inviting.
* Get advice from young adults about what game systems and games
the library should collect. Remember that, like any other library
collection, a development policy should be created for the game
collection, including procedures for handling challenges.
* Consider incorporating games into existing library programs (e.g.,
summer reading) as well as developing programs where the focus is
purely on games.
* Remember to advertise gaming events using a variety of venues,
including speaking with young people in the community, visiting
local schools and spots, and utilizing social media. Engage young
adults in planning, promoting, and presenting programs. Encourage
them to bring their friends!

Program ideas:

* *Geeking out!* A get-together to share and learn more about information sources for improving your game. Get advice on how to find
tips, codes, and other game-related information online from experienced gamers and your librarian.
* *Get your game on!* A game club that provides technology, space,
and a social atmosphere and supports a variety of game types in a
safe environment.
* *Beyond play.* A game design workshop where young adults learn to
use video game design software and work in groups to design, develop, and play games of their own creation.

Notes:

a. Scott Nicholson, "Playing in the Past: A History of Games, Toys,
and Puzzles in North American Libraries," *Library Quarterly*
83, no. 4 (2013): 341–61.
b. Ron T. Brown and Tamara Kasper, "The Fusion of Literacy and
Games: A Case Study in Assessing the Goals of a Library Video
Program," *Library Trends* 61, no. 4 (2013): 755–78.
c. Angela M. Vanden Elzen and Jacob Roush, "Brawling in the
Library: Gaming Programs for Impactful Outreach and Instruction at an Academic Library, Library," *Library Trends* 61, no. 4
(2013): 802–13.
d. Kat Werner, "Bringing Then In: Developing a Gaming Program
for the Library," *Library Trends* 61, no. 4 (2013): 790–801.

e. Charlene O'Hanlon, "Don't Play It, Make It!" *Technical Horizons in Education Journal* 38, no. 8 (2011): 16, 18; Kathy Sanford, and Leanna Madill, "Understanding the Power of New Literacies through Video Game Play and Design," *Canadian Journal of Education* 30, no. 2 (2007): 432–55.

f. Nicholson, "Playing in the Past."

PRIVACY, IDENTITY, AND SAFETY

Whether teens are using media for schoolwork, to follow personal interests, to socialize, or to play, it is important that they know how to protect themselves. They need specific knowledge to protect their personal safety and privacy as well as to understand the importance of managing their online identities. Research tells us that most young adults are not worried about their online safety.[35] Research also reveals that young adults online are confronted by hate speech,[36] perpetrate and are victims of bullying,[37] perpetrate and are victims of cyber dating abuse,[38] do not necessarily know how to handle being harassed online,[39] and may share personally identifying information with strangers.[40]

In recognition of the potential risks that online activity can pose, adults have sought to control young adult behavior online by setting up rules and restricting access, but this does not always work. It is not uncommon for young adults to find work-arounds and hide their activities to achieve the access that they need to meet their informational, social, and recreational needs.[41] Even though many services restrict registration to users 13 and older, this does not always keep younger teens and tweens from signing up.[42]

Online safety, like learning to cross the street and to stay safe in the shopping mall, is one of those areas where adults may need to anticipate young adults' information needs and work to build their competence in knowing how to comport themselves online. Young adults need to be aware that they do not have full control of personal content online. Users need to be careful with all personally identifying information, such as full name, physical address, phone numbers, and social security numbers. Being careful with this information will help them avoid identity theft and the potential that their personally identifying information will be used in ways that could prove harmful to their personal reputation or safety.

A good rule of thumb is not to post content unless the poster is going to be comfortable when he or she finds out that parents, teachers, potential future schools and employers, government agents, and others have accessed the post now or in the future. Limiting public access on SNSs to personal data is a good idea, but young adults should remember that "friends" may take content and repost it without asking permission. In some cases, data that have been deleted may still exist in archives, on friends' phones, and in files kept by people and organizations that the original poster does not personally know. Users may think that they own their content, when in fact it may legally belong to the service where they are posting and, under the right conditions, could be subject to subpoena. Young adults can benefit by sharing their concerns about privacy, as well as what they know about how to protect personal data, with friends. Friends and family can help protect one another's privacy by asking permission before reposting content and before posting content that identifies others (such as pictures, names, and quotes).

All users of electronic media need to be aware that content shared electronically has a way of following people into aspects of their lives that they may not have contemplated or predicted. For this reason, it is important for users to consider how they portray themselves, their activities, and their interests and the consequences that online behavior can have on important life choices and goals, such as admittance to schools and employment opportunities.

This reality can be difficult to accept and to conform to at a time in life when it is natural and even expected that young people are trying on new identities and roles as part of figuring out who they are and who they want to be in the future. After all, the point of social media and gaming is to socialize, make new friends, explore identities, and have fun. Librarians at the University of British Columbia have developed an interesting website called Digital Tattoo (digitaltattoo.ubc.ca/), which contains information and tools for understanding personal presence online. The site provides links to other sites that allow young adults to see what kind of identities they are forming on the Internet. The site also provides quizzes and other tools to help young people think about and construct the kind of presence they want to build for themselves online.

Cyberbullying

While many concerns have been voiced about the danger of sexual predators online, the incidence of this kind of activity is less pervasive than what many think.[43] Cyberbullying, however, is an online danger that affects a significant number of youth. A review of studies of cyberbullying in peer-reviewed journals demonstrates a range of victimization rates, from 5.5 to 72 percent.[44] Cyberbullying is bully behavior perpetrated online and can include threats, libel, angry or offensive language, harassment, impersonation, making secrets public, excluding someone from an online group, stalking, posting humiliating photos, and perpetrating other forms of willful harm.[45] Work by Sticca and Perren[46] has shown that cyberbullying may be more harmful than in-person bullying due to the extremely public nature of online attacks as well as the relative ability of bullies to hide their identities in online contexts.

The effects of cyberbullying can be quite severe and include feeling embarrassed, sad, fearful, or angry and engaging in behaviors such as suicidal thoughts, drug use, fighting, dropping out of school, and bringing weapons to school.[47] The news media have verified the devastating effect that cyberbullies can have on their victims, with heartbreaking reports of young people who have committed suicide after invasions of their privacy and public cruelty inflicted on them through electronic media.[48]

What can be done? Young people should react to witnessing bullying by telling a trusted adult, by defending the victim, and by not doing anything that might reinforce this kind of behavior on the part of the bully. The response of bystanders to bullying is an important influence on the prevalence of bullying behavior. Research has shown that when peers do not accept bullying behavior and adults do not sanction it, bullying behavior declines.[49] It is also important that bullies not be allowed to be anonymous. Tracing IP addresses and outing bullies can restore a sense of control for victims and reduce incentives for bullies to continue this type of behavior. Another way to combat bullying is through building strong bonds between adults and young people and using the power of the group to influence behavior.[50] Positive youth development, discussed in chapter 2, is an example of this kind of effort.

SPOTLIGHT!

Internet Safety

The Internet provides lots of fun and informative things to do, but it also has a dark side. Libraries can help inform young adults on how to respond to negative content, protect privacy, and build a community of users who know how to respect and support themselves and one another when interacting on the web, sharing content, and seeking information. Furthermore, these goals may be best achieved through education rather than by restricting access. The competencies that youth need to achieve to be lifelong learners and to master 21st-century literacies require engaging with social media and other interactive web tools.[a]

Tips:

* Young people aren't necessarily concerned about Internet safety. They think that they know what they need to know about Internet safety. Engaging young people in presenting content or incorporating true life stories may help to make programming more relevant.

- Remember that technology changes rapidly and that new Internet services and media are constantly being produced. These changes need to be monitored for their effect on the knowledge and skills needed for Internet safety.
- Libraries should have an Internet safety policy in place that reflects the needs of the local community. The policy should be posted in the library and made widely available to users.
- Parents and other adults who work with youth may also need education regarding how to stay safe on the Internet.

Program ideas:

- *What's your rep? Building the online identity you want.* What does your digital footprint say about you? Explore the nature of online identity using tools from the Digital Tattoo website and social media profiles.
- *He/she loves me; he/she loves me not*: Learn the signs of cyber dating abuse and how to promote healthy relationships online and off.
- *Cover up your digital footprint!* Learn how the privacy settings on Facebook and other social media work, what Internet sites can do with your data, and how to protect yourself and the people you care about online.

Note:

    a. Barbara A. Jansen, "Internet Filtering 2.0: Checking Intellectual Freedom and Participative Practices at the Schoolhouse Door," *Knowledge Quest* 39, no. 1 (2010): 46–53.

Cyber Dating Abuse

While less is known about cyber dating abuse—psychological or emotional abuse and attempts at control between dating partners via technology—this is an area that research is starting to address. A recent study supported by the National Institute of Justice[51] looked at the prevalence of cyber dating abuse and its relationship to other forms of teen dating violence. More than 25 percent of the 5,647 respondents reported being the victim of cyber dating abuse within the last year, and about 10 percent self-identified as perpetrators of cyber dating abuse.

    Cyber dating abuse is perpetrated by young men and young women and is described as reciprocal in some relationships. The most common form of abuse reported by perpetrators and victims was using a partner's Facebook account without his or her knowledge.[52] Victims reported getting unwanted e-mail about engaging in sexual acts, being pressured to send naked photos of themselves, and receiving threatening texts and e-mail that made them feel unsafe. Victims talked about partners who bombarded them with texts and e-mail, said mean things about them online, and posted embarrassing photos so that others could see them. Perpetrators also reported that they had made mean public statements and posted embarrassing photos of their partners online.

Among respondents, victims of cyber dating abuse were more likely than nonvictims to have experienced sexual coercion offline, and perpetrators were more likely than nonperpetrators to have sexually coerced someone offline. In response to all these findings, the study authors suggest the development of prevention programs administered through schools and the use of technology to spread awareness, change attitudes, and report occurrences of cyber sexual abuse.

A good resource for young adults to know about is the website loveisrespect.org, which provides a variety of information and help. Assistance is provided one-on-one in a chat room environment, by text ("love is" to 77054), and by toll-free phone service (866-331-9474 or 866-331-8453 TTY).

SUMMARY

Whether hanging out, messing around, or geeking out, young people are media users, and trends show that an increasing number of young adults own and use mobile devices. Electronic media provides venues for identity development and connection to peers and family, and it contributes to the development of reading and writing skills. However, immersion in media brings with it the need for specific knowledge and skills to protect privacy and identity and to keep young adults safe online. It is important for young adults to understand what the risks to their well-being are, how to avoid potential dangers, and what to do if confronted with messages of hate and other offensive behavior and content online. This is an area where adults interested in the welfare of youth will want to proactively provide for these information needs and help young people build a culture of support in which cyberbullying, cyber dating abuse, and breaches of privacy are considered unacceptable.

IMPLICATIONS FOR PRACTICE

- SNSs, apps, and other media can be used to extend the reading experience as well as connect young adults to books.

- Young adults continue to need education and guidance on how to present (and protect) themselves online.
- Young adults may need training to understand what constitutes cyberbullying and cyber dating abuse as well as training to know what to do if they are a victim or a witness.

QUESTIONS TO THINK ABOUT AND DISCUSS

1. What literacies are required to be competent users of SNSs and games?
2. What is the best way to help young adults build online relationships that are respectful?
3. In what ways do various electronic media facilitate the development of identity?
4. Virtual worlds and games are being increasingly incorporated into education. What might be the long-term effects of this on education, professional training, and recreational games?

NOTES

1. Mary Madden, Amanda Lenhart, Maeve Duggan, Sandra Cortesi, and Urs Gasser, *Teens and Technology* (Washington, DC: Pew Research Center, 2013); Andrea Pieters and Christine Krupin, "Youth Online Behavior," Harris Interactive for McAfee, June 1, 2010, http://safekids.com/mcafee_harris.pdf; Victoria Rideout, "Social Media, Social Life: How Teens View Their Digital Lives. A Common Sense Media Research Study," June 26, 2012, http://www.commonsensemedia.org/research/social-media-social-life.

2. Rideout, "Social Media, Social Life"; "How Teens Use Media: A Nielsen Report on the Myths and Realities of Teen Media Trends," June 2009, http://www.nielsen.com/us/en/reports/2009/How-Teens-Use-Media.html.

3. "How Teens Use Media: A Nielsen Report on the Myths and Realities of Teen Media Trends," June 2009, http://www.nielsen.com/us/en/reports/2009/How-Teens-Use-Media.html.

4. Pieters and Krupin, "Youth Online Behavior."

5. Victoria J. Rideout, Ulla G. Foehr, and Donald F. Roberts, "Generation M2: Media in the Lives of 8- to 18-Year Olds: A Kaiser Family Foundation Study," January 2010, http://kff.org/other/poll-finding/report-generation-m2-media-in-the-lives/.

6. Mizuko Ito et al., *Hanging Out, Messing Around, and Geeking Out: Kids Living and Learning with New Media* (Cambridge, MA: MIT Press, 2009).

7. Rideout et al., "Generation M2."

8. Rideout et al., "Generation M2."

9. Danah M. Boyd and Nicole B. Ellison, "Social Networking Sites: Definitions, History, and Scholarship," *Journal of Computer-Mediated Communication* 13, no. 1 (2008): 210–30.

10. Pieters and Krupin, "Youth Online Behavior"; Rideout, "Social Media, Social Life."

11. Pieters and Krupin, "Youth Online Behavior."

12. Rideout, "Social Media, Social Life."

13. Victor Luckerson, "Is Facebook Losing Its Cool? Some Teens Think So," *Time*, March 8, 2013, http://business.time.com/2013/03/08/is-facebook-losing-its-cool-some-teens-think-so/.

14. Ilya Povin, "Teens Drive Pheed to #1," *Forbes*, February 20, 2013, http://www.forbes.com/sites/ilyapozin/2013/02/20/teens-drive-pheed-to-1-social-app/.

15. Amazon.com, "Press Release: Amazon.com to Acquire Goodreads," http:// phx.corporate-ir.net/phoenix.zhtml?c=176060&p=irol-newsArticle&ID=1801563&highlight=.

16. Heather Brewer, *Eighth Grade Bites*, book 1 of *The Chronicles of Vladimir Tod* (New York: Dutton, 2007).

17. Linden Research, "History of Second Life," June 25, 2013, http://wiki.secondlife.com/ wiki/History_of_Second_Life.

18. Numedeon, "Whyville Demographics," 2009, http://b.whyville.net/top/pdf/whyville_demographics.pdf.

19. Pieters and Krupin, "Youth Online Behavior."

20. Rideout, "Social Media, Social Life."

21. Ito et al., *Hanging Out, Messing Around*.

22. Ito et al., *Hanging Out, Messing Around*, 22.

23. Ito et al., *Hanging Out, Messing Around*, 220.

24. Ito et al., *Hanging Out, Messing Around*.

25. Nick Yee, "The Dedalus Gateway: The Psychology of MMORPGs, Avatar and Identity," 2004, http://www.nickyee.com/daedalus/gateway_identity.html.

26. Titan Books, *Halo: The Art of Building Worlds* (London: Titan Books, 2011).

27. Nick Yee, "The Dedalus Gateway: The Psychology of MMORPGs Playing Together," last updated 2004, accessed June 27, 2013, http://www.nickyee.com/daedalus/gateway_playtogether.html

28. Nick Yee, "The Dedalus Gateway: The Psychology of MMORPGs, Player Demographics," 2004, http://www.nickyee.com/daedalus/gateway_demographics.html.

29. Yee, "The Dedalus Gateway: Player Demographics."

30. James Paul Gee, *What Video Games Have to Teach US about Learning and Literacy* (New York: Macmillan, 2003), 205.

31. Christopher J. Ferguson, "Video Games and Youth Violence: A Prospective Analysis in Adolescents," *Journal of Youth & Adolescence* 40 (2011): 377–91; Jose J. Valadez and Christopher J. Ferguson, "Just a Game after All: Violent Video Game Exposure and Time Spent Playing Effects on Hostile Feelings, Depression, and Visuospatial Cognition," *Computers in Human Behavior* 28, no. 2 (2012): 608–16.

32. Paul J. C. Adachi and Teena Willoughby, "More Than Just Fun and Games: The Longitudinal Relationships between Strategic Video Games, Self-Reported Problem Solving Skills, and Academic Grades," *Journal of Youth and Adolescence* 42, no. 7 (2013): 1041–52.

33. Christopher J. Ferguson, Adolfo Garza, Jessica Jerabeck, Raul Ramos, and Mariza Galindo, "Not Worth the Fuss after All? Cross-Sectional and Prospective Data on Violent Video Game Influence on Aggression, Visuospatial Cognition and Mathematics Ability in a Sample of Youth," *Journal of Youth and Adolescence* 42, no. 8 (2013): 109–22.

34. Daniel Erikson, *The Art and Making of "Star Wars": The Old Republic* (San Francisco: Chronicle Books, 2011).

35. Pieters and Krupin, "Youth Online Behavior."

36. Rideout, "Social Media, Social Life."

37. Pieters and Krupin, "Youth Online Behavior."

38. Janine M. Zweig, Meredith Dannk, Jennifer Yahner, and Pamela Lachman, "The Rate of Cyber Dating Abuse among Teens and How It Relates to Other Forms of Teen Dating Violence," *Journal of Youth and Adolescence* 42, no. 7 (2013): 1063–77.

39. Pieters and Krupin, "Youth Online Behavior."

40. Pieters and Krupin, "Youth Online Behavior."

41. Ito et al., *Hanging Out, Messing Around*; Pieters and Krupin, "Youth Online Behavior."

42. Denise E. Agosto and June Abbas, "Youth and Online Social Networking: What Do We Know So Far?" in *The Information Behavior of a New Generation*, ed. Jamshid Beheshti and Andrew Large (Lanham, MD: Scarecrow Press, 2013), 117–41.

43. Denise E. Agosto and June Abbas, "Teens, Social Networking, and Safety and Privacy Issues," in *Teens, Libraries, and Social Networking: What Librarians Need to Know*, ed. Denise E. Agosto and June Abbas (Santa Barbara: Libraries Unlimited, 2011), 59–76; Annette Lamb, "Social Networking: Teen Rights, Responsibilities, and Legal Issues," in *Teens, Libraries, and Social Networking*, 77–96.

44. Sameer Hinduja and Justin W. Patchin, "Social Influences on Cyberbullying Behaviors among Middle and High School Students," *Journal of Youth and Adolescence* 42 (2013): 711–22.

45. Agosto and Abbas, "Teens, Social Networking"; Hinduja and Patchin, "Social Influences."

46. Fabio Sticca and Sonja Perren, "Is Cyberbullying Worse Than Traditional Bullying? Examining the Differential Roles of Medium, Publicity, and Anonymity for the Perceived Severity of Bullying," *Journal of Youth and Adolescence* 42 (2013): 739–50.

47. Hinduja and Patchin, "Social Influences."

48. Doug Stanglin and William M. Welch, "Two Girls Arrested on Bullying Charges after Suicide," *USA Today*, October 16, 2013, http://www.usatoday.com/story/news/nation/2013/10/15/florida-bullying-arrest-lakeland-suicide/2986079/; Aisha Sultan, "Has Bullying Gotten Worse? *Bismark Tribune*, November 12, 2013; John Schwartz, "Bullying, Suicide, Punishment," *New York Times*, October 2, 2010, http://www.nytimes.com/2010/10/03/weekinreview/03schwartz.html?_r=0.

49. Hinduja and Patchin, "Social Influences"; Sticca and Perren, "Is Cyberbullying Worse?"

50. Hinduja and Patchin, "Social Influences."

51. Zweig et al., "The Rate of Cyber Dating Abuse."

52. Zweig et al., "The Rate of Cyber Dating Abuse."

Chapter Five

Fiction and Fan Fiction

This chapter discusses fiction for young adults and fan fiction:

- Fiction, reading, and young adults
- Fantastic fiction
- Realistic fiction
- Fan fiction
- Evaluating and promoting fiction
- Spotlight! Booktalks
- Spotlight! Readers' advisory
- Implications for practice
- Questions to think about and discuss

Graphic novels and other formats are discussed in chapter 8.

FICTION, READING, AND YOUNG ADULTS

Fiction, according to the *Oxford Concise Dictionary of Literary Terms*, is "the general term for invented stories, now usually applied to novels, short stories, novellas, romances, fables and other narrative works in prose."[1] Like adult fiction, the world of young adult fiction consists of a variety of genres and subgenres, including fantasy, horror, science fiction, adventure, suspense, sports, romance, and so-called problem novels. There is something to appeal to almost every taste and interest. Young adults read fiction for recreational, informational, and educational purposes (e.g., school assignments, personal interest). As Rudine Sims Bishop memorably pointed out, a work of fiction can serve as a mirror, reflecting a reader's culture and experiences, or as a window, opening up vistas onto other cultures and other experiences.[2]

Bishop was discussing, in particular, the importance of African American youth having fiction available that can serve as a mirror, reflecting their culture and experiences as members of a microculture within a predominantly white society. More broadly speaking, her analogies provide an apt way of looking at how fiction can work for all readers. The best fiction arguably serves as both a mirror and a window, validating and broadening their experiences.

Fiction can also help address young adults' developmental needs by providing models of behavior and information related to physical, sexual, cognitive, emotional, and social maturation. As such, reading fiction aids in young adults' identity development by allowing them to try out various identities vicariously. As Paulette Rothbauer says, reading stories helps young adults "both to imagine new possibilities and to establish recognized boundaries for identity. The nature of this kind of reading affords a certain pleasure in finding oneself in the text while also functioning as a way to gather and organize information about the larger world and one's place in it."[3] At the same time, Rothbauer notes that there are gender-based differences in young adults' reading preferences, with most girls liking romances and most boys liking suspense stories with lots of action.

On a basic level, though, a good story is a good story. Much has been written about the appeal of stories, about humans' deep-seated psychological needs that stories speak to. From the time that we are small children, most of us are enthralled by a good story that is told well. While not all young adults become avid fiction readers (or, indeed, avid readers period), most retain a fascination with narratives, whether in the form of movies, television shows, or video games. What is it about stories that so captures our imaginations? What is it that makes us want to know what happens next? Lisa Zunshine argues that reading fiction allows us to practice our "mind-reading" skills— that is, those skills that allow us to "explain people's behaviors in terms of their thoughts, feelings, beliefs, and desires."[4] We may not always attribute "states of mind" correctly, but the acuity of our mind-reading skills help us to exist more or less successfully as social beings. (By way of comparison, these skills are typically deficient in people with autism spectrum disorder.) Christopher Booker, in discussing the appeal of stories, puts it this way: "the hidden language of stories provides us with a picture of human nature and the inner dynamics of human behaviour which nothing else can present to us with such objective authority."[5]

Reading fiction also can help foster critical thinking skills along with an understanding of and appreciation for the elements of literature. Analytical skills acquired through recreational reading can often transfer to the reading of literary texts assigned in school, and it is not unusual for young adult titles to be taught side by side with literary classics in secondary school classrooms. The key elements of fiction are evident across all narratives, and part of the pleasure of reading any particular story is the intellectual game of entering the author's universe and seeing how she or he makes use of these elements in relating the story. These literary elements include plot, characters, setting, theme, narrative viewpoint, and narrative structure. We examine each of these in more detail a bit later, in the section "Evaluating and Promoting Fiction."

While readers generally agree that the pleasure of reading a "good" story arises from what happens and how the story is told, what they do not always agree on is what makes a story "good." For that, we need to turn to a consideration of genre, by which is meant "a type, species, or class of composition. A literary genre is a recognizable and established category of written work employing such common conventions as will prevent readers or audiences from mistaking it for another kind."[6] Different readers prefer different genres, or what might be more properly called "subgenres." We consider the broad subgenres of fantastic fiction and realistic fiction along with a discussion of more specialized subtypes within each of those categories.

To be sure, there are many ways of looking at a work of literature, aside from genre. One obvious way is to consider theme, but there are a number of other critical/interpretive strategies as well. In *Critical Approaches to Young Adult Literature*, Kathy Latrobe and Judy Drury discuss not only genre criticism but also formal, psychological, sociological, historical, gender, archetypal/mythological, and reader-response criticism.[7] This provocative book attests to the richness of much young adult literature in lending itself to a variety of critical approaches. We, however, use genre criticism as the framework for our discussion, as we feel that it serves particularly well librarians engaged in collection development and readers' advisory, for it provides a useful way for thinking and talking about the wide range of stories available to meet various readers' interests and tastes.

FANTASTIC FICTION

Scholars and writers of fantastic fiction generally agree on one thing: that there is no agreed-on definition of fantasy. In the *Encyclopedia of Fantasy*, John Clute defines fantasy as "a self-coherent narrative. When set in this world, it tells a story which is impossible in this world as we perceive it . . . when set in an otherworld, that otherworld will be impossible, though stories set there may be possible in its terms."[8] Carl Tomlinson and Carol Lynch-Brown describe fantasy like this: "stories . . . in which the events, settings, or characters are outside the realm of possibility. A fantasy is a story that cannot happen in the real world, and of this reason this genre has been called the literature of the fanciful impossible."[9] For our purposes, we define fantastic fiction as stories that contain one or more elements that are impossible in our world as we know it. This definition should be elastic enough to cover the wide range of fantastic subgenres, including modern fantasy, horror, and science fiction, as well as their various subtypes.

Modern fantasy is the term used for the kinds of stories that most people think of when they hear the word "fantasy," but in fact, there are several types of stories within this broad category. *High fantasy* is typically set in an otherworld, involves magic and magical creatures (such as dragons and unicorns), and often makes use of the quest motif. These stories are often told over several volumes, allowing readers to get to know and enjoy the characters and otherworldly settings over an extended period. A classic of the genre is J. R. R. Tolkien's *The Lord of the Rings* trilogy,[10] which tells the story of a Dark Lord, the all-powerful Ring that he creates, and the epic quest by various inhabitants of Middle-earth to possess the Ring. Other examples include Lloyd Alexander's *The Chronicles of Prydain;*[11] Ursula K. Le Guin's *Earthsea* cycle;[12] Anne McCaffrey's *Dragonriders of Pern* series, beginning with *Dragonflight*[13] and continuing with more than 20 additional titles; Philip Pullman's *His Dark Materials* trilogy—*The Golden Compass, The Subtle Knife,* and *The Amber Spyglass;*[14] J. K. Rowling's enormously popular *Harry Potter* series;[15] Rick Riordan's mythology-inspired *Percy Jackson and the Olympians;*[16] and Christopher Paolini's boy-and-dragon novels, the *Inheritance* cycle.[17]

Anthropomorphized animal stories feature animals that talk, think, and experience humanlike emotions. In any given story, these animals may or may not interact with actual human characters. Richard Adams's *Watership Down,*[18] for example, relates the epic adventure of a group of rabbits in southern England. Terry Pratchett's *The Amazing Maurice and His Educated Rodents*[19] depicts a clever cat and his mice minions in a retelling of "The Pied Piper of Hamlin." *Modern folk tales* draw on traditional folk and fairy tales; they may be modern adaptations of well-known folk tales, or they may simply employ the familiar folk-tale structure to tell a new story. Pratchett's *Maurice* is one such example of the former. Others are *Beauty,*[20] Robin McKinley's retelling of "Beauty and the Beast"; *Briar Rose,*[21] Jane Yolen's version of "Sleeping Beauty"; *Confessions of an Ugly Stepsister,*[22] Gregory Maguire's take on "Cinderella"; and *Tender Morsels,*[23] Margo Lanagan's re-creation of "Snow White and Rose Red."

Historical fantasy is set in some recognizable period of the past but involves one or more magical elements. Walter Mosley's *47* is set during the American Civil War and tells the story of a teenaged slave who is befriended by a "slave" from another time and galaxy.[24] *Sword and sorcery* is a type of historical fantasy that uses a medieval setting as its backdrop. Tales of King Arthur and the Knights of the Roundtable have been a source of fascination for a number of fantasy writers. Some examples include T. H. White's *The Once and Future King,*[25] Marion Zimmer Bradley's *The Mists of Avalon,*[26]

Katherine Paterson's *Parzival: The Quest of the Grail Knight*,[27] Jane Yolen's *Sword of the Rightful King: A Novel of King Arthur*,[28] and Diana Wynne Jones's *The Merlin Conspiracy*.[29]

Magical realism is a mode that employs realistic, recognizable settings but introduces an element of magic into this setting via an extraordinary character or event. David Almond's novels often involve elements of magical realism. The characters in *Kit's Wilderness*,[30] for example, see ghostly children in an abandoned mine shaft, while the protagonists of *Clay*[31] bring a clay man to life. Isabel Allende makes use of magical realism in her Alexander Cold books—*City of the Beasts*, *Kingdom of the Golden Dragon*, and *Forest of the Pygmies*.[32] Francesca Lia Block also employs the mode in her *Weetzie Bat* books,[33] creating a magically tinged view of her native Los Angeles.

Horror is a type of fantasy (sometimes called "dark fantasy") in which characters are threatened by some sort of supernatural, often evil, force. A popular type of horror fiction involves *supernatural beings* such as vampires, werewolves, ghosts, and zombies. Rick Yancey's *The Monstrumologist*[34] is about a boy who must save his town from monsters who eat people. A popular subgenre of horror blends the supernatural with romance. Annette Curtis Klause's *Blood and Chocolate*,[35] for example, tells the story of a female werewolf who falls in love with a human boy. Stephenie Meyer's popular *Twilight* series[36] flips that conceit and relates the story of a teenaged girl who falls in love with a "boy" vampire. Another, albeit closely related, type of horror focuses on the *occult* and tells stories of demons and other satanic forces. A refreshing take on that theme is A. M. Jenkins's *Repossessed: A Novel*,[37] written from the point of view of a demon that inhabits a slacker teen's body. The genesis of horror fiction is the Gothic novel, which became popular in the mid-18th century with the publication of Horace Walpole's *The Castle of Otranto*.[38] Gothic novels, sometimes called Gothic romances, told stories "of terror or suspense" and were "usually set in a gloomy old castle or monastery."[39] A contemporary example of Gothic horror is *Beautiful Creatures*[40] and its sequels by Kami Garcia and Margaret Stohl. Set in a small town in the American South, these books tell the story of telepathic teenagers battling dark magic.

Science fiction is often described as "speculative fiction," in the sense that it tells stories about what could happen once science is advanced enough. As the science fiction writer Arthur C. Clarke memorably noted, "any sufficiently advanced technology is indistinguishable from magic."[41] A science fiction story typically involves some explanation of the "science" behind the phenomena depicted and the dazzling technology described, but the extent to which these elements are evident depends very much on the type of science fiction that the story represents. Science fiction, perhaps more than fantasy, often uses imaginative descriptions of what the future could be like to make comments about the present state of society and the world. Like modern fantasy, science fiction can be divided into several subtypes, although these "subtypes" might be more properly described as motifs, with quite a bit of overlap possible.

Space opera or *space travel* involves travel to other worlds and, usually, encounters with other extraterrestrial beings. Larry Niven and Jerry Pournelle's *The Mote in God's Eye*,[42] set far in the future, tells of the first contact between humans and a species from another world. Douglas Adams's *The Hitchhiker's Guide to the Galaxy*[43] relates the story of the main characters' travel to the planet Magrathea, and it is notable for being a humorous parody of space travel stories.

The other side of the space travel coin is the *alien invasion* story, in which beings from other worlds—friendly or otherwise—travel to Earth. *Interstellar Pig*,[44] by William Sleator, tells of a teenager's encounter with aliens living next door to his parents' summer rental house. Rick Yancey's *The Fifth Wave*[45] describes waves of alien invasions, each more terrifying than the last. And Orson Scott Card's *Ender's Game*[46] depicts a young prodigy who is trained by the military to fight an alien species that is threatening Earth.

Yet another kind of travel that appears in some science fiction is *time travel*, which is sometimes combined with travel to other worlds (not just the past or future of Earth). H. G. Wells's *The Time Machine*,[47] a classic of the genre, tells of the Time Traveller's visit to the year 802–701, where he encounters two races locked in an interdependent struggle. In Nancy Etchemendy's *The Power of Un*,[48] the main character discovers a device that allows him to erase mistakes.

Science fiction of various types may include *robots and artificial intelligence,* sophisticated machines created by humans who serve as both characters and technology. Isaac Asimov's *I, Robot*[49] is a collection of stories that sets forth the three laws of robotics and traces the development of a robot. Sometimes, however, stories take as their main focus sentient machines that become the agents of conflict and action, and these stories may thus be considered as a separate subtype. Philip K. Dick's *Do Androids Dream of Electric Sheep?*[50] for example, tells of a bounty hunter who must locate and destroy six rogue androids. Another kind of science fiction story focuses on the dangers of *science gone awry*, whether by accident or through evil intent. Usually, a key topic of these kinds of stories is the ethics of science and, in particular, the proper limits of humans' manipulation of nature and technology. Nancy Farmer's *The House of the Scorpion*[51] examines the ethics of cloning through the eyes of a young boy who discovers that he is the clone of a powerful drug lord. *Eva,*[52] by Peter Dickinson, explores the conflict that a teenaged girl experiences when, after a terrible accident, her consciousness is transplanted into a chimpanzee's body. And William Sleator's *House of*

Stairs[53] tells the story of five teenaged orphans who are subjected to a psychological and social experiment by being placed in a house made of nothing but endless stairs.

An especially popular type of science fiction is *dystopian fiction,* which depicts a society under the oppression of a totalitarian government. Sometimes, dystopian stories appear to depict utopian societies at first—that is, societies where people live in harmony and work together for the good of all members. But these apparent utopias are usually shown to be dystopias whose members have little freedom or autonomy. Lois Lowry's *Giver* quartet[54] depicts just such a society, where freedom and choice have been sacrificed in the name of peace and security. Scott Westerfeld's *Uglies* series[55] describes a society where 16-year-olds are surgically altered to transform them into beautiful people. And Suzanne Collins's *Hunger Games* Trilogy[56] tells the story of a powerful Capitol that keeps its districts subservient by forcing them to send teenaged tributes to participate in annual battles to the death. Dystopian novels sometimes describe *postapocalyptic scenarios,* showing characters' struggle to survive following a wide-scale catastrophic disaster. In Susan Beth Pfeffer's *Life As We Knew It,*[57] the catastrophe is caused by an asteroid hitting the moon and moving it closer to Earth. Robert C. O'Brien's *Z for Zachariah*[58] focuses on the survivors of a nuclear holocaust.

Steampunk is a type of science fiction that features steam-powered technology and is usually set in an alternative history version of the 19th or early 20th century or in a postapocalyptic future. Kenneth Opel's *Airborn*[59] and its sequels, though set in the early 20th century, portray a time that never existed, when the preferred mode for long-distance travel was airships. *Cyberpunk* focuses on advanced technologies but usually in deteriorating, often dystopian, settings. *Neuromancer,*[60] by William Gibson, is an acknowledged classic of the genre and features a virtual reality database called the "Matrix." In M. T. Anderson's *Feed,*[61] citizens are equipped with a "feednet," a computer link implanted in their brains, to feed them commercial advertisements and make them easily manipulated consumers. And Ernest Cline's *Ready Player One*[62] is set in the near future and describes a race to find three keys to a fortune in OASIS, a virtual reality world.

REALISTIC FICTION

While young adult readers sometimes like to embark on flights of imagination to magical kingdoms, at other times they may wish to take more realistic journeys that depict life in the here and now. Realistic fiction can meet that recreational reading need, providing insight into how other people have dealt with the changes, emotions, frustrations, and decisions that all young adults face. *Realism*—that is, "literary realism"—is defined as "a mode of writing that gives the impression of recording or 'reflecting' faithfully an actual way of life."[63] In contrast to fantastic fiction, *realistic fiction* consists of stories that are possible, although not always probable, in the world as we perceive it. *Coming-of-age stories* are frequent in young adult fiction, especially in realistic fiction for young adults. As the name suggests, a coming-of-age story relates a character's maturation, often as the result of a significant life event or encounter. Sometimes the term *Bildungsroman* is used to describe these kinds of stories, but, strictly speaking, a Bildungsroman, or "formation-novel,"[64] recounts the main character's childhood, adolescence, and entry into adulthood. The typical young adult coming-of-age story, however, usually does not cover so much ground but instead focuses on a particular experience that has a significant impact on the main character's development from a child to an adolescent or from an adolescent to an adult. As is the case with fantastic fiction, realistic fiction has a number of subgenres, which are not, of course, mutually exclusive. The most common subgenres are sports and adventure, mystery and suspense, romance, contemporary issues, urban fiction, and historical fiction.

Stories that focus on *sports and adventure* tend to be plot driven, although there is often a subplot involving friendships, rivalries, and/or the importance of teamwork. Both kinds of stories typically involve characters' developing physical and mental skills to achieve the stamina and agility required to excel at a particular sport or activity. Chris Crutcher is a master of the sports story, and he often uses sports as a way for his characters to overcome other challenges in their lives. In *Staying Fat for Sarah Byrnes*,[65] the sport is swimming, but the key issues are weight, body image, friendship, and an abusive father. Crutcher's book *Athletic Shorts: Six Short Stories*[66] looks at the transformative role that sports play in the lives of six young people. Edward Bloor's *Tangerine*[67] tells the story of a visually impaired soccer player and his abusive older brother. Gary Paulsen is the author of numerous adventure novels, with *Hatchet*[68] perhaps being his best known. *Hatchet* tells the story of a 13-year-old boy who, after being the sole survivor of a plane crash, must face the Canadian wilderness with nothing but his hatchet. Geraldine McCaughrean's *The White Darkness*[69] relates the adventures of a 14-year-old girl who must survive the harsh climate of Antarctica, where she has gone on an expedition with her demented uncle.

Like sports stories, *mysteries* represent a kind of game too, but this game is more intellectual than physical. The pleasure in reading a mystery comes from trying to figure out "whodunit" before the identity of the villain is revealed. Mysteries have been popular with young adults going back at least as far the Stratemeyer Syndicate's successful series of books, including Nancy Drew, the Hardy Boys, the Bobbsey Twins, and Tom Swift. The fact that mysteries usually follow a predictable formula might suggest that this subgenre is rather pedestrian, but for fans there is great fun in seeing how various writers employ and modify the formula to tell their own unique stories. John Green's *Paper Towns*[70] involves a boy trying to discover why his neighbor has gone missing. In *A Northern Light*,[71] Jennifer Donnelly reimagines the events surrounding a real-life murder that took place in 1906 in upstate New York (a crime that also inspired Theodore Dreiser's novel *An American Tragedy*). Mark Haddon's *The Curious Incident of the Dog in the Night-Time*[72] tells the story of a 15-year-old boy who appears to have a condition similar to high-functioning autism and his quest to solve the mystery of who killed his neighbor's dog and why.

Suspense stories are closely related to mysteries. Suspense, like a good mystery, can make readers' pulses race by building a sense of threat. The thrill of reading a suspense story is similar to the thrill that one gets from bungee jumping or riding roller coasters. Lois Duncan's *I Know What You Did Last Summer*[73] tells of four friends who kill a boy in a hit-and-run accident and then are later terrorized by someone claiming to know what they did last summer. Her novel *Killing Mr. Griffin*[74] is about a group of high school students whose plot to kidnap their English teacher goes terribly awry, resulting in his death. Strictly speaking, mystery and suspense stories depict threats that turn out to have a rational explanation; in other words, they are of this world. If the threat turns out to be supernatural, then we generally classify that as an example of horror.

Romance stories focus on love relationships (though often not explicitly sexual relationships), and for that reason they tend to be more character than plot driven. Romance stories can focus on girl-boy or same-gender relationships, and they typically involve the two main characters' discovering their mutual attraction, getting to know each other, encountering some sort of obstacle or threat to the relationship, and achieving a resolution, though not always one that preserves their status as a couple. Judy Blume's *Forever*,[75] a perennial favorite, explores the theme of teenage sexuality and shows that love does not always last forever. Rachel Cohn and David Levithan's *Nick and Norah's Infinite Playlist*[76] relates the romantic adventures of a boy and girl as they drive around New York City looking for an elusive indie band. Levithan's *Boy Meets Boy*[77] plays off the usual "boy meets girl" plotline to tell the romantic story of two boys. Nancy Garden's *Annie on My Mind*,[78] a groundbreaking work in the same-gender romance genre, tells a "girl meets girl" story and the difficulties that they face. Jacqueline Woodson's *The House You Pass on the Way*[79] depicts the evolving relationship between two girls, one who is certain of her sexual identity and other who is questioning hers. Sometimes two characters are brought together because of unusual, even traumatic circumstances. John Green's *The Fault in Our Stars*,[80] for example, tells the story of two teenagers with terminal cancer who meet through a support group.

Nonsexual friendship stories belong in this category as well, and these might be thought of as "platonic" romances. (The nonsexual male friendship version is sometimes called the "bromance.") The point here is that the vicissitudes of friendship can be as complicated as those of love relationships. Such is the case in Sherman Alexie's *The Absolutely True Diary of a Part-Time Indian*,[81] in which the main character, Junior, experiences a rift in the relationship with his best friend, Rowdy, when Junior begins attending a school off the reservation where they both live.

Whatever else they may do, many young adult novels deal with *contemporary issues*, including teen pregnancy, bullying, sexual/physical/psychological abuse, substance abuse, eating disorders, parental problems (such as divorce), coming out, physical and/or mental challenges, terminal illness . . . the list goes on. At one time, these kinds of books were called "problem novels," because they typically dealt with one or more problems, and they were prevalent in the young adult literature published in the 1960s and 1970s. In fact, scholars consider some of these books to be young adult classics and largely responsible for ushering in the golden age of young adult literature in the late 1960s. At the same time, many of these books have fallen out of favor for being excessive in their melodramatic tone and pedantic in their depiction of social problems. While this kind of excess still exists, more recent young adult novels have presented a more nuanced—and more realistic—view of the issues that young adults face. Angela Johnson's *The First Part Last*[82] depicts both the joys and the trials of a teenage father who is raising his infant daughter. Walter Dean Myers's *Monster*[83] focuses on issues of race, identity, and crime as the novel moves between an accused teenager's journal entries and the screenplay he is writing about his trial. Rape, and its devastating consequences, is the topic of Laurie Halse Anderson's *Speak*.[84] Her novel *Wintergirls*[85] addresses the issues of anorexia and bulimia. Jay Asher's *Thirteen Reasons Why*[86] deals with the suicide of a victim of bullying.

Another subgenre that tends to be issues focused is *urban fiction*, also known as "street lit." Urban fiction is defined as literature "where the stories, be they fiction or non-fiction, are consistently set in urban, inner-city enclaves. Street Literature of yesteryear and today, by and large, depicts tales about the daily lives of people living in lower income city neighborhoods. This characteristic spans historical timelines, varying cultural identifications, linguistic associations, and various format designations."[87] Not surprising, the tone is often dark, and the stories grapple with difficult subjects, such as violence, drugs, sex, poverty, and incarceration.[88] The roots of street lit can be found in autobiographical works from the 1960s,[89] such as Malcolm X's *The Autobiography of Malcolm X*[90] and Claude Brown's *Manchild in the Promised Land*.[91] The genre enjoyed a resurgence in the 1990s[92] with the publication of *Flyy Girl*,[93] by Omar Tyree, which tells the coming-of-age story of an African American girl in Philadelphia, and Sister Souljah's *The Coldest Winter Ever*,[94] which relates the story of a spoiled but tough teenaged daughter of a Brooklyn drug dealer.

Though the books are usually written with an adult audience in mind, they often focus on young adult characters, between the ages of 16 and 23.[95] *Tyrell*,[96] by Coe Booth, for example, is the story of a 14-year-old boy dealing with poverty, homelessness, and a father who is in jail. Teri Woods's *True to the Game*[97] is about a young girl from the projects who falls in love with a wealthy drug dealer. *Yummy: The Last Days of a Southside Shorty*,[98] by G. Neri and Randy Duburke, is a graphic novel that relates the mostly true story of Robert "Yummy" Sandifer, an 11-year-old boy who was killed by members of his own gang in Chicago in the mid-1990s. In a similar vein, Walter Dean Myers and Christopher Myers's *Autobiography of My Dead Brother*[99] is an illustrated novel that tells the story of a young artist in Harlem who, through his sketches, tries to make sense of his friend's involvement in drugs, gangs, and violence.

Multicultural literature is usually realistic literature that focuses on members of one or more minority groups, or microcultures—defined on the basis of race and ethnicity, religion, sexuality, ability, family status, and so on. A work of multicultural literature can play an important role in providing a mirror to members of the minority group depicted, reflecting and validating its experiences, and in providing a window to members of other groups, offering a view of the minority group and its culture. Moreover, as Sandra Hughes-Hassell points out, multicultural literature for young adults can also serve as kind of "counter-storytelling," in which these "counter-stories challenge the stereotypes often held by the dominant culture, give voice to marginalized youth, and present the complexity of racial and ethnic identify formation."[100]

Multicultural literature for young adults often depicts a teenage member of a minority group grappling with identity issues related to being both a member of that microculture and a member of the larger culture as well. The previously mentioned *The Absolutely True Diary of a Part-Time Indian*,[101] for example, explores the main character's struggles with his Native American identity as he enrolls in a predominantly white high school. Cynthia Kadohata's *Kira-Kira*[102] depicts the challenges faced by two Japanese American girls when their family moves from Iowa to Georgia in the late 1950s. Pam Muñoz Ryan's *Esperanza Rising*[103] relates the emigration experiences of a young girl and her mother who move from Mexico to California during the Great Depression. In *The Glory Field*,[104] Walter Dean Myers explores, among other things, the evolving ethnic identity of an African American family over many generations.

Multicultural literature is not limited to racial and ethnic groups. An increasing number of young adult novels focus on the challenges faced by

LGBTQ youth in developing their identities in a predominantly straight world. M. E. Kerr's *Deliver Us from Evie*[105] relates the story of a 17-year-old lesbian in rural Missouri as seen through the sympathetic eyes of her younger, straight brother. Julie Anne Peters's *Luna*[106] tells the story of a 17-year-old transgender boy as seen through the sympathetic eyes of his younger sister. And Benjamin Alire Sáenz's *Aristotle and Dante Discover the Secrets of the Universe*[107] deals with the developing friendship between two boys, one who is comfortable with his sexuality and one who is not.

Some consider *international literature* to be a subset of multicultural literature. However, strictly speaking, international literature is defined as a work published in one country and subsequently published in another. Sometimes, this involves translating the work from one language to another. A work of international literature may or may not focus on one or more microcultures within the country of origin. A few examples illustrate the complexity of the notion of international literature. The *Harry Potter* series is an example of an international publishing phenomenon, although it is not defined as an "international" series in England, where it was originally published. Jean Claude Mourlevat's *The Pull of the Ocean*, a reworking of Charles Perrault's "Hop o' My Thumb" story, was originally published in France (in French) and then translated into English.[108] Marjane Satrapi's graphic memoirs *Persepolis: The Story of a Childhood* and *Persepolis 2: The Story of a Return*,[109] which depict Satrapi's Iranian childhood and adolescence during the time of the Islamic Revolution, were originally published in France (in French) and then translated into several other languages. Allan Stratton's book *Chanda's Secrets*[110] is a Canadian book, although it tells the story of a young adult dealing with the AIDS/HIV epidemic affecting her family and community in sub-Saharan Africa.

Historical fiction may combine any of these genres. Although we are discussing it in the context of realistic fiction, in some ways it is a special case. It might be seen as the generic antithesis of science fiction in that, whereas (most) science fiction represents imaginative speculation about the future, historical fiction represents imaginative speculation about the past. Just as it is fun and intellectually engaging to think about what it might be like to live at some period in the future, it is also fun and intellectually engaging to imagine what might have been like to live at some period in the past. Avi's *Crispin: The Cross of Lead*[111] tells the story of a poor orphan boy in 14th-century England who must run for his life when he is accused of a crime that he did not commit. Geraldine McCaughrean's *The Kite Rider*,[112] set in 13th-century China, focuses on a boy who becomes a kite rider to escape extreme poverty. *Chains*,[113] by Laurie Halse Anderson, tells of two teenage sisters who are sold as slaves in New York City in 1776, ironically the year of American independence. Julius Lester's *Day of Tears: A Novel in Dialogue*[114] is an account of a slave auction in Savannah, Georgia, in the late

1850s. And *Code Name Verity*,[115] by Elizabeth Wein, is set during World War II and presents the story of a young woman who has been captured by the Nazis and her and her friend's involvement in the Resistance.

Most historical fiction is realistic in the sense that it attempts to employ a historically accurate backdrop for a fictional story. However, it should be remembered that there is a fairly small subgenre known as historical fantasy, which we have already discussed in the section on fantastic fiction.

FAN FICTION

Fan fiction is fiction written by fans of a particular story or series, using the characters created by the original author but creating new stories, situations, and relationships. Fan fiction is also known as an example of "transformative works," defined by Jen Scott Curwood, Alecia Marie Magnifico, and Jayne C. Lammers as "the kinds of writing and designing practices that take an original artifact and turn it into something with a new function or expression."[116] Fan fiction includes characters from all genres and formats—fantastic fiction, realistic fiction, manga and anime, comics, movies, television shows, and games.

Most of these stories are shared via Internet sites devoted to fan fiction, and most of the readers also write fan fiction and reviews of fan fiction themselves. Not limited to teens by any means, these sites attract writers and readers of all ages. Fanfiction.net is one the largest sites of this sort, featuring stories, communities, and forums devoted to particular titles and interests. Archiveofourown.org, sponsored by the Organization for Transformative Works, bills itself as "a fan-created, fan-run, non-profit, non-commercial archive for transformative fanworks, like fanfiction, fanart, fan videos, and podfic" (i.e., fan fiction that is audiorecorded).[117]

Moviefanficchains.com is devoted specifically to movie- and television-related fan fiction. Other sites are even more specific, focusing on a particular series, such as *Harry Potter* (HarryPotterFanFiction.com is just one of many sites devoted to the popular boy wizard), *Star Trek* (TrekFanFiction.net), *Doctor Who* (A Teaspoon and an Open Mind: A Doctor Who Fan Fiction Archive: www.whofic.com), *Lord of the Rings* (Lord of the Rings Fanfiction: A Tolkien Loving Community: www.lotrfanfiction.com), the *Twilight* series (Twilighted: www.twilighted.net), and the *Dragon Ball* manga and anime series (Dragon Ball Fanfiction Library: www.dbfl.gokugirl.com). And these are just a few of the many fan fiction sites available.

What's the appeal of fan fiction? For avid readers (or viewers) of a particular series, participating in fan fiction is a way of extending the stories, filling in gaps, or taking the characters in completely new directions. James

Paul Gee calls these fan fiction sites "affinity spaces," places where people can come together based on similar interests and skills and engage in informal learning.[118] It is an opportunity to participate in the creative process, to read additional stories about your favorite characters, and to be part of a community with similar interests and tastes. As media scholar and critic Henry Jenkins explains,

> fans write stories because they want to share insights they have into the characters, their relationships, and their worlds; they write stories because they want to entertain alternative interpretations or examine new possibilities which would otherwise not get expressed through the canonical material. These interpretations are debatable—indeed, fans spend a great deal of time debating the alternative interpretations of the characters which appear in their stories.[119]

For Jenkins, "all fan fiction constitutes a form of critical commentary on the original texts."[120]

Writing fan fiction, then, fosters not only writing skills but also critical thinking skills. Moreover, in addition to writing and posting stories based on favorite characters, fan fiction enthusiasts contribute to discussion boards on a variety of topics, from engaging in debates about characters' motivations to offering tips on writing. Authors and publishers, of course, are always concerned about protecting their properties and potential profits, but many have apparently come to recognize that fan fiction, rather than detract from their profits, because it is freely produced and distributed, can actually serve to enhance a franchise, attracting even more readers or viewers.

EVALUATING AND PROMOTING FICTION

Evaluating fiction involves understanding that narratives can appeal to young adults on both a visceral level and an intellectual level. Louise Rosenblatt's concept of reader response provides a useful way for understanding the relationship between readers and texts.[121] She argues that meaning is created through a transactional process between the reader and the text. In addition, she sees responses to any given text as occurring on a continuum between efferent (nonliterary) and aesthetic (literary) reading. A reader who is engaged by a text (efferent response) is more likely to be able to appreciate its literary qualities (aesthetic response). It is important, then, in working with young adults to acknowledge and honor their efferent reading experiences. It is also important in evaluating any given work of fiction to consider how the various literary elements are employed, for these are the elements that either will or will not engage individual readers:

1. Plot—The plot is what happens in the story. Typically, a plot will involve some sort of conflict that leads to rising action and eventually some sort of resolution. Some stories feature episodic plots, which consist of a series of short plots (or scenes) strung together. Other stories feature more sustained plots that build up to a climax, followed by a resolution of some sort. In his book *Seven Basic Plots: Why We Tell Stories*, Christopher Booker provides a useful framework for discussing different kinds of narratives. Drawing on the psychological theories of Carl Jung as well as others, Booker identifies seven basic plots that are evident in the seemingly infinite variety of stories throughout the world:

   a. Overcoming the monster—the protagonist faces and defeats an evil force.
   b. Rags to riches—the protagonist starts with little and achieves much.
   c. The quest—the protagonist searches for something of great value.
   d. Voyage and return—the protagonist undertakes an adventure and returns home.
   e. Comedy—two protagonists are thwarted by an antagonist in their attempt to form a (usually) romantic relationship, but in the end they defeat the antagonist.
   f. Tragedy—the protagonist has a flaw that leads to her or his downfall.
   g. Rebirth—the protagonist has a flaw and is heading toward a downfall but manages to reverse course.

   Booker sums it up by saying that "the plot of a story is that which leads its hero or heroine either to a 'catastrophe' or an 'unknotting'; either to frustration or liberation; either to death or to a renewal of life."

2. Characters—These are the people (or, in some cases, animal or robots) to whom the events in the story happen and/or who cause the events to happen. They have personalities (as conveyed through speech, behavior, and appearance); they interact with one another; and they often come into conflict. The main character is called the "protagonist"; the protagonist's rival or nemesis is called the "antagonist."

3. Setting—This refers to the place and time in which the story is set. Setting provides the context in which the characters engage in actions and experience events.

4. Theme—The theme is the (usually implicit) comment that the author is making about the characters and events of the story. In a broader

sense, this comment may be taken as a comment about life or society. Often, more than one theme is evident in a work of fiction, although a single theme may predominate. A common theme in many works of fiction for young adults is coming of age—that is, stories that depict the maturation process. Sometimes authors use one or more symbols or motifs to help convey the theme. The recurring image of a flower, for example, may connote the beautiful yet transitory nature of life.

5. Narrative viewpoint—This refers to the position of the narrator in relation to the story and the characters in the story. A narrator who is a character in the story will probably tell the story in first person. A narrator who is outside the story will probably tell the story in third person. A third-person narrator may be omniscient—that is, all knowing about what is going to happen and what motivates each character. Or, a third-person narrator may be limited in her or his knowledge and may be "focalized" on one particular character. In some cases, multiple narrators are used to present multiple viewpoints. Usually, though not always, these are written in first person and represent the viewpoints of various characters within the story.

6. Narrative structure—This refers to the time strategies that the narrator (and, by extension, the author) uses to tell the story. A story may be told in chronological order, with the events being relayed in the order in which they happened, or a story may be told as a series of flashbacks, alternating between the story's present and past—and, in some cases, even the future (flash-forwards, perhaps?).

In evaluating works of fiction, these basic literary elements can be useful. However, there is no magic formula for determining what works and what does not. Reading preferences are as diverse as readers themselves. The key is to look for an engaging story, told in an interesting way, and involving believable characters (even if those characters are nonhuman, as is sometimes the case with fantasy). Few people enjoy a didactic story or a story that talks down to its readers, and young adults are no exception in this respect.

In addition to reading and evaluating as much fiction as one can, it is equally important to be familiar with review sources. *VOYA* (*Voice of Youth Advocates*) focuses on books for young adults, as does *Teenreads.com*. *School Library Journal*, *The Horn Book*, *The Bulletin of the Center for Children's Books*, the Cooperative Children's Book Center, and *Booklist* are broader in scope, but they do have extensive sections of reviews for young adult books. And *Goodreads.com* offers reviews in a variety of "genres," including young adult.

Another excellent way of keeping up with what librarians, teachers, and other professionals have deemed especially worthy of attention is by consulting lists of award winners (including "honor books") and "best books."

YALSA, a division of the American Library Association, sponsors several annual awards for young adult books. The Michael L. Printz Award is given for the best book written for young adults during the previous year. The Margaret A. Edwards Award is given to an author in recognition of a significant body of high-quality work written for young adults. The William C. Morris Young Adult Debut Award is for the best young adult book written by a previously unpublished author. And the Alex Awards are for 10 adult books judged to have "crossover" interest for young adults. Additional information can be found on the YALSA website, in the section "Book Awards."

Though not devoted exclusively to young adult books, three awards that are administered by the Association for Library Service to Children worth keeping an eye on are the Newbery Award, which is given to authors of books for readers up to age 14; the Pura Belpré Awards, for outstanding Latino/Latina authors and illustrators; and the Mildred L. Batchelder Award, for an outstanding international children's book, defined as a book "originally published in a language other than English in a country other than the United States, and subsequently translated into English for publication in the United States."[122] The Coretta Scott King Awards, administered by the Ethnic and Multicultural Information Exchange Round Table, is given to outstanding African American authors and illustrators. These latter three awards are sometimes given to books intended for young people (12 and up), so it is worth being aware of the selections for each year. Finally, the Street Literature Book Award Medal has recently implemented a young adult fiction category. Additional information about each award, including lists of current and past winners and honor books, can be found on the award's website (see appendix 1).

In addition to the aforementioned awards, YALSA sponsors several book lists, and these can be excellent resources for outstanding fiction for young adults. Best Fiction for Young Adults lists the best fiction written for young adults over the previous 16 months. Outstanding Books for the College Bound is designed for older teens who are planning to go to college, and it is updated every 5 years. Popular Paperbacks for Young Adults focuses on books with lots of teen appeal. The lists are typically divided into four thematic categories, although the categories change from year to year. Quick Picks for Reluctant Young Adult Readers identifies books with broad appeal for teens who are not avid readers. Readers' Choice is the list of titles that YALSA members have voted as their favorites for the year. Teens' Top Ten is the list of books that teens have selected as their favorites for the year. More information about how these lists are compiled as well as access to current and past lists is available on the YALSA website, in the "Booklists" section.

Selecting a variety of high-quality works of fiction for young adults is important, but it is not enough; it is just as important to promote the collection effectively. Fortunately, there are a number of strategies at our disposal for doing so that can be divided into three basic types. (By the way, these same strategies work well with nonfiction too, as we will see in chapter 6.)

Presentational strategies are so named because they mostly present fiction to young adults for the purpose of raising their awareness about what is available. Such strategies include booktalks (brief teasers designed to pique interest in a particular title) delivered by a librarian or teacher, book displays (either physical or virtual), storytelling sessions (in contrast to booktalks, storytelling relates a complete story), and visits from authors of young adult fiction.

SPOTLIGHT!

Booktalks

Booktalks are short, spoken "teasers" intended to get young adults interested in reading books. Typically, a booktalk is actually a series of several talks (6–10), each focusing on a title with transitions linking one talk to the next. Booktalks can be given by librarians, teachers, or young adults themselves. Carol Littlejohn advises anyone who is planning a booktalk to "think of yourself as a salesperson sharing the love of reading. The booktalk is the advertisement, the book is the product, and the reader is the consumer."[a] Booktalks offer a number of potential benefits. They encourage reading, of course, but they may also entice reluctant readers to check out a particular title.[b] In addition, they can help to promote a positive image of librarians among young adults,[c] which can lead to increased use of libraries and library services. Booktalks also have the advantage of being consistently effective promotional strategies that do not require additional funding.[d]

Booktalks are traditionally performed live and face-to-face, but with the widespread availability of technology, they can now be recorded and posted online to be viewed whenever and wherever. These are basically video recordings of talks that have been performed live. Another technology-based option is the book trailer, a short video that uses images, transitions, and sound to offer an impressionistic introduction to a particular book.[e] Book trailers can be produced by young adults, offering a way for reluctant readers to participate in book promotions, as well as others who may not feel comfortable presenting a talk to their peers.[f] Plus, it facilitates visual and technology literacies in addition to the more traditional literacy skills.[g] Like booktalks, book trailers should be short, and they shouldn't give too much away. After all, the point is to get readers interested in reading the book, not to spoil it for them!

Tips:

- Choose books that you like and can talk about enthusiastically. If you're interested in the book, you can probably get at least some of the young adults in your audience interested in it as well.
- Select a variety of books based on what you know about your audience. Consider different genres and different formats, as well as different reading levels. An effective way to organize a talk is to choose a theme and then select books that somehow relate to that theme.
- Choose a focus for each book that you talk about. Michele Gorman and Tricia Suellentrop describe four possible approaches: focus on the mood of the book, focus on the plot (but don't give too much away), focus on a character (perhaps give the talk in that character's voice or from that character's perspective), or focus on a scene (again taking care not to give too much away).[h]
- In delivering the talk, pay attention to the body language of your audience, and consider getting feedback on your performance via a short survey. Ruth Cox Clark, in a research project involving 160 booktalkers giving 800 booktalks to nearly 3,000 young adults, discovered that young adults generally preferred first-person talks given from the perspective of a character in a book and were generally less enthusiastic about talks that involved discussion (i.e., a lot of interaction) with the audience.[i]
- In developing a book trailer or helping young adults develop their own, create a storyboard, and be sure to include the title and author of the book, an image of the cover, images that help to convey the mood or plot, text or voice-over, and music.[j]

Notes:

a. Carol Littlejohn, *Talk That Book*, vol. 1 of *Booktalks to Promote Reading* (Worthington, OH: Linworth, 1999), 1.
b. Carol Littlejohn, *Keep Talking That Book!* vol. 2 of *Booktalks to Promote Reading* (Worthington, OH: Linworth, 2000), 3.
c. Littlejohn, *Keep Talking That Book!* 3.

d. Rosemary Chance and Teri Lesesne, "Rethinking Reading Promotion: Old School Meets Technology," *Teacher Librarian* 39 (June 2012): 26–28.

e. Sara Kajder, "The Book Trailer: Engaging Teens through Technologies," *Educational Leadership* 65 (March 2008), http://www.ascd.org/publications/educational-leadership/mar08/vol65/num06/The-Book-Trailer@-Engaging-Teens-Through-Technologies.aspx.

f. Kajder, "The Book Trailer."

g. Kajder, "The Book Trailer."

h. Michele Gorman and Tricia Suellentrop, *Connecting Young Adults and Libraries,* 4th ed. (New York: Neal-Schuman, 2009), 176–77.

i. Ruth Cox Clark, "Listening to Teens Talk Back: Teen Responses to Booktalking Styles," *Voice of Youth Advocates* 31 (February 2009): 501–4.

j. Chance and Lesesne, "Rethinking Reading Promotion," 28.

Interactive strategies for promoting fiction involve more interaction with the audience and may include the aforementioned strategy, with the primary difference being that the audience is invited to interact with the leader, storyteller, or author. Someone delivering a booktalk, for example, might ask young adults to guess what a book is about based on the cover art. Book discussion groups can be organized by an adult but can involve a great deal of interaction among the young adult participants, including providing advice on what to read and discuss next. Readers' advisory is a (usually) one-on-one form of interaction, in which a librarian provides reading recommendations to a young adult. In providing readers' advisory, a librarian will typically conduct a readers' advisory interview, asking about reading likes, reading dislikes, recent books read, favorite authors, favorite plot types, and so on.

SPOTLIGHT!

Readers' Advisory

Readers' advisory is the process of recommending resources to young adults based on their stated reading interests and needs. Heather Booth describes it as "reference work for recreational reading" and notes that it involves "a skill that is part science and part art, with a healthy dash of mind reading."[a] A familiarity with various genres and formats is important, as is a familiarity with specific titles that young adults are reading.[b] Young adults' reading interests are as diverse as young adults themselves, and reading is one way that they explore various identities and create their own identities.[c] The point of readers' advisory is not to "push" resources onto young adults but rather to find out what they're interested in and what they find entertaining and then connect them with those kinds of resources.

The readers' advisory interview will depend on whether the young adult is looking for recommendations for recreational reading or needing help in finding an appropriate book for a school assignment. In the case of the former, it's useful to ask about the kinds of books (plots, characters, formats) that the teen enjoys and doesn't enjoy. You might ask about favorite movies, television shows, and hobbies, too, as those can give insight into the teen's interests and preferences. In the case of a school assignment, it's important to ask about the assignment instructions. Meeting the requirements of the assignment is the first priority, but if you can find out what the teen is interested in, then you might be able to help her or him find a resource that is both engaging and appropriate for the assignment.

Tips:

- Be approachable and friendly. If you see a young adult wandering in the stacks, offer to help but don't be pushy.
- Read as many young adult resources as possible, and try to read widely in terms of genre and format. Gorman and Suellentrop recommend developing a core list of authors and titles in your mental rotation: have at least three authors and three titles each in various genres and formats that you can recommend off the top of your head.[d]
- Talk to young adults as well as professional colleagues to find out what they're reading and enjoying.
- Keep up with the latest authors and titles by consulting Teenreads.com, Goodreads.com, NoveList, YALSA's various book lists, and review journals such as *Voice of Youth Advocates*, *Booklist*, and *School Library Journal*.
- Don't be judgmental when talking with young adults about their reading interests. Their tastes may not be the same as yours. The goal is to connect them with resources that they'll find useful and enjoyable.

Notes:

a. Heather Booth, *Serving Teens Through Readers' Advisory* (Chicago: American Library Association, 2007), 19–20.

b. Michele Gorman and Tricia Suellentrop, *Connecting Young
Adults and Libraries: A How-to-Do-It Manual for Librarians*,
4th ed. (New York: Neal-Schuman, 2009), 65.
c. Gorman and Suellentrop, *Connecting Young Adults and Libraries*, 21.
d. Gorman and Suellentrop, *Connecting Young Adults and Libraries*, 66.

Finally, *participatory* strategies elicit the highest degree of interaction and
activity on the part of the young adult audience. Young adults can (as we
have seen) write fan fiction, participate in collaborative fiction writing projects, create illustrations for published works or their own original works,
post reviews of books they have read, and lead their own book discussion
groups (in person or online). They can also deliver their own booktalks,
participate in storytelling sessions, and develop marketing campaigns for
particular fiction titles.

Special book-themed events are another popular way to promote fiction
reading and library use. Many libraries, for example, hosted *Harry Potter*
events to coincide with the release of each book in J. K. Rowling's best-
selling series. Participants dressed as their favorite characters, played *Harry
Potter*–themed games, and ate *Harry Potter*–themed food. Similar strategies
were used with Stephenie Meyer's *Twilight* series and Suzanne Collins's
Hunger Games series.

Another way that young adults can participate directly in selecting fiction
for their library's collection is by becoming members of the teen advisory
board. Though not devoted exclusively to promoting fiction, such boards can
make recommendations about collection development, help in developing
programs, assist in delivering those programs, and provide advice about upgrades to facilities and technology.

In secondary schools, librarians and teachers can work together to promote fiction by using any of the strategies listed here and by developing
lesson plans incorporating fiction into various curricular units. A history unit
on the American Civil War might use a work of historical fiction set in that
period. A literature lesson might pair a "classic" work with a more contemporary young adult book dealing with the same theme. Librarians can provide instruction in locating works of fiction, as well as literary biographies
and works of criticism.

SUMMARY

Young adult fiction offers a variety of genres and subgenres to appeal to a
wide range of tastes and to meet recreational, informational, and educational

needs. Any individual work of fiction can serve as a mirror, reflecting a reader's own culture and experiences, or as a window, providing a view of other cultures and experiences. Moreover, reading fiction facilitates young adults' identity development by allowing young adults to try out various identities vicariously by identifying with fictional characters. Reading fiction can also foster critical thinking skills by allowing young adults to experience the pleasure of entering the author's fictional world and thinking about how the author has made use of various literary elements in creating that world. At its heart, reading fiction offers the appeal of a good story, with vivid characters and an engaging plot. In addition to reading fiction, many young adults also enjoy writing their own fiction, particularly fan fiction. By promoting fiction, through strategies such as readers' advisory, book talks, and book discussion groups, librarians can promote the development of multiple literacy skills as well as the joys of getting lost in a good book.

IMPLICATIONS FOR PRACTICE

- Recognize that different young adult readers will have different preferences in what kinds of fiction they choose to read. For that reason, it is vital to have a balanced collection that includes a variety of genres.
- Talk to young adults about what they read, what they like to read, and what they do not like to read.
- Be on the alert for opportunities to recommend new titles to young adults, perhaps encouraging them to try a genre that they have not tried before.
- Regularly consult review sources, award lists, and "best book" lists.
- Maintain a network of professional colleagues with whom you can share information about the latest young adult fiction.
- Enlist the help of young adults in developing programs to promote fiction reading, and always be sure to incorporate some sort of evaluation into whatever programs you offer.
- Look for opportunities to work with local teachers. They can help you in developing your collection, and you, in turn, can help them in developing assignments and instructional units.

QUESTIONS TO THINK ABOUT AND DISCUSS

1. Did you read fiction when you were a young adult? If so, what kind of fiction did you like to read and why? What kind of fiction did you not like to read and why?
2. How can librarians and teachers help young adults effectively analyze, evaluate, and respond to fiction?

3. How might web resources be used to supplement fiction resources in print, and vice versa?

4. What kinds of activities can be used to make connections between fiction resources and nonfiction works on the same topic?

5. What role should libraries and schools play in promoting nonbook fiction resources (magazines, fan fiction sites, other websites, blogs, etc.)?

NOTES

1. Chris Baldick, *Oxford Concise Dictionary of Literary Terms* (New York: Oxford University Press, 2004), 96.

2. Rudine Sims Bishop, "Mirrors, Windows, and Sliding Glass Doors," *Perspectives: Choosing and Using Books for the Classroom* 6, no. 3 (1990), http://www.rif.org/us/literacy-resources/multicultural/mirrors-windows-and-sliding-glass-doors.htm.

3. Paulette M. Rothbauer, "Young Adults and Reading," in *Reading Matters: What the Research Reveals about Reading, Libraries, and Community,* ed. Catherine Sheldrick Ross, Lynne McKechnie, and Paulette M. Rothbauer (Westport, CT: Libraries Unlimited, 2006), 101–31.

4. Lisa Zunshine, *Why We Read Fiction: Theory of Mind and the Novel* (Columbus: Ohio State University Press, 2006), 6.

5. Christopher Booker, *The Seven Basic Plots: Why We Tell Stories* (New York: Continuum, 2004), 8.

6. Baldick, *Oxford Concise Dictionary,* 104–5.

7. Kathy H. Latrobe and Judy Drury, *Critical Approaches to Young Adult Literature* (New York: Neal-Schuman, 2009).

8. John Clute and John Grant, eds., *Encyclopedia of Fantasy* (New York: St. Martin's Press, 1997), 338.

9. Carl Tomlinson and Carol Lynch-Brown, *Essentials of Young Adult Literature,* 2nd ed. (Boston: Pearson, 2010), 63.

10. J. R. R. Tolkien, *The Fellowship of the Ring*; *The Two Towers*; *The Return of the King* (London: Allen & Unwin, 1954–1955).

11. Lloyd Alexander, *The Book of Three*; *The Black Cauldron*; *The Castle of Lyr*; *Taran Wanderer*; *The High King* (New York: Holt, Rinehart and Winston, 1964–1968).

12. Ursula K. Le Guin, *A Wizard of Earthsea* (Berkeley, CA: Parnassus, 1968); *The Tombs of Atuan* (New York: Atheneum, 1971); *The Farthest Shore* (New York: Atheneum, 1972); *Tehanu* (New York: Atheneum, 1990); *Tales from Earthsea* (New York: Harcourt Brace, 2001); *The Other Wind* (New York: Harcourt Brace, 2001).

13. Anne McCaffrey, *Dragonflight* (New York: Ballantine, 1968).

14. Philip Pullman, *The Golden Compass* (London: Scholastic Point, 1995); *The Subtle Knife* (London: Scholastic Point, 1997); *The Amber Spyglass* (London: Fickling, 2000).

15. J. K. Rowling, *Harry Potter and the Sorcerer's Stone*; *Harry Potter and the Chamber of Secrets*; *Harry Potter and the Prisoner of Azkaban*; *Harry Potter and the Goblet of Fire*; *Harry Potter and the Order of the Phoenix*; *Harry Potter and the Half-Blood Prince*; *Harry Potter and the Deathly Hallows* (New York: Scholastic, 1998–2007).

16. Rick Riordan, *The Lightning Thief*; *The Sea of Monsters*; *The Titan's Curse*; *The Battle of the Labyrinth*; *The Last Olympian* (New York: Disney Hyperion, 2005–2009).

17. Christopher Paolini, *Eragon*; *Eldest*; *Brisingr*; *Inheritance* (New York: Knopf, 2002–2011).

18. Richard Adams, *Watership Down* (London: Rex Collings, 1972).

19. Terry Pratchett, *The Amazing Maurice and His Educated Rodents* (New York: Doubleday, 2001).

20. Robin McKinley, *Beauty: A Retelling of the Story of Beauty and the Beast* (New York: HarperCollins, 1978).

21. Jane Yolen, *Briar Rose* (New York: Doherty, 1992).

22. Gregory Maguire, *Confessions of an Ugly Stepsister* (New York: Regan, 1999).

23. Margo Lanagan, *Tender Morsels* (New York: Knopf, 2008).

24. Walter Mosley, *47* (New York: Little, Brown, 2005).

25. T. H. White, *The Once and Future King* (London: Collins, 1958).

26. Marion Zimmer Bradley, *The Mists of Avalon* (New York: Ballantine, 1982).

27. Katherine Paterson, *Parzival: The Quest of the Grail Knight* (New York: Lodestar, 1998).

28. Jane Yolen, *Sword of the Rightful King: A Novel of King Arthur* (San Diego, CA: Harcourt, 2003).

29. Diana Wynne Jones, *The Merlin Conspiracy* (New York: Greenwillow, 2003).

30. David Almond, *Kit's Wilderness* (New York: Delacorte, 2000).

31. David Almond, *Clay* (New York: Delacorte, 2006).

32. Isabel Allende, *City of the Beasts*; *Kingdom of the Golden Dragon*; *Forest of the Pygmies*; trans. Margaret Sayers Peden (New York: HarperCollins, 2002–2005).

33. Francesca Lia Block, *Weetzie Bat*; *Witch Baby*; *Cherokee Bat and the Goat Guys*; *Missing Angel Juan*; *Baby Be-Bop* (New York: HarperCollins, 1989–1995).

34. Rick Yancey, *The Monstrumologist* (New York: Simon & Schuster, 2009).

35. Annette Curtis Klause, *Blood and Chocolate* (New York: Delacorte, 1997).

36. Stephenie Meyer, *Twilight*; *New Moon*; *Eclipse*; *Breaking Dawn* (New York: Little, Brown, 2005–2008).

37. A. M. Jenkins, *Repossessed: A Novel* (New York: HarperTeen, 2007).

38. Horace Walpole, *The Castle of Otranto* (New York: Oxford University Press, 2009).

39. Baldick, *Oxford Concise Dictionary*, 106.

40. Kami Garcia and Margaret Stohl, *Beautiful Creatures*; *Beautiful Darkness*; *Beautiful Chaos*; *Beautiful Redemption* (New York: Little, Brown, 2009–2012).

41. Arthur C. Clarke, *Profiles of the Future: An Enquiry into the Limits of the Possible* , rev. ed. (New York: Harper & Row, 1973), 21n1.

42. Larry Niven and Jerry Pournelle, *The Mote in God's Eye* (New York: Simon & Schuster, 1974).

43. Douglas Adams, *The Hitchhiker's Guide to the Galaxy* (London: Pan, 1979).

44. William Sleator, *Interstellar Pig* (New York: Bantam, 1984).

45. Rick Yancey, *The Fifth Wave* (New York: Putnam, 2013).

46. Orson Scott Card, *Ender's Game* (New York: Tor, 1985).

47. H. G. Wells, *The Time Machine* (London: Heinemann, 1895).

48. Nancy Etchemendy, *The Power of Un* (Honesdale, PA: Front Street/Cricket, 2000).

49. Isaac Asimov, *I, Robot* (New York: Gnome, 1950).

50. Philip K. Dick, *Do Androids Dream of Electric Sheep?* (New York: Doubleday, 1968).

51. Nancy Farmer, *The House of the Scorpion* (New York: Atheneum, 2002).

52. Peter Dickinson, *Eva* (London: Victor Gollancz, 1988).

53. William Sleator, *House of Stairs* (New York: Dutton, 1974).

54. Lois Lowry, *The Giver*; *Gathering Blue*; *Messenger*; *Son* (New York: Houghton Mifflin, 1993–2012).

55. Scott Westerfeld, *Uglies*; *Pretties*; *Specials*; *Extras* (New York: Simon & Schuster, 2005–2007).

56. Suzanne Collins, *The Hunger Games*; *Catching Fire*; *Mockingjay* (New York: Scholastic, 2008–2010).

57. Susan Beth Pfeffer, *Life As We Knew It* (New York: Harcourt, 2006).

58. Robert C. O'Brien, *Z for Zachariah* (New York: Atheneum, 1974).

59. Kenneth Oppel, *Airborn* (New York: HarperCollins, 2004).

60. William Gibson, *Neuromancer* (New York: Ace, 1984).

61. M. T. Anderson, *Feed* (Somerville, MA: Candlewick, 2002).

62. Ernest Cline, *Ready Player One* (New York: Random House, 2011).

63. Baldick, *Oxford Concise Dictionary*, 212.

64. Baldick, *Oxford Concise Dictionary*, 27.
65. Chris Crutcher, *Staying Fat for Sarah Byrnes* (New York: Greenwillow, 1993).
66. Chris Crutcher, *Athletic Shorts: Six Short Stories* (New York: Greenwillow, 1991).
67. Edward Bloor, *Tangerine* (New York: Scholastic, 1997).
68. Gary Paulsen, *Hatchet* (New York: Bradbury, 1987).
69. Geraldine McCaughrean, *The White Darkness: A Novel* (New York: HarperTempest, 2007).
70. John Green, *Paper Towns* (New York: Dutton, 2008).
71. Jennifer Donnelly, *A Northern Light* (New York: Harcourt, 2003).
72. Mark Haddon, *The Curious Incident of the Dog in the Night-Time* (New York: Doubleday, 2003).
73. Lois Duncan, *I Know What You Did Last Summer* (New York: Little Brown, 1973).
74. Lois Duncan, *Killing Mr. Griffin* (New York: Little, Brown, 1978).
75. Judy Blume, *Forever* (New York: Bradbury, 1975).
76. Rachel Cohn and David Levithan, *Nick and Norah's Infinite Playlist* (New York: Knopf, 2006).
77. David Levithan, *Boy Meets Boy* (New York: Knopf, 2003).
78. Nancy Garden, *Annie on My Mind* (New York: Farrar, Straus and Giroux, 1982).
79. Jacqueline Woodson, *The House You Pass on the Way* (New York: Delacorte, 1997).
80. John Green, *The Fault in Our Stars* (New York: Dutton, 2012).
81. Sherman Alexie, *The Absolutely True Diary of a Part-Time Indian* (New York: Little, Brown, 2007).
82. Angela Johnson, *The First Part Last* (New York: Simon & Schuster, 2003).
83. Walter Dean Myers, *Monster*, illus. Christopher Myers (New York: HarperCollins, 1999).
84. Laurie Halse Anderson, *Speak* (New York: Farrar, Straus and Giroux, 1999).
85. Laurie Halse Anderson, *Wintergirls* (New York: Viking, 2009).
86. Jay Asher, *Thirteen Reasons Why* (New York: Razorbill, 2007).
87. Vanessa Irvin Morris, *The Readers' Advisory Guide to Street Literature* (Chicago: American Library Association, 2011), 2.
88. Vanessa J. Morris et al., "Street Lit: Flying Off Teen Fiction Bookshelves in Philadelphia Public Libraries," *Young Adult Library Services* (fall 2006): 16–23.
89. Morris et al., "Street Lit."
90. Malcolm X, *The Autobiography of Malcolm X* (New York: Grove, 1965).
91. Claude Brown, *Manchild in the Promised Land* (New York: MacMillan, 1965).
92. Morris et al., "Street Lit."
93. Omar Tyree, *Flyy Girl* (New York: Simon & Schuster, 1993).
94. Sister Souljah, *The Coldest Winter Ever* (New York: Simon & Schuster, 1999).
95. Morris et al., "Street Lit."
96. Coe Booth, *Tyrell* (New York: Scholastic, 2007).
97. Teri Woods, *True to the Game* (New York: Grand Central, 2007).
98. G. Neri, *Yummy: The Last Days of a Southside Shorty*, illus. Randy Duburke (New York: Lee and Low, 2010).
99. Walter Dean Myers, *Autobiography of My Dead Brother*, illus. Christopher Myers (New York: HarperTempest, 2005).
100. Sandra Hughes-Hassell, "Multicultural Young Adult Literature as a Form of Counterstorytelling," *Library Quarterly* 83 (July 2013): 212–28.
101. Alexie, *The Absolutely True Diary*.
102. Cynthia Kadohata, *Kira-Kira* (New York: Atheneum, 2004).
103. Pam Muñoz Ryan, *Esperanza Rising* (New York: Scholastic, 2000).
104. Walter Dean Myers, *The Glory Field* (New York: Scholastic, 1994).
105. M. E. Kerr, *Deliver Us from Evie* (New York: HarperCollins, 1994).
106. Julie Anne Peters, *Luna* (New York: Little, Brown, 2004).
107. Benjamin Alire Sáenz, *Aristotle and Dante Discover the Secrets of the Universe* (New York: Simon & Schuster, 2012).

108. Jean Claude Mourlevat, *The Pull of the Ocean*, trans. Y. Maudet (New York: Delacorte, 2006).

109. Marjane Satrapi, *Persepolis: The Story of a Childhood* (New York: Random House, 2003); *Persepolis 2: The Story of a Return* (New York: Random House, 2004).

110. Allan Stratton, *Chanda's Secrets* (Toronto: Annick, 2004).

111. Avi, *Crispin: The Cross of Lead* (New York: Hyperion, 2002).

112. Geraldine McCaughrean, *The Kite Rider: A Novel* (New York: HarperCollins, 2002).

113. Laurie Halse Anderson, *Chains* (New York: Atheneum, 2008).

114. Julius Lester, *Day of Tears: A Novel in Dialogue* (New York: Hyperion, 2005).

115. Elizabeth Wein, *Code Name Verity* (New York: Hyperion, 2012).

116. Jen Scott Curwood, Alecia Marie Magnifico, and Jayne C. Lammers, "Writing in the Wild: Writers' Motivation in Fan-Based Affinity Spaces," *Journal of Adolescent and Adult Literacy* 56 (2013): 677–85.

117. Archive of Our Own, "Welcome to the Archive of Our Own!" 2013, http://archiveofourown.org/.

118. James Paul Gee, *Situated Language and Learning: A Critique of Traditional Schooling* (New York: Routledge, 2004).

119. Henry Jenkins, "Confessions of an Aca-Fan: The Official Weblog of Henry Jenkins," September 27, 2006, http://henryjenkins.org/2006/09/fan_fiction_as_critical_commen.html.

120. Jenkins, *Confessions of an Aca-Fan*.

121. Louise Rosenblatt, *Literature as Exploration* (New York: Modern Language Association of America, 1995).

122. Association for Library Service to Children, "Welcome to the (Mildred L.) Batchelder Award home page," 2013, http://www.ala.org/alsc/awardsgrants/bookmedia/batchelderaward.

Chapter Six

Nonfiction

This chapter covers key aspects of nonfiction resources for young adults:

- Definition and characteristics of nonfiction
- Nonfiction, reading, and young adults
- Types of nonfiction
- Evaluating and promoting nonfiction
- Spotlight! Reference services
- Implications for practice
- Questions to think about and discuss

Nonfiction is more popular than fiction with some young adults. Moreover, in most school libraries, the allotment for nonfiction materials accounts for the majority of the materials budget.[1] Young adults turn to nonfiction resources for a variety of information needs, including research for school assignments, information related to hobbies, instruction, inspiration, and recreational reading, just to name a few. The topics for nonfiction are as vast as human history, knowledge, and achievement, and there is seemingly no limit to the kinds of nonfiction resources being produced in our information- and media-rich world. Understanding the array of nonfiction resources available for young adults can help information professionals and other educators better meet the informational and recreational needs of the young adults with whom they work.

DEFINITION AND CHARACTERISTICS OF NONFICTION

Nonfiction may be defined as fact-based texts intended primarily to inform. This apparently straightforward definition, when examined closely, proves to be more complex than it first appears. One issue is the term itself. *Nonfiction* implies *not fiction* to many people, and, as such, they think of nonfiction as referring to poetry and drama as well as informational texts. Strictly speaking, however, poetry and drama are separate genres, just as fiction is, and nonfiction is yet a different genre altogether, one that focuses more on factual rather than imaginative writing.

Another issue is that many textbooks on young adult literature define nonfiction as consisting of two broad categories—biographical writing and informational writing. This division unnecessarily complicates the term and suggests, incorrectly, that biography is somehow different from informational texts, that it does not contain information, or that it contains a special kind of information that sets it apart. This false dichotomy most likely stems from the observation that most biographies have a strong narrative arc and, in that sense, are closely akin to fiction. However, other kinds of informational texts employ narrative structure as well, including history, current events, true crime, and even some books on science. In fact, many of the best informational texts are those in which the author has found the story lurking beneath or emerging from the seemingly disparate collection of facts. So nonfiction, as we define it, is writing based on facts intended primarily to inform. This definition is broad and flexible enough to encompass both biographical writing (including autobiography and memoir) and what are often called "informational texts."

A third issue is the notion that nonfiction writing is intended primarily to inform. To say that nonfiction informs is not, however, to suggest that it cannot also provide pleasure in reading. As we shall see, many of the most well-respected authors of young adult fiction have mastered the ability to convey facts in a way that is informative and entertaining, enlightening and engaging at the same time. Again, it is often a matter of the author finding the story (or the drama) within the mound of facts, bringing it to the fore, and telling it in a compelling way.

Aside from the basic definition, then, what are the specific characteristics of nonfiction? Most nonfiction texts have significant paratextual elements. The paratext, as Gerard Genette explains, comprises those parts of a book that surround the text proper and connect it to the world.[2] Two such elements provide access to the various topics covered in the book: the table of contents, at the beginning of the text, provides an outline of the text that follows; the index, at the end of the text, provides more specific access via keywords and phrases. These two paratextual elements can be especially useful if a reader wants to look up information on a particular topic, for example, in compiling notes for a research project.

Some nonfiction works have a preface or foreword—sometimes written by the author, sometimes by someone else. Usually, these elements serve to introduce the material that follows and thus pave the way for the reader to enter the text itself. By the same token, an afterword can provide a summary of the material presented in the text and perhaps point to future research that needs to be done or issues that need to be resolved. A bibliography or list of source notes connects what appears in the text to other texts and provides documentation for readers who want to consult the sources that were used. Similarly, some nonfiction books include suggestions for further reading, in addition to a list of the sources used in compiling the book. These suggested readings can be particularly useful to someone wanting to do further research or further reading on the topic.

Nonfiction resources typically contain nontextual elements within the text that help to convey the information visually. It is not unusual for nonfiction books to contains photographs, illustrations, diagrams, graphs, tables, and so forth, that supplement and strengthen the material covered by the writing. Photographs may include images of people, places, things, or scenes or reproductions of artifacts such as letters or newspaper articles. Illustrations and diagrams may be used to convey technical information in a way that is easier to see and understand than that which a photograph would provide. Graphs and tables can convey statistical information, for example, in a way that allows for easier comparison across instances than what would be possible in straight textual form. These visual elements are not simply nice decorations but rather key parts of the information that is provided in the written text. It is important that visual elements be labeled appropriately (with captions, call-out boxes, etc.) and that they be clearly connected to information presented in the text. As with written material, visual material should be carefully documented to identify sources and creators.

None of this is to say that fiction texts cannot contain the same kinds of paratextual and nontextual elements, but it is much more unusual to find such elements in works of fiction. It should also be noted that autobiography and memoir do not often contain bibliographies or lists of source notes, as the author is basing the information on the facts of her or his life rather than secondary sources. Autobiography and memoir may not contain as many—or, indeed, any—visual elements either, with graphic memoirs being an obvious exception.

Nonfiction is often distinguished from fiction as being fact based rather than imaginative writing. While this is true in the sense that nonfiction is not "made up" in the way that the other genres are, there is certainly a creative aspect to nonfiction. The nonfiction author does not just present facts in a rote manner. Few people would find that interesting. Instead, good nonfiction writers select and arrange facts in a skillful, artful way to present a compelling account of the topic, whether it be a person's life, a historical event, a current social issue, or a scientific phenomenon. Nonfiction writers must make decisions about which facts to present, which to omit, and how to arrange them. Add to this a consideration of the style in which the material is written, and it becomes apparent how "imaginative" good nonfiction writers must be. Style involves matters of sentence structure, vocabulary, and tone. There is no one style that is appropriate for nonfiction, just as there is no single style appropriate for fiction. It depends on the author, the topic, and the intended audience. As with fiction, part of the pleasure of reading nonfiction is enjoying the style in which it is written. Humor has its place in nonfiction, as do sorrow, wonder, suspense, and joy. What's to be avoided at all costs is a dry-as-dust style that young adults associate with many textbooks.

Finally, we should say a word about objectivity. It is commonplace to think that works of nonfiction should be free of bias, and, generally speaking, there is merit to this view. However, it raises the question of whether any work—fiction or nonfiction—can be completely objective and, moreover, whether this would be desirable if it could be achieved. Authors cannot help but bring their own understandings, views, and background to any creative activity, including the writing of nonfiction. In the facts that they select, the words that they use to phrase them, and the ways that they arrange them, authors bring their own viewpoints to bear—viewpoints related to their subject, their audience, and their sense of language. If an author could achieve complete objectivity, the presentation might very well come off in the dry-as-dust manner mentioned earlier.

Given authors' inability to not insert their own viewpoints in the ways that they shape their material, is it even possible to provide young adults with nonfiction materials that are (relatively) unbiased? Four points should be kept in mind. First, it is important to avoid works with known inaccuracies. While the reason may be more a matter of sloppy homework than intentional bias, incorrect information should not be perpetrated on an unsuspecting audience. Second, it is important to be wary of books that deliberately distort or suppress key facts, for incomplete information can be as harmful as incorrect information. Third, it is important to recognize that no single book can do it all and, therefore, to strive for a balanced collection that contains multiple works on any given topic. Fourth, information professionals should avoid nonfiction books that have obvious bias or are written for didactic purposes. At the same time, they should help young adults develop the skills to be discerning readers in detecting bias and in comparing the ways that different authors address the same subject.

NONFICTION, READING, AND YOUNG ADULTS

Nonfiction resources can meet young adults' informational and recreational reading needs, as well as help them address imposed and self-generated information tasks.[3] Nonfiction can help young adults in completing assignments for school, but more broadly, it can help satisfy curiosity by answering the questions *How?* and *Why?* As discussed in chapter 2, the brain experiences an intense period of growth just before puberty in the area related to planning, memory, mood regulation, and organizing.[4] Faris[5] notes that this period of very active brain development is an optimal time to provide preteens with nonfiction books that both respond to those questions and encourage further inquisitiveness.

It is also during this time that young adults are typically introduced to the research process in school and, as such, are expected to consult secondary sources (usually nonfiction) to complete research projects. Students quickly move beyond simply collecting factual information to analyzing, interpreting, and synthesizing information from a variety of sources. Nonfiction is crucial in helping students complete these kinds of assignments. This is also the time when young people are developing hobbies and interests that often spur them to look for more information so that they can become more adept at and more knowledgeable about whatever they're pursuing. Again, nonfiction resources provide valuable information, whether it's how to become a better soccer player or why there may once have been life on Mars.

Nonfiction can help support young adults' various developmental tasks, as discussed in chapter 2. The young adult years are a time of tremendous changes in terms of physical development. Resources on sports, physical fitness, nutrition, health, and sexuality can help young adults better understand the changes they are experiencing in their bodies as well as how properly to care for themselves and to develop their bodies to be healthy and active individuals. Books about other individuals' physical challenges— whether great athletes, differently abled individuals, or people who have faced serious illness—can provide role models for young adults and help them to become more comfortable in their own skin.

By the same token, the act of reading nonfiction can help promote cognitive growth by encouraging learning, analysis, and critical thinking. Reading nonfiction can aid in emotional development by, for example, providing information about how other people have developed emotionally or faced emotional challenges. Many self-help books, for example, address this need, as do biographies and memoirs.

Nonfiction can also promote social development by providing information on such diverse topics as friendship, romantic relationships, team sports, bullying, safe Internet practices, and many more. Finally, nonfiction can promote moral development in young adults who may be starting to question their parents' and society's values. Advice books may or may not have a religious component, but they often discuss the "right" thing to do in a given situation. Similarly, biographies and memoirs, through either positive or negative examples, can provide models of people who have developed their own particular ethos and may have struggled with their own moral dilemmas.

It is certainly the case that the bulk of school library budgets, especially in middle and high school libraries, is devoted to nonfiction resources.[6] It is also the case that some young adults actually prefer nonfiction to fiction. Nonfiction seems to be particularly popular with boys[7] and with many reluctant readers.[8] Why should this be the case? One explanation might be a general preference for factual information, as is evident in the popularity of so-called reality television. Regardless of what one may think of this phenomenon, it is clear that the public—and young adults are no exception—currently has a taste for the "real," in all of its messy glory.

Boys especially seem to prefer practical information that they can apply to real-world problems. Smith and Wilhelm[9] capture this attitude memorably in the title of their book on boys and reading: *Reading Don't Fix No Chevys*. Unless, of course, one is reading a book on how to fix Chevys! And that is precisely the point. When many boys read, it's for the purpose of learning how something works, how to do something, and how to improve one's skills (at, say, playing video games).

Reluctant readers also often find nonfiction more appealing than fiction. The reason is not that nonfiction is "easier" but rather that it focuses on topics related to real life, contains appealing graphics as well as text, is organized into manageable chunks of information, and doesn't have to be read from beginning to end.[10] Many young adults find real stories about real people overcoming hardship or achieving great feats to be more compelling than fictional stories on similar topics. And, of course, some young adults don't make a strong distinction between the two genres. After all, a good story on a high-interest topic is enticing, whether fiction or nonfiction.

In addition to helping young adults meet their developmental needs, informational needs (whether imposed or self-generated), and recreational needs, nonfiction has an important role to play in meeting the various standards related to analytical reading and critical thinking that are being emphasized in education today. The *Common Core State Standards*, for example, emphasizes increased use of informational texts especially in grades 6–12. Developed by the National Governors Association Center for Best Practices and the Council of Chief State School Officers with input from a variety of constituent groups, the *Common Core State Standards* provide specific standards for each grade level (K–12), intended to ensure that students are equipped to succeed in college and the workforce.[11] According to these standards, required reading lists of informational texts should include "the subgenres of exposition, argument, and functional text in the form of personal essays, speeches, opinion pieces, essays about art or literature, biographies, memoirs, journalism, and historical, scientific, technical, or economic accounts (including digital sources) written for a broad audience."[12] Similarly, the Partnership for 21st Century Skills has set forth five *21st Century*

Standards, all of which relate in one way or another to students' ability to engage with informational texts. Specifically, the standards

- focus on 21st-century skills, content knowledge, and expertise;
- build understanding across and among core subjects as well as 21st-century interdisciplinary themes;
- emphasize deep understanding rather than shallow knowledge;
- engage students with the real-world data, tools, and experts they will encounter in college, on the job, and in life—students learn best when actively engaged in solving meaningful problems; and
- allow for multiple measures of mastery. [13]

The American Association of School Librarians' *Standards for the 21st Century Learner* [14] also emphasize the role of reading and research in the educational process. These standards state that learners use skills, resources, and tools to

1. Inquire, think critically, and gain knowledge.
2. Draw conclusions, make informed decisions, apply knowledge to new situations, and create new knowledge.
3. Share knowledge and participate ethically and productively as members of our democratic society.
4. Pursue personal and aesthetic growth. [15]

While informational texts are not mentioned specifically in these standards, the focus on reading, writing, and the research process suggests an underlying expectation—namely, that students be able to analyze, evaluate, and use information from a variety of nonfiction resources.

TYPES OF NONFICTION

The range of topics covered by nonfiction is as broad and diverse as human knowledge and experience. Categorizing this enormous mass of information is challenging, to say the least, but there are existing frameworks at our disposal. One way to think about nonfiction resources is in terms of the three broad academic disciplines: science and technology, the social sciences, and arts and humanities. Another way is to use the framework provided by the Dewey decimal classification system: [16]

000 Generalities
100 Philosophy and psychology
200 Religion
300 Social sciences

400 Language
500 Natural sciences and mathematics
600 Technology (applied sciences)
700 The arts
800 Literature and rhetoric
900 Geography and history

It should be noted that the 800s contain both fiction and nonfiction. Poetry and riddles are included there, as are critical works of literary analysis. For our purposes, we consider various types of nonfiction and representative titles in terms of popular categories among young adult readers: biography, autobiography, and memoir; history; science and technology; health and sexuality; and self-development.[17]

In this chapter, we focus on the traditional print format (although many of these titles are available electronically as well). In the next chapter, we consider graphic formats, including graphic nonfiction. And books aren't the only kind of nonfiction young adults read. In summarizing the research on young adults and their reading preferences, Paulette Rothbauer[18] notes that many young adults read magazines and newspapers, both of which contain mostly nonfiction writing, and we might add that they are increasingly accessing those sources in electronic format.

Biography, Autobiography, and Memoir

Biography, autobiography, and memoir are types of nonfiction writing that cut across all fields and disciplines. As Bernard Lukenbill points out, biography can play a variety of important roles in the lives of young adults, including "transmitting vital cultural information," helping young adults "understand options and consequences of choices in terms of such areas as gender and social roles, relationships, and achievement," and modeling and facilitating the various developmental tasks that young adults must undertake.[19] In summary, Lukenbill says that biography "plays an important role in preparing youth for adulthood. It provides social and psychological support, enabling and encouraging youth to achieve to the best of their potential."[20]

Biography resonates with many young adults because it foregrounds issues related to developing an identity, a key developmental task for adolescents. Biography provides instructive information through both positive and negative examples and encourages young adults to think critically about what it means to take one's place in adult society. Biography can also encourage young adults to think critically about how the process of selecting facts and suppressing others can color the portrait of a given subject. Reading and comparing two (or more) biographies on the same individual can be highly instructive in illustrating different writers' emphases and biases, as well as a powerful way to demonstrate the importance of consulting more than one source on any topic. Biographical writing typically makes use of narrative but may also include expository modes, such as cause and effect, analysis, and comparison and contrast.

Political figures, national leaders, and infamous individuals are popular subjects for biographies. Russell Freedman's *Lincoln: A Photobiography*[21] is an award-winning biography of the 16th president of the United States that makes ample use of period photographs and facsimiles of historical documents. Similarly, James Cross Giblin includes a number of photographs and the occasional political cartoon to present *The Rise and Fall of Senator Joe McCarthy*,[22] about the rabid anticommunist senator from Wisconsin. Candace Fleming's *Our Eleanor: A Scrapbook Look at Eleanor Roosevelt's Remarkable Life*[23] goes even further than Freedman's or Giblin's book, offering a rich portrait of its subject through reproductions of photographs, newspaper clippings, speeches, letters, drawings, posters, and advertisements. In contrast, Steve Sheinkin uses few visuals and relies instead on a well-paced chronological account to tell the compelling story of *The Notorious Benedict Arnold: A True Story of Adventure, Heroism, and Treachery*.[24]

Other famous people who are popular subjects of biographies include entertainers and sports figures. Of perennial interest to young adults are musicians, especially those who made a significant impact and died young. Ann Angel's *Janis Joplin: Rise Up Singing*[25] uses a clever design and colorful graphics from the 1960s to tell the remarkable yet tragic story of the hard-living rock star from Port Arthur, Texas. Angel clearly admires her subject and appreciates the important contributions that she made to rock music, but she does not shy away from presenting Joplin as someone who struggled with inner demons and sometimes made bad choices. Elizabeth Partridge takes a similar approach to her subject in *John Lennon: All I Want Is the Truth*.[26] Partridge presents an appreciative yet honest account of the musician's innovative contributions to pop music and courageous stance against the Vietnam War but also his drug use, mistreatment of his first wife, and somewhat distant attitude toward their son.

Biographies of ordinary young people facing extraordinary situations are also of great interest to many young adults. One example is Andrea Warren's *Surviving Hitler: A Boy in the Nazi Death Camps*.[27] Warren's book focuses on the coming-of-age story of Janek "Jack" Mandelbaum, who spent three years as a teenager in Hitler's concentration camps and survived to tell the horrors that he experienced there. Phillip Hoose's *Claudette Colvin: Twice toward Justice*[28] relates the story of an African American teenager in Montgomery, Alabama, who, months before Rosa Parks's famous act of civil disobedience, refused to relinquish her seat on the bus to a white person. Both Warren's and Hoose's books recover a part of history that had heretofore been mostly forgotten. Both depict "typical" teenagers who face and conquer great challenges through courage, determination, and strength of character.

Autobiographies and memoirs can be especially appealing to young adults who enjoy hearing peoples' life stories in their own words. These accounts can also provide role models for young adults who are grappling with making their own decisions and forming their own identities. Memoirs by writers that young adults know and admire can be especially effective. Walter Dean Myers, for example, is the author of numerous young adult books featuring African American, usually male, protagonists. *Bad Boy: A Memoir*,[29] Myers's account of his own childhood and adolescence, tells of his development as a reader and a writer. Growing up in a society thinking that African American males were suitable only for sports or physical labor and with a father who saw reading as a waste of time, Myers became a "closeted reader," quickly progressing from comic books to works of classic literature.[30] Because of his sensitive, intelligent nature, Myers did not have an easy adolescence. However, the message of *Bad Boy* is that reading and education are valuable and that one should not be afraid to go against the grain of family or society.

Jack Gantos, an author best known for his children's books, recounts his development as a writer in his memoir *Hole in My Life*.[31] This book focuses on a roughly two-year period in Gantos's life when he was arrested for smuggling drugs into the country, was tried and convicted, and spent 18 months in prison. During this time, Gantos grew up and developed his writing ability, partly as a way to ward off boredom and fear. Young adults who, perhaps as children, enjoyed the Joey Pigza books might be surprised to learn that Gantos served time in prison, and they will likely be fascinated by his story of bad decisions and personal redemption.

An even more dramatic example of self-destructive behavior is provided by Brent Runyon's *The Burn Journals*.[32] In this memoir, Runyon tells the gripping story of his painful physical and emotional recovery from self-inflicted wounds he received when, as a 14-year-old, he deliberately set himself on fire.

Additional recommendations on biographies and autobiographies for young adults can be found in Bernard Lukenbill's insightful book *Biography in the Lives of Youth: Culture, Society, and Information* and in appendix 2.[33]

History

Historical writing is closely related to biography; in fact, one genre is often found in the other. A vivid biography usually must include historical context so that readers can fully appreciate the subject's life, challenges, and achievements. By the same token, history is made up of the lives of people, and a compelling historical account must include enough biographical information to make the players come alive. History can focus on particular places, periods, movements, peoples, and events—or some combination thereof. Authors typically draw on both primary (if available) and secondary sources in constructing their accounts, and they often use reproductions of primary materials, such as photographs, letters, newspaper clippings, cartoons, and so on, to help bring their subjects to life. In addition, authors of historical nonfiction can use various modes of writing, with the most common being narrative, causal analysis, and comparison and contrast.

One common kind of historical writing for young adults examines the history of a particular group of people. Sometimes these are stories of people who have asserted themselves in spite of the prejudice and even persecution they faced. *Gay America: Struggle for Equality*, by Linas Alsenas,[34] for example, looks at the history of gay and lesbian people in the United States from the late 19th century to the present, successfully demonstrating that there was a vibrant gay culture before and after the famous Stonewall riots of 1969. In *Almost Astronauts: 13 Women Who Dared to Dream*,[35] Tanya Lee Stone recounts the story of 13 highly skilled women pilots who met overwhelming resistance when they tried to gain admission to the astronaut training program in the early 1960s. Susan Campbell Bartoletti's *Hitler Youth: Growing Up in Hitler's Shadow*[36] draws on a variety of primary sources to relate the sinister story of how the Nazis recruited millions of naïve young people to serve the Third Reich. In *They Called Themselves the KKK: The Birth of an American Terrorist Group*,[37] Bartoletti again draws on primary source material, this time to tell the equally horrific story of the genesis, evolution, and nefarious deeds of the Ku Klux Klan.

Some histories focus on specific events that have had a significant impact on humanity. Calamities are especially popular topics—some of them of natural origins, others human-made. Jim Murphy's *An American Plague: The True and Terrifying Story of the Yellow Fever Epidemic of 1793*[38] vividly describes the devastating effects of and medical response to the yellow fever epidemic in Philadelphia, at that time the nation's capital. In *Titanic: Voices from the Disaster*,[39] Deborah Hopkinson uses archival materials to allow people who survived or witnessed the sinking of the great ship to tell their own stories. Russell Freedman, in *The War to End All Wars: World War I*,[40] provides a realistic, unflinching look at the human costs of the Great War. And in *Bomb: The Race to Build—and Steal—the World's Most Dangerous Weapon*,[41] Steve Sheinkin details the gripping story of the secrecy and intrigue surrounding the development and deployment of the world's first atomic bomb.

Other histories focus on social or artistic movements. Marc Aronson's *Art Attack: A Short Cultural History of the Avant-Garde*[42] examines the creative forces on the leading edge of modern art from the late 19th century onward. *Harlem Stomp! A Cultural History of the Harlem Renaissance*,[43] by Laban

Carrick Hill, discusses the art, music, and literature of that 20th-century cultural movement. Women's liberation is the topic of *Wheels of Change: How Women Rode the Bicycle to Freedom (with a Few Flat Tires along the Way),*[44] by Sue Macy, while *Freedom Riders: John Lewis and Jim Zwerg on the Front Lines of the Civil Rights Movement,*[45] by Ann Bausum, looks at the civil rights movement through the experiences of two participants, one black and one white.

Some histories, rather than focusing on people or events, take as their focus a specific phenomenon. Such is the case with Marc Aronson and Marina Budhos's *Sugar Changed the World: A Story of Magic, Spice, Slavery, Freedom, and Science.*[46] Through the use of oral histories, photographs, and maps, the authors trace the fascinating and often brutal history of sugar cane. A chapter on how the authors researched and wrote the book effectively models the research process for young adult readers.

A very different kind of phenomenon book is *The Good, the Bad, and the Barbie: A Doll's History and Her Impact on Us,*[47] by Tanya Lee Stone. Part history, part cultural studies, the book examines the influence of the iconic doll that has generated both affection and controversy for more than 50 years. Stone includes numerous cleverly posed photographs of the different incarnations of Barbie, as well as testimony from both young people and adults who talk about the doll's impact on their lives.

A special type of historical writing that is popular with some young adults is the true crime book. From Jack the Ripper and Lizzie Borden to Charles Manson and Ted Bundy, murderers, serial killers, and other criminals hold a fascination for many young adults—and, indeed, for many adults as well. Part of the appeal of such books, aside from the thrill of a gripping story, is the intellectual gratification of gaining insight into the criminal mind and solving, or trying to solve, a mystery. Usually, though not always, true crime books focus on crimes that had societal impact beyond the boundaries of the local communities in which they occurred. One such book is Chris Crowe's *Getting Away with Murder: The True Story of the Emmett Till Case,*[48] which looks at the effect that this murder had on energizing the civil rights movement. Some true crime accounts focus on forensic science techniques, and those are discussed in the "Science" section. Other true crime stories are presented in graphic format and are discussed in the next chapter.

Science and Technology

Science writing examines the natural world and employs various modes, including description, casual analysis, comparison and contrast, and problem/solution. Some of the most compelling science writing also employs narrative in telling the stories behind phenomena, discoveries, and processes in the physical sciences, life sciences, and earth and space sciences. Writing on technology examines machines and processes developed by humans and typically includes the same modes used in science writing, including narrative. There are, of course, numerous biographies on scientists and inventors. *Charles and Emma: The Darwins' Leap of Faith*,[49] by Deborah Heiligman, for example, explores the relationship between the father of evolution and his religious wife. And Russell Freedman's *The Wright Brothers: How They Invented the Airplane*[50] presents the story of the famous siblings and their flying machine. However, since we've already discussed biography, we now focus on informational texts that examine the phenomena and processes of science and technology.

Science nonfiction can help meet young adults' information needs related to cognitive development, particularly their understanding of how the world works, and it can also help them achieve science literacy, as defined by the National Research Council's *A Framework for K–12 Science Education*.[51] The framework specifies skill development along three dimensions: scientific and engineering practices (e.g., asking questions, developing models, conducting investigations, analyzing results), crosscutting concepts (e.g., recognizing patterns, analyzing cause and effect, understanding systems and structures), and disciplinary core ideas (in the physical sciences, life sciences, earth and space sciences, and technology and applied sciences).[52]

The best books on science not only explore interesting questions but also illustrate the passion and process involved in scientific inquiry, or as Zarnowski and Turkel (2011) put it, "how real people solve real problems."[53] Going beyond the simple presentation of facts, these books reveal what Zarnowski and Turkel elsewhere call the "nature of science," by which they mean "the philosophical, historical, and sociological essence of what [science] is."[54]

Several books that exemplify these characteristics of good science writing focus on different kinds of animals, a perennially popular topic among young adults. Nic Bishop has a series of books on animals featuring his vivid and stunning photographs. Among the titles are *Spiders, Frogs, Marsupials, Butterflies and Moths, Lizards*, and *Snakes*.[55] Sy Montgomery and Bishop have collaborated on several books on the interactions of humans and exotic animals, including *The Tarantula Scientist, The Quest for the Tree Kangaroo: An Expedition to the Cloud Forest of New Guinea*, and *Kakapo Rescue: Saving the World's Strangest Parrot*.[56] Books focusing on similar topics are Phillip Hoose's *Moonbird: A Year on the Wind with the Great Survivor B95*[57] and Loree Griffin Burns and Ellen Harasimowicz's *The Hive Detectives: Chronicle of a Honey Bee Catastrophe*.[58]

Another topic of great interest for young adults is forensic science, combining the elegance of scientific principles with the thrill of a good mystery. No doubt motivated by the popularity of forensics-focused television programs, young adults are exploring forensic science in both their science classes[59] and their recreational reading. Richard Platt's *Forensics*[60] takes readers inside a crime laboratory to demonstrate how science helps investigators solve crimes. *Dusted and Busted: The Science of Fingerprinting*,[61] by D. B. Beres, is part of *Scholastic's 24/7: Science behind the Scenes—Forensics* series and examines a familiar but not necessarily well-understood aspect of crime scene investigations. Anna Prokos's *Guilty by a Hair! Real-Life DNA Matches!*[62] is part of the same series and focuses on the role of DNA evidence in solving crimes. Young adults interested in forensics might also be intrigued by *Every Bone Tells a Story: Hominin Discoveries, Deductions, and Debates*,[63] by Jill Rubalcaba and Peter Robertshaw. This book recounts the discoveries of four human ancestors and the resulting scientific research and heated debates that ensued among paleontologists and archaeologists.

Books on science are as rich and diverse as the scientific phenomena they address. Other topics that hold high interest for young adults include dinosaurs, space and astronomy, climate change, the environment, and natural disasters. Many young adults are also interested in books that offer guidance on developing science fair projects and books that pose and discuss intriguing math puzzles.

Books on technology are equally diverse, but many of them take as their focus explaining how something works. An excellent example of this kind of book is David Macaulay and Neil Ardley's *The New Way Things Work*,[64] which examines the mechanisms behind many everyday machines, including computers. Macaulay also has published several classic books offering astonishing views of how architectural structures "work," that is, how they are put together; *Cathedral*, *Castle*, and *Mosque*[65] are just a few examples. Marshall Brain, the founder and CEO of HowStuffWorks, has written a reference guide, *How Stuff Works*,[66] addressing that question on more than 100 topics. Not strictly limited to technology (one topic, for example, is viruses), the book nonetheless offers clear explanations on the workings of scores of machines, from toasters to airplanes.

Some books on technology also include a historical perspective. *Secrets of a Civil War Submarine: Solving the Mysteries of the H. L. Hunley*,[67] by Sally M. Walker, provides a detailed account of the design and construction of the submarine and the expedition to recover it from Charleston Harbor more than 130 years later. DK Publishing's *Ideas That Changed the World: Incredible Inventions and the Stories behind Them*[68] examines more than 80 inventions and their impact on the world. DK also has a number of books on specific inventions, ranging from cars to robots and from trains to space exploration. Though appropriate for intermediate readers, these books offer a wealth of information, through text and visuals, that young adults would find useful and appealing as well.

Many young adults also seek how-to information, some of which is technology focused. The myriad topics in this category are as diverse and specific as young adults' hobbies and interests. These include how to use a particular software program (Adobe Photoshop, for instance), upgrade a computer, build a robot, or repair a car (maybe reading can help fix Chevys after all!). While how-to books rarely win awards or make best-seller lists and become outdated rather quickly, they can help address young adults' information needs related to building, maintaining, and using technology. A number of the books in the *Complete Idiot's Guide* and the *Dummies* series relate specifically to technology.

Health and Sexuality

Young adults consult health resources for a variety of reasons in response to imposed and self-generated information tasks. Books on human anatomy and physiology can satisfy curiosity about the human body and can help in completing research projects for school. An excellent example of this kind of book is David Macaulay and Richard Walker's *The Way We Work: Getting to Know the Amazing Human Body*,[69] a detailed and beautifully illustrated guide to human anatomy.

Young adults may also be interested in particular diseases, either because they have a chronic disease or they have a friend or family member with one. Maureen J. Hinds's *Fighting the AIDS and HIV Epidemic: A Global Battle*[70] provides information about prevention and treatment. Maintaining good health through a healthy lifestyle is also a topic of great interest to many young adults. Books on nutrition, obesity, and weight loss abound and range from the practical, such as Matthew Locricchio's cookbook *Teen Cuisine*,[71] to the polemical, such as Eric Schlosser and Charles Wilson's *Chew on This: Everything You Didn't Want to Know about Fast Food.*[72]

Health resources also include mental health resources, and there are a number of books dealing with mental health issues, such as eating disorders, depression, anxiety, suicide, and substance abuse. Social issues affecting mental health are also the topic of many books. A recent *New York Times* article stated that books on bullying, for both adults and young people, had become a cottage industry.[73] Other social issues affecting mental health include sexual, physical, and emotional abuse; homophobia; and body image, just to name a few. An excellent resource on health information resources and services is Bernard Lukenbill and Barbara Immroth's *Health Information for Youth: The Public Library and School Library Media Center Role.*[74]

Of particular interest to most young adults is information about sex, sexuality, dating, and relationships. Robie H. Harris and Michael Emberley's controversial classic *It's Perfectly Normal: A Book about Changing Bodies, Growing Up, Sex, and Sexual Health*[75] has been updated for the 21st century and is still one of the best on this topic—but there are plenty of others as well. Some take a "frequently asked question" approach and present useful information in a matter-of-fact way. One example is Faith Hickman Brynie's *101 Questions about Sex and Sexuality . . . with Answers for the Curious and Confused*.[76] Other books present sexual information specifically for girls or boys, while still others focus on ways to prevent sexually transmitted diseases, unwanted pregnancies, and unwanted advances. It should be noted that the most effective books on sex and sexuality deal with the emotional and social aspects of sexual behavior in addition to the physical. It should also be noted that making these books easily accessible to young adults is important because some of them will be too embarrassed or self-conscious to ask for this kind of information. This can be a particularly sensitive issue for LGBTQ young people.

Self-Development

Self-development represents a broad category, and admittedly, almost any kind of informational book could be used for self-actualization. However, we're using the term *self-development* to refer to self-help/advice and how-to books as well as (some) books on sports, hobbies, and other recreational activities. Under the heading of self-help/advice, there's Jack Canfield, Mark Victor Hansen, and Kimberly Kirberger's *Chicken Soup for the Teenage Soul: 101 Stories of Life, Love, and Learning*,[77] and there are books in the series dealing with such diverse topics as growing up, negotiating relationships, dealing with difficult situations, getting into college, and so on. There's also an installment of the popular *7 Habits* series specifically for young adults: Sean Covey's *The 7 Habits of Highly Effective Teens: The Ultimate Teenage Success Guide*.[78]

The topics of young adult advice books reflect the diversity of the activities that young adults engage in; there are books on dating, etiquette, Internet safety, fashion, faith, financial management—you name it, and there's a book on it. Young adults also read books and other information sources on sports, hobbies, and other recreational activities. There are plenty of biographies on famous athletes and histories of particular sports and sports teams, but there are also a number of how-to books on improving one's performance in a given sport, whether an individual sport such as golf or tennis or a team sport such as baseball or volleyball.

How-to books extend to other activities as well. As noted here, some of these activities, such as repairing a car or building a computer, are technology focused, and certainly these activities can enhance self-development. But young adults engage in many other activities too, such as playing the guitar, quilting, cooking, gardening, woodworking, dancing, bodybuilding, gymnastics, writing, drawing—the list is endless—and there are numerous books available to meet young adults' related information needs. As Rothbauer[79] points out, the assertion that young adults don't read because they're too busy doing other things is incorrect, for, in fact, many young adults read materials directly related to their hobbies and other recreational activities. An activity of interest to many young adults is travel, and even if they're not currently in a position to travel widely, they enjoy reading about other places and other people's adventures. There are a number of travel memoirs on the market and an even greater number of travel guides. The DK *Eyewitness Travel Guides* are a notable example, clearly written and replete with beautiful color illustrations.

EVALUATING AND PROMOTING NONFICTION

In evaluating nonfiction resources, there's no substitute for a close examination of the resources themselves. Donelson and Nilsen[80] suggest focusing on setting/scope, theme, tone, and style when evaluating nonfiction. Tomlinson and Lynch-Brown[81] recommend considering specific aspects of structure, theme, and style. The criteria used by the Orbis Pictus Award for Nonfiction Committee are accuracy, organization, design, and style.[82] We suggest the following as useful criteria:

Content: Is it accurate? Is it interesting? Does it avoid any obvious bias?

Graphics: Do they effectively supplement the text? Are they easy to read and understand?

Readability: Is the text clearly written? Is it engaging? Is it at an appropriate level for the intended audience?

Documentation: Are sources, including sources for graphics, clearly identified? Are suggestions for further reading provided?

Usability: Are chapters and sections clearly organized? Are headings and subheadings used appropriately? Is the table of contents useful and appropriately detailed? Is the index useful and appropriately detailed?

Of course, given that it's impossible to read everything, it's helpful to be familiar with review sources that regularly review nonfiction for young adults. These include *VOYA* (*Voice of Youth Advocates*), *School Library Journal, The Horn Book, The Bulletin of the Center for Children's Books*, the Cooperative Children's Book Center's *Books for Middle and High School Age, Booklist*, and *Teenreads.com*.

It is also helpful to keep an eye on various awards and "best of" lists for young adult nonfiction, although a word of caution is in order. Most award committees tend to prefer biography, autobiography, and history, with the occasional science book receiving some recognition. If a library's collection development policy were guided only by awards lists, there would be no how-to, self-help, travel, or sports books in the collection. At the same time, of course, it's important to know which nonfiction books have been judged meritorious by various award committees. Some to keep an eye on follow:

YALSA Award for Excellence in Nonfiction: Sponsored by YALSA, this award is given annually to a nonfiction book just to be the best among the nonfiction books for young adults published the previous year.

Robert F. Sibert Informational Book Medal: Sponsored by the Association for Library Service to Children, "the Sibert Award is presented annually to the author, author/illustrator, co-authors, or author and illustrator named on the title page of the most distinguished informational book for children published in the United States in English during the preceding year."[83] The association defines "children" as birth to 14 years. In practice, most of the award winners and honor books have been works for older children, so there is (usually) overlap with the interests of at least younger young adults.

Orbis Pictus Award: Sponsored by the National Council of Teachers of English, the Orbis Pictus Award recognizes "excellence in the writing of nonfiction for children."[84] Like the Sibert Medal, the Orbis Pictus Award is for books intended for younger readers, specifically grades K–8; however, the winners and honor books are often appropriate for middle schoolers.

Other awards for young adult books may sometimes be given to nonfiction books. For a list of awards and related URLs, see appendix 2.

Evaluating and selecting nonfiction materials is only one factor in the equation. Equally important is promoting nonfiction resources to young adults (and to teachers and other adults). After all, there's no point having a robust nonfiction collection if no one is aware of it or using it. Fortunately, the strategies that work in promoting fiction and other genres can work with nonfiction as well. Booktalks—brief teasers designed to entice people to read—can include nonfiction titles or focus on them exclusively. Sometimes it's possible to pair a nonfiction book and a work of fiction. For example, Jim Murphy's *An American Plague: The True and Terrifying Story of the Yellow Fever Epidemic of 1793*[85] pairs nicely with Laurie Halse Anderson's fictional account *Fever 1793.*[86] Booktalks can be especially effective in relation to special recognitions, such as Women's History Month, and particular class projects in school.

The same is true with book displays. These can be used in conjunction with special recognitions and can include nonfiction titles. Young adult volunteers, perhaps from a youth services advisory board, can be recruited to help develop and deliver booktalks and design book displays. The library's website can also be used to promote nonfiction materials, featuring, for instance, a nonfiction title of the week. Librarians and students can create resource guides on particular topics that can incorporate nonfiction resources. Book discussion groups can occasionally focus on a nonfiction title, as can special interest groups, such as a gaming club. Librarians and teachers should always be looking for opportunities to collaborate to enhance young adults' learning, and one way to do this is through assignments and other activities that promote the use of nonfiction resources.

Nonfiction resources can be especially important to students working on homework assignments. Libraries can provide homework help centers within the library. As Meghan Harper explains, the purpose of such centers is "to gather informational resources that students may access in one easy location to complete homework assignments or to study for specific academic tests."[87] Libraries can also offer peer and adult tutoring services, in house and online, and provide access to online subscription services such as Tutor.com (http://www.tutor.com), Brainfuse (http://home.brainfuse.com), or Virtual-Tutor Center (http://www.virtualtutorcenter.com).

Information professionals working with young adults should be aware of a few potential issues related to providing homework help. One is that students working on homework assignments that involve consulting sources are engaged in imposed information-seeking tasks.[88] Because this kind of task has been given (or imposed) by another person (i.e., the teacher), students may not have a clear sense of what they need or what the assignment requires, and some will not be highly motivated to undertake the task. Librarians may very well feel torn between wanting to provide help in locating "answers" and wanting to provide guidance in helping students locate answers on their own.[89] An even more challenging situation is when parents are undertaking information-seeking tasks for their teenager. Parents are likely to know less about the assignment and are almost certainly not interested in learning how to locate the information on their own.[90] In providing homework help, librarians should interact with the young adult if at all possible, always offer courteous service, and be aware of and responsive to the teachable moment.

SPOTLIGHT!

Reference Services

The Reference and User Services Association defines reference work as follows: "Reference Transactions are information consultations in which library staff recommend, interpret, evaluate, and/or use information resources to help others to meet particular information needs."[a] Very often, when young adults are searching for information in a library setting (traditional or virtual), it is for an imposed query, such as a school assignment. However, this isn't the only reason why young adults use reference services. The search for information can just as easily reflect information to satisfy personal interests and goals as well as personal situations that young adults face.

Today reference work is performed in a variety of settings and through a variety of media. It is important to ensure that traditional and virtual reference services are as available to young adults as other populations served by the library. Equity of access continues to be an important value in youth librarianship and should be promoted by all library staff.

Tips:

- When performing reference services, work with the user to identify the query type. Differentiate between imposed queries that young adults are transacting for someone else (teacher, parent, sibling, etc.) and self-generated questions that reflect their personal interests, situation, or goals. Knowing how the information is to be used can affect how the question is transacted and what selection of sources best suit the situation.
- Use open questions (questions that start with who, what, why, etc.) rather than closed questions (yes/no) to make sure you fully understand the user's information need.
- Remember to be approachable, encouraging, objective, and nonjudgmental when working with any user.
- Be prepared for young people to approach the reference desk in groups as well as individually.
- Don't assume that young adults have been taught information literacy skills. Model good information-seeking skills, and consider that reference work includes information literacy instruction. Teach as you respond to information needs.
- If traffic at the desk is slow, get up and see if there are users in the stacks or at the computers who need assistance.
- Consider incorporating various types of social media when planning reference services for young adults.
- Try to get ahead of school assignments by establishing relationships with teachers. This will help you manage access to resources as well as gain an understanding of the assignments from the teachers' perspectives.
- If a young adult is asking for help with a school assignment and has a handout from the teacher, ask if you can make a copy. Chances are, other students are on the way looking for similar information.
- Be sure to always ask if the young adult has more questions!

Note:

a. Reference and User Services Association, "Definitions of Reference," 2008, http://www.ala.org/rusa/resources/guidelines/definitionsreference.

SUMMARY

Nonfiction resources can help meet young adults' informational, developmental, and recreational needs. While many young adults enjoy nonfiction and some actually prefer it, librarians and teachers are often more comfortable with recommending and discussing fiction. More and more, however, educational standards, such as the *Common Core State Standards*, are emphasizing reading, analyzing, and writing about nonfiction texts. To help young adults meet these standards and to address their reading interests and needs, librarians and teachers need to understand how the basic components and structure of nonfiction resources differ from those of fictional works. They also need to understand the popular types of nonfiction, including biography and memoir, history, science and technology, health and sexuality, and self-development. And, finally, they need to be well versed in the criteria used to evaluate nonfiction and the strategies that can be employed to promote it.

IMPLICATIONS FOR PRACTICE

- Recognize the importance of nonfiction resources in promoting critical literacies among young adults and in meeting their informational, developmental, and recreational needs.
- Don't be judgmental about a young adult's reading preferences; recognize that reading nonfiction such as self-help and how-to books is still "real" reading.
- Make resources on sensitive topics such as health and sexuality readily available so that young adults don't have to approach anyone else to access these materials.
- Remember that young adults have everyday responsibilities, problems, and concerns that nonfiction books can help address.
- If you don't already, include nonfiction in your regular reading of young adult books.
- Look for opportunities to collaborate with other professionals (teachers and librarians, for instance) as well as young adults to promote nonfiction resources.

QUESTIONS TO THINK ABOUT AND DISCUSS

1. Did you read nonfiction when you were a young adult? If so, what did you read and why?
2. How can librarians and teachers help young adults effectively evaluate nonfiction resources?
3. How might web resources be used to supplement nonfiction resources in print, and vice versa?
4. What kinds of activities can be used to make connections between nonfiction resources and fictional works on the same topic?
5. What role should libraries and schools play in promoting nonbook nonfiction resources (such as magazines, newspapers, websites, blogs, etc.)?

NOTES

1. Kenneth L. Donelson and Alleen Pace Nilsen, *Literature for Today's Young Adults*, 7th ed. (Boston: Pearson, 2005).

2. Gérard Genette, *Paratexts: Thresholds of Interpretation*, trans. Jane E. Lewin (New York: Cambridge University, 1997).

3. Melissa Gross, "The Imposed Query," *Reference Quarterly* 35 (1995): 236–43.

4. Jay N. Giedd, "The Teen Brain: Insights from Neuroimaging," *Journal of Adolescent Health* 42 (2008): 335–43.

5. Crystal Faris, "Nonfiction and Young Readers," in *Nonfiction Readers' Advisory*, ed. Robert Burgin (Westport, CT: Libraries Unlimited, 2004), 143–55.

6. Donelson and Nilsen, *Literature for Today's Young Adults*.

7. Jeffrey D. Wilhelm and Michael Smith, *"Reading Don't Fix No Chevys": Literacy in the Lives of Young Men* (Portsmouth, NH: Heinemann, 2002).

8. Jamie Watson and Jennifer Stencel, "Reaching Reluctant Readers with Nonfiction," *Young Adult Library Services* 4, no. 1 (2005): 8–11.

9. Smith and Wilhelm, *"Reading Don't Fix No Chevys."*

10. Watson and Stencel, "Reaching Reluctant Readers."

11. National Governors Association Center for Best Practices, Council of Chief State School Officers, "Implementing the Common Core State Standards," http://www.corestandards.org/.

12. National Governors Association Center for Best Practices, Council of Chief State School Officers, "English Language Arts Standards, Standard 10: Range, Quality, and Complexity, Range of Text Types for 6–12," http://www.corestandards.org/ELA-Literacy/standard-10-range-quality-complexity/range-of-text-types-for-612.

13. Partnership for 21st Century Skills, "21st Century Standards," http://www.p21.org/overview/skills-framework/351.

14. American Association of School Librarians, *Standards for the 21st-Century Learner* (Chicago: American Library Association, 2007).

15. American Association of School Librarians, *Standards for the 21st Century Learner*.

16. University Library, University of Illinois at Urbana-Champaign, "Dewey Decimal Classification System," http://www.library.illinois.edu/ugl/about/dewey.html.

17. Jennifer Burek Pierce, "Picking the Flowers in the 'Fair Garden': The Circulation, Noncirculation, and Disappearance of Young Adult Nonfiction Materials," *School Libraries Worldwide* 9, no. 2 (2003): 62–72.

18. Paulette M. Rothbauer, "Young Adults and Reading," in *Reading Matters: What the Research Reveals about Reading, Libraries, and Community*, ed. Catherine Sheldrick Ross,

Lynne McKechnie, and Paulette M. Rothbauer (Westport, CT: Libraries Unlimited, 2006), 101–31.

19. W. Bernard Lukenbill, *Biography in the Lives of Youth: Culture, Society, and Information* (Westport, CT: Libraries Unlimited, 2006), 2, 3.

20. Lukenbill, *Biography in the Lives of Youth*, 6.

21. Russell Freedman, *Lincoln: A Photobiography* (New York: Clarion, 1987).

22. James Cross Giblin, *The Rise and Fall of Senator Joe McCarthy* (Boston: Clarion, 2009).

23. Candace Fleming, *Our Eleanor: A Scrapbook Look at Eleanor Roosevelt's Remarkable Life* (New York: Atheneum, 2005).

24. Steve Sheinkin, *The Notorious Benedict Arnold: A True Story of Adventure, Heroism and Treachery* (New York: Roaring Brook, 2010).

25. Ann Angel, *Janis Joplin: Rise Up Singing* (New York: Amulet, 2010).

26. Elizabeth Partridge, *John Lennon: All I Want Is the Truth* (New York: Viking, 2005).

27. Andrea Warren, *Surviving Hitler: A Boy in the Nazi Death Camps* (New York: HarperCollins, 2011).

28. Phillip Hoose, *Claudette Colvin: Twice towards Justice* (New York: Melanie Kroupa Books / Farrar, Straus and Giroux, 2009).

29. Walter Dean Myers, *Bad Boy: A Memoir* (New York: HarperCollins, 2001).

30. Don Latham, "The Reader in the Closet: Literacy and Masculinity in Walter Dean Myers' *Bad Boy: A Memoir*," *Children's Literature Association Quarterly* 35 (2010): 72–86.

31. Jack Gantos, *Hole in My Life* (New York: Farrar, Straus and Giroux, 2002).

32. Brent Runyon, *The Burn Journals* (New York: Knopf, 2004).

33. Lukenbill, *Biography in the Lives of Youth*.

34. Linas Alsenas, *Gay America: Struggle for Equality* (New York: Amulet, 2008).

35. Tanya Lee Stone, *Almost Astronauts: 13 Women Who Dared to Dream* (Somerville, MA: Candlewick, 2009).

36. Susan Campbell Bartoletti, *Hitler Youth: Growing Up in Hitler's Shadow* (New York: Scholastic. 2005).

37. Susan Campbell Bartoletti, *They Called Themselves the KKK: The Birth of an American Terrorist Group* (New York: Houghton Mifflin Harcourt, 2010).

38. Jim Murphy, *An American Plague: The True and Terrifying Story of the Yellow Fever Epidemic of 1793* (New York: Clarion, 2003).

39. Deborah Hopkinson, *Titanic: Voices from the Disaster* (New York: Scholastic, 2012).

40. Russell Freedman, *The War to End All Wars: World War I* (Boston: Clarion, 2010).

41. Steve Sheinkin, *Bomb: The Race to Build—and Steal—the World's Most Dangerous Weapon* (New York: Roaring Brook, 2012).

42. Marc Aronson, *Art Attack: A Short Cultural History of the Avant-Garde* (New York: Clarion, 1998).

43. Laban Carrick Hill, *Harlem Stomp! A Cultural History of the Harlem Renaissance* (New York: Little, Brown, 2003).

44. Sue Macy, *Wheels of Change: How Women Rode the Bicycle to Freedom (with a Few Flat Tires along the Way)* (Washington, DC: National Geographic, 2011).

45. Ann Bausum, *Freedom Riders: John Lewis and Jim Zwerg on the Front Lines of the Civil Rights Movement* (Washington, DC: National Geographic, 2005).

46. Marc Aronson and Marina Budhos, *Sugar Changed the World: A Story of Magic, Spice, Slavery, Freedom, and Science* (New York: Clarion, 2010).

47. Tanya Lee Stone, *The Good, the Bad, and the Barbie: A Doll's History and Her Impact on Us* (New York: Viking, 2010).

48. Chris Crowe, *Getting Away with Murder: The True Story of the Emmett Till Case* (New York: Phyllis Fogelman, 2003).

49. Deborah Heiligman, *Charles and Emma: The Darwins' Leap of Faith* (New York: Holt, 2009).

50. Russell Freedman, *The Wright Brothers: How They Invented the Airplane* (New York: Holiday House, 1991).

51. Committee on a Conceptual Framework for New K–12 Science Education Standards, *A Framework for K–12 Science Education: Practices, Crosscutting Concepts, and Core Ideas* (Washington, DC: National Academies Press, 2012).

52. Committee on a Conceptual Framework, *A Framework for K–12 Science Education*, 3.

53. Myra Zarnowski and Susan Turkel, "Nonfiction Literature that Highlights Inquiry: How Real People Solve Real Problems," *Journal of Children's Literature* 37, no. 1 (2011): 30–37.

54. Myra Zarnowski and Susan Turkel, "How Nonfiction Reveals the Nature of Science," *Children's Literature in Education* (published online January 16, 2013).

55. Nic Bishop, *Spiders* (New York: Scholastic, 2007); *Frogs* (New York: Scholastic, 2008); *Butterflies and Moths* (New York: Scholastic, 2009); *Marsupials* (New York: Scholastic, 2009); *Lizards* (New York: Scholastic, 2010); *Snakes* (New York: Scholastic, 2012).

56. Sy Montgomery and Nic Bishop, *The Tarantula Scientist* (Boston: Houghton Mifflin, 2004); *The Quest for the Tree Kangaroo: An Expedition to the Cloud Forest of New Guinea* (Boston: Houghton Mifflin, 2006); *Kakapo Rescue: Saving the World's Strangest Parrot* (Boston: Houghton Mifflin, 2010).

57. Phillip Hoose, *Moonbird: A Year on the Wind with the Great Survivor B95* (New York: Farrar, Straus and Giroux, 2012).

58. Loree Griffin Burns and Ellen Harasimowicz, *The Hive Detectives: Chronicle of a Honey Bee Disaster* (Boston: Houghton Mifflin, 2010).

59. Marcia A. Mardis, "It's Not Just Whodunnit, but How: 'The CSI Effect,' Science Learning, and the School Library," *Knowledge Quest* 35, no. 1 (2006): 12–17.

60. Richard Platt, *Forensics* (Boston: Kingfisher, 2005).

61. D. B. Beres, *Dusted and Busted: The Science of Fingerprinting* (New York: Franklin Watts, 2007).

62. Anna Prokos, *Guilty by a Hair! Real-Life DNA Matches!* (New York: Franklin Watts, 2007).

63. Jill Rubalcaba and Peter Robertshaw, *Every Bone Tells a Story: Hominin Discoveries, Deductions, and Debates* (Watertown, MA: Charlesbridge, 2010).

64. David Macaulay and Neil Ardley, *The New Way Things Work* (Boston: Houghton Mifflin, 1998).

65. David Macaulay, *Cathedral* (Boston: Houghton Mifflin, 1973); *Castle* (Boston: Houghton Mifflin, 1977); *Mosque* (Boston: Houghton Mifflin, 2003).

66. Marshall Brain, *How Stuff Works* (Edison, NJ: Chartwell, 2001).

67. Sally M. Walker, *Secrets of a Civil War Submarine: Solving the Mysteries of the H. L. Hunley* (Minneapolis, MN: Carolrhoda, 2005).

68. DK Publishing, *Ideas That Changed the World: Incredible Inventions and the Stories Behind Them* (New York: DK, 2010).

69. David Macaulay and Richard Walker, *The Way We Work: Getting to Know the Amazing Human Body* (Boston: Houghton Mifflin, 2008).

70. Maureen J. Hinds, *Fighting the AIDS and HIV Epidemic: A Global Battle* (Berkeley Heights, NJ: Enslow, 2007).

71. Matthew Locricchio, *Teen Cuisine* (Tarrytown, NY: Marshall Cavendish, 2010).

72. Eric Schlosser and Charles Wilson, *Chew on This: Everything You Didn't Want to Know about Fast Food* (Boston: Houghton Mifflin, 2006).

73. Leslie Kaufman, "Publishers Revel in Youthful Cruelty," *New York Times* (March 26, 2013), http://www.nytimes.com/2013/03/27/books/bullying-becomes-hot-and-profitable-topic-for-publishers.html?pagewanted=all&_r=0.

74. W. Bernard Lukenbill and Barbara Froling Immroth, *Health Information for Youth: The Public Library and School Library Media Center Role* (Westport, CT: Libraries Unlimited, 2007).

75. Robie H. Harris and Michael Emberley, *It's Perfectly Normal: A Book about Changing Bodies, Growing Up, Sex, and Sexual Health*, 3rd ed. (Cambridge, MA: Candlewick, 2009).

76. Faith Hickman Brynie, *101 Questions about Sex and Sexuality . . . with Answers for the Curious and Confused* (Brookfield, CT: Twenty-First Century, 2003).

77. Jack Canfield, Mark Victor Hansen, and Kimberly Kirberger, *Chicken Soup for the Teenage Soul: 101 Stories of Life, Love, and Learning* (Deerfield Beach, FL: Health Communications, 1997).

78. Sean Covey, *The 7 Habits of Highly Effective Teens: The Ultimate Teenage Success Guide* (New York: Simon & Schuster, 1998).

79. Rothbauer, "Young Adults and Reading."

80. Donelson and Nilsen, *Literature for Today's Young Adults*.

81. Carl M. Tomlinson and Carol Lynch-Brown, *Essentials of Young Adult Literature*, 2nd ed. (Upper Saddle River, NJ: Pearson, 2010).

82. National Council of Teachers of English, "NCTE Orbis Pictus Award for Outstanding Nonfiction for Children," http://www.ncte.org/awards/orbispictus.

83. Association for Library Service to Children, "Welcome to the Robert F. Sibert Informational Book Medal Home Page!" http://www.ala.org/alsc/awardsgrants/bookmedia/sibertmedal.

84. National Council of Teachers of English, "NCTE Orbis Pictus Award."

85. Murphy, *An American Plague*.

86. Laurie Halse Anderson, *Fever 1793* (New York: Simon & Schuster, 2000).

87. Meghan Harper, *Reference Sources and Services for Youth* (New York: Neal-Schuman, 2011), 17.

88. Gross, "The Imposed Query."

89. Michele Gorman and Tricia Suellentrop, *Connecting Young Adults and Libraries: A How-to-Do-It Manual*, 4th ed. (New York: Neal-Schuman, 2009).

90. Gorman and Suellentrop, *Connecting Young Adults*.

Chapter Seven

Poetry and Music

This chapter discusses poetry and music for young adults and by young adults:

- Young adults, poetry, and music
- Key terms
- Poetry resources
- Music and lyrics
- Young adults writing poetry and lyrics
- Evaluating and promoting poetry and music
- Spotlight! Poetry slams / open-mic events
- Spotlight! Writing workshops
- Implications for practice
- Questions to think about and discuss

YOUNG ADULTS, POETRY, AND MUSIC

Poetry, in the form of nursery rhymes and song, becomes a part of most people's lives at a very young age, providing pleasure then and fond memories in later years.[1] Some young adults enjoy reading poetry and even writing their own poems, and many regularly listen to music and write their own songs and lyrics. Yet if asked whether they like poetry, many young adults would say no. Why the disconnect? One reason may be that they think the word *poetry* sounds formal and forbidding and that they don't think of music lyrics as poetry. Another reason may have to do with the way that poetry is sometimes presented in school, with an overemphasis on analysis rather than focusing on the pleasure provided by the playfulness of language. In a study of preservice English teachers, Janette Hughes and Sue Dymoke discovered several misconceptions that these undergraduate students held about poetry, including that it is boring, elitist, inaccessible, a frill, and understandable only through detailed analysis.[2] No doubt, the views of these college students probably mirror the views of the young adults they will teach.

The purpose of this chapter is to discuss strategies for helping students and teachers (and other adults) become enthusiastic readers of poetry, especially poetry for and by young adults. We proceed under two assumptions: first, poetry should be experienced holistically and contextually rather than as an object isolated for dissection; second, accessible poems, valuable in their own right, can also be used to pave the way for the study of more challenging works. In other words, any poem that provides pleasure or yields a flash of insight is worth promoting.

KEY TERMS

Poetry includes many forms, and as such, a precise definition can be elusive. Chris Baldick defines poetry as "language sung, chanted, spoken, or written according to some pattern of recurrence that emphasizes the relationships between words on the basis of sound as well as sense: this pattern is almost always a rhythm or metre, which may be supplemented by rhyme or alliteration or both."[3] This definition emphasizes a key aspect of poetry—namely, that it was originally shared orally and that much poetry still needs to be heard to appreciate its full effect. Poetry, even in the case of long poems, also tends to reflect a concise use of language to convey feelings and ideas. Kathy Latrobe and Judy Drury define poetry as "a concise and compact form of literature that utilizes sounds and images to involve the reader emotionally."[4] Carl Tomlinson and Carol Lynch-Brown define it as "the concentrated expression of ideas and feelings through precise and imaginative words selected for their sonorous and rhythmic effects."[5] As these definitions imply, poetry is different from prose, although some poems, except for their unusual line breaks, read much like prose, while some prose is quite poetic. In looking at the various kinds of poetry, we see the range of possibilities that poets have at their disposal for conveying ideas and feelings through concise language, interesting images, and rhythmical sounds.

While people often think of poetry as consisting of rhythmic lines that rhyme, such is not always the case. Poems written in *blank verse* have a regular rhythmic pattern, but they do not rhyme.[6] William Shakespeare made frequent use of blank verse in his plays. Poems written in *free verse* have neither a regular rhythmic pattern nor a particular rhyme scheme; in fact, they may not rhyme at all.[7] Robert Louis Stevenson's "The Light-Keeper" and "The Light-Keeper II" are examples of poems that make use of free verse.

Poetry can be divided into three basic types: narrative, dramatic, and lyric.[8] *Narrative poetry*, as the name implies, tells a story. *Dramatic poetry* is essentially a play in which characters speak in verse; it is generally intended for theatrical performance, although some dramatic poetry is intended for reading only, not for performance. *Lyric poetry* is primarily descriptive, tends to be highly personal, and expresses a mood or feeling. Each of those basic types can be divided into further subtypes. That may be as much as many people care to know about the formal aspects of poetry; indeed, developing a love for poetry and inspiring a love for poetry in other people does not require an intimate familiarity with various poetic forms and technical terms. In fact, some would argue that the terminology often gets in the way of enjoyment and genuine appreciation. However, such knowledge can come in handy when working with teens on school assignments or working with teachers on developing assignments and identifying appropriate resources. Moreover, teens who write their own poetry may be interested in learning more about the formal aspects of their craft. Being able to talk with them and point them to helpful resources will be easier for librarians who have some knowledge of the topic. In any case, the following terms and definitions are offered as a reference, to be used or ignored as desired.

Narrative Poetry

* *Ballads* are poems that tell stories of (usually) tragic events and are often intended to be sung. Edgar Allan Poe's "Annabel Lee," which tells the story of the tragic death of the narrator's beloved, is an example of a ballad. A more lighthearted example is Ernest L. Thayer's "Casey at the Bat," which tells of the mock tragedy of a great baseball player who strikes out and loses the game for his team.
* *Epics* are long poems that tell stories of heroes and gods and often involve great battles or journeys. A well-known example is the Old English poem *Beowulf*, which relates the story of how the warrior Beowulf defeated the monster Grendel and Grendel's mother.
* *Verse romances* usually involve elements of fantasy—idealized characters, enchanted settings, and allegorical meanings.[9] A notable example is *Sir Gawain and the Green Knight*, which tells of a beheading game involving one of King Arthur's knights and a magical green knight.
* *Verse novels* are novels written in verse, typically as a series of poems, and are a relatively new innovation. The poems, which taken together constitute a story, may be made of narrative poems or lyric poems. Karen Hesse's *Out of the Dust* uses the point of view of a 14-year-old girl to tell of an Oklahoma farming family's struggles during the Great Depression and Dust Bowl.

Dramatic Poetry

- *Verse drama* is a play in verse form. Many of Shakespeare's plays, for example, are in verse, as is T. S. Eliot's *Murder in the Cathedral*, about the assassination of Thomas Becket, archbishop of Canterbury, in the 12th century.
- *Dramatic monologues*, sometimes called "interior monologues," are spoken by an individual character, usually a persona, not the poet, for the purpose of conveying thoughts, feelings, attitudes in what is presented as a "private" confession. The purpose of a dramatic monologue is to offer insights into a particular individual's personality and motivations. Robert Browning wrote many dramatic monologues. In "Soliloquy of the Spanish Cloister," for instance, the speaker reflects on his intense loathing for his fellow monk, the congenial Brother Lawrence. In doing so, though, he also reveals his own pettiness and hypocrisy.

Lyric Poetry

Lyric poems appear in a variety of forms and on a variety of topics. We consider some of the more common ones here.[10]

> *Sonnet*—A sonnet is composed of 14 lines, and there are two main types of sonnets. The *Italian sonnet* consists of 8 lines (an octet) with a rhyme scheme of *abbaabba*, followed by 6 lines (a sestet) with a rhyme scheme of either *cdcdcd* or *cdecde*. Elizabeth Barrett Browning's "How Do I Love Thee?" is an example of an Italian sonnet, in which the speaker describes the breadth, depth, and intensity of her love for her beloved. The *English sonnet* consists of three groupings of 4 lines each (quatrains), followed by 2 lines (a couplet), with a rhyme scheme of *ababcdcdefefgg*. Each line is in *iambic pentameter*, five sets of an unstressed syllable followed by a stressed syllable. William Shakespeare's "Shall I compare thee to a summer's day" is an example of an English sonnet, in which the speaker suggests that his true love's beauty exceeds that of a glorious day in summer. Modern sonnets do not necessarily adhere to strict iambic pentameter.
>
> *Ode*—An ode is a formal poem in praise of a person or thing and addressed directly to that person or thing. John Keats's "Ode to a Nightingale" reflects on the fact that the nightingale, though mortal, will live eternally through its song. The bird, of course, is a parallel to the poet, who hopes to gain immortality through his poetry.
>
> *Elegy*—An elegy is an elaborate poem reflecting on someone's death or on the impermanence of life in general. Walt Whitman's "When Lilacs Last in the Dooryard Bloom'd" is an elegy written on the occa-

sion of Abraham Lincoln's assassination. A. E. Housman's "To an Athlete Dying Young" laments the death of a young man.

Haiku—Haiku, a Japanese poetic form, generally consists of three lines, not rhymed, of five, seven, and five syllables, respectively. Haiku typically conveys the speaker's impression of a particular scene or object. The 17th-century poet Basho Matsuo was a master of haiku. One example of his impression of a natural scene is "An Old Silent Pond."

Limerick—A limerick is a type of *light verse* (i.e., humorous verse) in which there are five lines with the rhyme scheme *aabba*. Lines 1, 2, and 5 have three stresses (or beats), while lines 3 and 4 have two stresses. Edward Lear's *Book of Nonsense* offers numerous examples of limericks. Many limericks contain bawdy humor.

Concrete poetry—Concrete poetry is a type of poetry in which the words are arranged on the page to suggest an image related to the topic of the poem. A notable example is "The Mouse's Tale," which appears in the form of a long tail with increasingly smaller type font in Lewis Carroll's *Alice's Adventures in Wonderland.*

POETRY RESOURCES

Poetry for young adults can be found in several kinds of resources, including anthologies, collections of an individual poet's work, verse novels, illustrated editions of individual poems, and electronic resources.

Anthologies

An *anthology* is a collection of poems, usually representing the work of a number of different poets and focusing on a particular theme. Anthologies typically contain poems on a variety of subjects and may include classic and/or contemporary works. With an anthology, the compiler, or editor, plays an important role in selecting the poems, grouping them into sections, arranging them within sections, and writing an introduction to the collection as a whole and possibly one for each section as well.

Not surprising, a popular theme of poetry anthologies for young adults is the theme of growing up and becoming an adult. Liz Rosenberg's *The Invisible Ladder: An Anthology of Contemporary American Poems for Young Readers*[11] contains not only poems but also commentary from the poets as well as photographs of them as children and as adults. The term *young readers* in the title is a bit misleading, for the poems can be enjoyed by people of all ages, especially older children and young adults. Lori M. Carlson's *Cool Salsa: Bilingual Poems on Growing Up Latino in the United States*[12] and *Red Hot Salsa: Bilingual Poems on Life, Love, and Victory*[13] present poems about Latino young people and their experiences coming of age in the United States.

A popular theme for readers of all ages is love, and this is especially true for young adults who may be experiencing their first serious love relationship. Paul B. Janeczko's *Blushing: Expressions of Love in Poems and Letters*[14] offers a variety of poems on this timeless topic. And in *Love Speaks Its Name: Gay and Lesbian Love Poems*, J. D. McClatchy[15] collects love poems from nearly 150 poets, from Michelangelo to May Swenson and Walt Whitman to Elizabeth Bishop.

Poetry anthologies, of course, can be organized around any number of themes or emphases. Naomi Shihab Nye's collection *Time You Let Me In: 25 Poets under 25*,[16] for example, highlights the talents of 25 up-and-coming poets. Jan Greenberg's *Heart to Heart: New Poems Inspired by Twentieth-Century American Art*[17] pairs reproductions of American art works with poems about those works and is organized into four sections: stories, voices, impressions, and expressions. Lillian Morrison's *Way to Go! Sports Poems*[18] celebrates various sports with poems and illustrations. And Janeczko's *A Poke in the I: A Collection of Concrete Poems*[19] provides a wealth of examples of a particular form of poetry.

A number of anthologies are organized around the experiences of a particular ethnic group or gender. In *A Thousand Peaks: Poems from China*, Siyu Liu and Orel Protopopescu[20] present 35 splendid examples from 2,000 years of Chinese poetry. In *I, Too, Sing America: Three Centuries of African American Poetry*, Catherine Clinton[21] focuses on the contributions of African American voices to American poetry. Clinton's *A Poem of Her Own: Voices of American Women Yesterday and Today*[22] does the same for women's contributions to American poetry. And Nye and Janeczko's *I Feel a Little Jumpy around You: A Book of Her Poems and His Poems Collected in Pairs*[23] offers paired works on a variety of themes reflecting the sometimes different and sometimes similar viewpoints of women and men.

Collections of Individual Poets

Another excellent source of poetry can be found in the collections of individual poets. Like anthologies, these collections are often organized around a particular theme or motif. Kathi Appelt's *Poems from Homeroom: A Writer's Place to Start*,[24] for example, includes poems dealing with various young adult experiences related to growing up. Similarly, Nikki Grimes's *A Dime a Dozen*[25] contains poems on such topics as dealing with parents and discovering/creating one's identity. Naomi Shihab Nye looks at the issues of growing up from a girl's point of view in *A Maze Me: Poems for Girls*.[26] One important aspect of young adult development is exploring the possibilities and complexities of romantic relationships. Sara Holbrook and Allan Wolf's

More Than Friends: Poems from Him and Her[27] employs a variety of poetic forms to depict the evolving relationship between a girl and a boy from the perspective of each.

Another popular topic among poets is the influence of place, for better or worse, on young adult development. In Angela Johnson's *The Other Side: Shorter Poems*,[28] for example, a young woman recounts her experiences growing up in Shorter, Alabama. Walter Dean Myers presents the viewpoints of a number of Harlem residents in *Here in Harlem: Poems in Many Voices*.[29] Curtis L. Crisler assumes the voices of African American males growing up in Gary, Indiana, in *Tough Boy Sonatas*,[30] while Eve Merriam examines the more difficult aspects of coming of age in an urban environment in *The Inner City Mother Goose*.[31]

Some poets, perhaps in addition to focusing on a single theme, organize their collections around a particular form of poetry. In *Neighborhood Odes*,[32] Gary Soto re-creates the culture of an entire neighborhood through a series of odes. Linda Sue Park in *Tap Dancing on the Roof: Sijo*[33] brings new insights to everyday things through sijo, a form of Korean poetry similar to haiku, in which the last line offers a witty surprise on the topic. And in *Blue Lipstick: Concrete Poems*,[34] John Grandits assumes the voice of a 15-year-old girl to reflect on various aspects of teenage life through concrete poems.

Verse Novels

Verse novels have become quite popular among authors and poets who write for young adults, perhaps because verse novels offer not only an innovative way to tell a story but also a way of using the natural appeal of narrative to make poetry more palatable to young adults who may think that they do not like it. Verse novels often present a slice-of-life view of young adults in typical or not-so-typical situations. Mel Glenn's *Jump Ball: A Basketball Season in Poems*[35] focuses on the experiences of an urban basketball team. Walter Dean Myers's *Street Love*[36] relates the story of an academically smart boy who falls in love with a street-smart girl.

Sometimes verse novels focus on stories of different periods or cultures. The Depression-era Oklahoma Dust Bowl is the backdrop for Karen Hesse's *Out of the Dust*.[37] In free verse poems, the 14-year-old narrator tells of the challenges that she and her family face in the relentless dust storms. Nepal is the setting for Patricia McCormick's *Sold*,[38] in which the 13-year-old narrator describes her ordeal after having been sold into prostitution. Yet other verse novels portray difficult situations faced by teens closer to home. Thalia Chaltas's *Because I Am Furniture*[39] is told in the voice of a teenage girl whose sister and brother are being abused by their father. Juan Felipe Herrera, in *CrashBoomLove: A Novel in Verse*,[40] relates the story of a Mexican teen dealing with drugs, gangs, and racism in his American high school.

Helen Frost, in *Keesha's House*,[41] presents the gut-wrenching experiences of a group of young adults living in a house for runaway youth.

Some works written in verse are inspired by real people or events. *Your Own Sylvia: A Verse Portrait of Sylvia Plath*,[42] by Stephanie Hemphill, offers an intimate look at the famous poet. Hemphill's *Wicked Girls: A Novel of the Salem Witch Trials*[43] examines the tragic events caused by impressionable young people and mass hysteria. Paul B. Janeczko's *World's Afire*[44] presents views of another tragic event, the 1944 Hartford, Connecticut, circus fire, from the perspectives of various people who were there.

Illustrated Poems

Another highly appealing kind of poetry resource is the illustrated poem. Edgar Allan Poe's *The Raven*, often encountered in school, is nevertheless a perennial favorite among young adults. Ryan Price's illustrated version,[45] with its black cross-hatching and shadowy gradations, provides an appropriately creepy take on the classic poem. Joe Morse uses an urban setting and multiracial characters for his illustrated version of Ernest L. Thayer's baseball poem *Casey at the Bat*.[46] Both these books are part of the *Visions in Poetry* series from Kids Can Press, a series that offers a new look at classic poems through illustrated editions. More contemporary poems sometimes appear with illustrations as well. Walter Dean Myers and Christopher Myers's *Harlem*[47] conveys the people of Harlem's spirit and pride as well as their struggles against discrimination. And Marilyn Nelson and Philippe Lardy's *A Wreath for Emmett Till*[48] presents a crown of sonnets, a sequence of sonnets each on a particular aspect of the theme, as a memorial to a 14-year-old African American boy lynched in Mississippi in 1955 for allegedly whistling at a white woman.

Online Poetry Resources

In addition to print resources, there are several noteworthy online poetry resources. The Poetry Foundation (http://www.poetryfoundation.org/) provides access to a wealth of poems; although a number of them are more adult focused, many are suitable for young adults as well. There is, however, a section devoted to children's poetry, including poetry for middle school ages (http://www.poetryfoundation.org/children/). Poetry.org (http://www.poetry.org/) also provides access to poems on a variety of subjects and includes a "Poetry Resources for Teens" section (http://www.poets.org/page.php/prmID/394). The Poetry Foundation and Poetry.org offer video and audio clips in addition to text. A list of poetry resources in print can be found in the "Poetry" section of the Young Adult Library Services Association's Outstanding Books for the College Bound and Lifelong Learners, available at http://www.ala.org/yalsa/booklistsawards/booklists/outstandingbooks/poe-tryoutstanding. There are also several websites where teens can post their own writing, including poetry. We look at some of these sites in the section "Young Adults Writing Poetry and Lyrics."

MUSIC AND LYRICS

As noted earlier in this chapter, many young adults are leery of poetry, but very few do not like music of some kind or another. Sources for music are as varied as the types of music that young adults listen to. Print books are available containing lyrics only or lyrics and music notation (usually vocal, piano, and guitar). One example of a book of lyrics is Bob Dylan's *Lyrics 1961–2001*,[49] arranged album by album and song by song. Another is Adam Bradley and Andrew DuBois's compilation *The Anthology of Rap*,[50] which brings together more than 300 rap and hip-hop lyrics written over a period of 30 years. A particularly innovative anthology of poems and lyrics is Alan Sitomer and Michael Cirelli's *Hip-Hop Poetry and the Classics*,[51] which pairs "classic" poems with thematically or formally related hip-hop poems and which includes interpretation guides and student worksheets.

Books with lyrics and music notation are also popular, and many options are available representing artists, bands, and soundtracks of various styles and periods. There are, for example, numerous books of Beatles' songs, one of which is *The Beatles Best: More Than 120 Great Hits*.[52] For pianists, there is a collection of songs from the popular *Lord of the Rings* movies, Howard Shore's *The Lord of the Rings Trilogy: Music from the Motion Pictures Arranged for Solo Piano*.[53] Many music publishers as well as other distributors have websites where fans can download sheet music (for a fee). One such site is Sheet Music Plus (http://www.sheetmusicplus.com/).

There are numerous online stores, of course, where music files can be downloaded (again, for a price) and CDs purchased. The complexities of music formats are beyond the scope of our discussion; however, note while CD sales have decreased dramatically, some users still prefer acquiring music in that format, especially if the CD packaging offers interesting cover art and includes lyrics. A close look at various music genres is also beyond the scope of our discussion, but a list of genres as well as the bestsellers in different categories is available at Billboard.com (http://www.billboard.com/charts). Billboard breaks down music albums into these broad categories: pop, country, rock, R&B/hip-hop, dance/electronic, Latin, Christian/gospel, "additional" (e.g., blues, classical, jazz, reggae, soundtracks), and international.

In addition to recorded music and books with lyrics and music notation, there is a wealth of books about music and musicians. Walter Dean Myers has two such books honoring the contributions of African Americans to American music. Written as a series of poems, *Blues Journey*[54] celebrates the blues in the midst of hardship, while *Jazz*[55] presents a brief history of jazz complete with a glossary. Both books are beautifully illustrated by Myers's son Christopher, and while the books work quite nicely with younger readers, young adults can enjoy them as well. A book that works well with both young adults and adults is Alexs D. Pate's *In the Heart of the Beat: The Poetry of Rap*.[56] Mark Flowers, in an article in *Young Adult Library Services*, provides a useful bibliography of books that either document the contributions of women to rock music or offer advice on how to start a band.[57] In an article in *Voice of Youth Advocates*, Elsworth Rockefeller and Rollie Welch identify several books that make use of music as a backdrop and have lots of "guy" appeal.[58] Biographies of individual musicians are often popular among young adults and often include at least some of the lyrics associated with the artist. Two award-winning examples are Elizabeth Partridge's *John Lennon: All I Want Is the Truth*[59] and Ann Angel's *Janis Joplin: Rise Up Singing*.[60]

YOUNG ADULTS WRITING POETRY AND LYRICS

Many young adults enjoy writing their own poetry and lyrics, and, thanks to the Internet, there are many places where they can share their work and receive feedback on their creative compositions. TeenInk (http://www.teenink.com/) is a literary website (there is a print magazine available as well) with poetry, fiction, nonfiction, and reviews written by teens. The poetry section is divided into several categories based on poetic form: free verse, song lyrics, sonnet, haiku, limerick, and ballad. Teens can not only post their own works but also rate and comment on the works of others. YARN, Young Adult Review Network (http://yareview.net/), offers creative writing for young adults by adult writers and teens. Users can read and contribute poetry, as well as fiction and essays. In addition, there are interviews with writers and resources for teachers. Frodo's Notebook: A Journal of Teens, Literature, and the Arts (http://frodosnotebook.com/) allows for the posting of poetry, fiction, essays, and reviews. Protagonize (http://www.protagonize.com/) is another online creative writing community where users can post stories, poems, lyrics, exercises, and so on, and interact with other writers. Though not focused on young adults, teens as young as 13 years may sign up without a parent's or guardian's permission.

There are also published books of poetry written by teens. Betsy Franco, for example, presents poems that she collected from adolescent girls in *Things I Have to Tell You: Poems and Writing by Teenage Girls*[61] and poems from adolescent boys in *You Hear Me? Poems and Writing by Teenage Boys*.[62] From the work that WritersCorp has done with disadvantaged young people comes a collection by Bill Aguado and Richard Newirth, *Paint Me Like I Am: Teen Poems from WritersCorp.*[63] And Dave Johnson's *Movin': Teen Poets Take Voice*[64] offers a collection of poems written by teens as part of a workshop sponsored by Poets House and the New York Public Library.

Research indicates that writing poetry and lyrics has a number of positive benefits for young adults, in addition to allowing them to express themselves creatively. Korina M. Jocson, for example, found that writing poetry empowered urban high school students by helping them to find a voice and develop key literacies.[65] Jen Scott Curwood and Lora Lee H. Cowell discovered that encouraging students to engage in multimodal poetry writing fostered both "traditional" and digital literacies and helped bridge in-school and out-of-school literacy practices.[66] In their study, students created poetry with written text, audio clips, and visual images, and they used their poetry to explore issues related to identity and creativity. Angela Kinney, in a case study of one urban young adult male, found that writing song lyrics provided a "site of resilience" for him, allowing him to negotiate issues with his peers, family, and community.[67] And in a study of two songwriting partners (both males), Wendy R. Williams discovered that they felt writing songs helped them achieve several purposes: "to communicate, to relate to others, to help others, to preach . . . to create awe or inspiration, to fulfill themselves, to escape, or to vent" (p. 372).[68] In the following section, we consider how to promote not only the reading but also the writing of poetry and lyrics.

EVALUATING AND PROMOTING POETRY AND MUSIC

Good poetry, interesting poetry, is characterized by its vivid imagery, its interesting sounds and rhythms, and its tendency to make the familiar strange and the strange familiar. In evaluating any given poem, the following questions should be considered:

- Is the topic one that young adults would find interesting and engaging? Is it one to which they can relate?
- Is language used in a fresh, imaginative way? Is the language memorable, maybe even surprising?
- Are sounds used in a fresh, imaginative way? What does the poem sound like when read aloud? Does it have rhythm? Are individual word sounds memorable, maybe even surprising?

Reading professional reviews of poetry collections for young adults is another way of finding high-quality poetry resources, and professional journals such as *Voice of Youth Advocates, Young Adult Library Services,* and *School*

Library Journal publish full-length articles on young adult poetry from time to time.

Unfortunately, few awards currently exist for young adult poetry. The International Reading Association gives the Lee Bennett Hopkins Promising Poet Award every three years for people who have published no more than two books for children and/or young adults. The award was most recently given in 2013 to Guadalupe Garcia McCall for her free-verse novel *Under the Mesquite*.[69] The National Council of Teachers of English gives a poetry award every other year to a children's poet, which they define as someone writing for an audience between the ages of 3 and 13 years. The award was most recently given in 2013 to Joyce Sidman, author of *Dark Emperor and Other Poems of the Night*,[70] as well as other collections of poetry. See appendix 1 for more about these awards.

The National Book Award for Poetry is generally given to a poet writing for adults, but often the poems can be enjoyed by young adults as well. There is no award per se for lyricists or musicians writing and performing specifically for young adults, but an excellent resource for music awards across genres is the annual Grammy Awards, presented by the Recording Academy.

As for promoting poetry and music among young adults, a variety of strategies can be used, ranging from simply advertising the poetry that is available in your collection to engaging young adults in writing and performing their own poetry, lyrics, and songs. One way is to mount exhibits highlighting the poetry, lyrics, music, and books about music in your collection. Such exhibits would be especially appropriate during National Poetry Month (April in the United States and Canada), although poetry and music can be included in exhibits highlighting the contributions of various groups—women poets and musicians, for example, during Women's History Month (February in the United States, October in Canada). In addition, poems, lyrics, and books on poets, music, and musicians can be featured in booktalks as well as book discussion groups. In fact, groups can be set up that focus exclusively on poetry or music.

Another excellent way to promote interest in poetry or music is to invite poets and musicians to read, perform, and talk about their work with young adults. Not only do young adults get exposed to some interesting work, but they also gain unique insight into the creative process. Young adults themselves can perform poetry, either individually or as part of choral poetry readings. Paul Fleischman has published several collections of poetry intended to be read by multiple voices. Although in terms of content, the poems tend to skew toward the younger end of the young adult spectrum, they can certainly be performed and enjoyed by teens of all ages. *Joyful Noise: Poems for Two Voices*[71] features poems about insects and black-and-white illustrations, while *Big Talk: Poems for Four Voices*[72] provides color-coded text and color illustrations. Laura Amy Schlitz's *Good Masters! Sweet*

Ladies! Voices from a Medieval Village[73] is a beautifully illustrated book that presents a series of (mostly) monologues designed to be read aloud.

Of course, young adults can perform their own poetry or music. Libraries can host open-mic nights for poets and musicians; they can also sponsor friendly competitions known as *poetry slams*. Hearkening back to the spoken poetry of the Beat poets in local coffee houses, these competitions typically involve a panel of judges made up of members of the community—local teachers and poets, for example—and small prizes. Such friendly competitions can have many benefits. Lynn R. Rudd found that participating in a high school poetry slam group helped students in developing their identity as outcast artists, gave them a sense of a creative family, and enhanced their self-esteem through awards and recognition.[74]

SPOTLIGHT!

Poetry Slams / Open-Mic Events

Poetry slams and open-mic events are opportunities for young adults to perform poetry that they have written themselves. Poetry slams are competitions involving rules, judges, and prizes. Created by Marc Smith in Chicago in 1986, they were initially for adults and were held in bars.[a] Since then, this activity has become popular with young adults, who typically compete in libraries, classrooms, or community centers. As Scott Woods says, "a good slam is fun, loud, and filled with good poetry performed well."[b] A slam allows for participation from a diverse group of young people, involving not just the poets/performers but also the audience. As such, it offers a number of potential benefits: "[It] instills positive values to guide teens . . . , helps them develop life skills and social competencies . . . , and nurtures, celebrates, and affirms their positive identity."[c] Open-mic events are similar to slams, except that they are not competitions. Otherwise, they too give poets an outlet for their work and provide audiences with an opportunity to experience poetry in a nonacademic setting.

Tips:

- Whether hosting a poetry slam or an open-mic event, be sure to publicize it well in advance and through a variety of channels.
- Make sure that participants understand how much time they have. In the interest of not letting any one individual monopolize the event, it's usually a good idea to limit poems to about two or three per performer, three to five minutes each.

- If hosting a poetry slam, you need to consider the structure of the competition. Typically, there are three rounds, with half the contestants being eliminated after each of the first two rounds and with the top three being chosen after the last round.[d]
- Again, with a poetry slam, make a plan for selecting judges. They can be adults chosen in advance or from the audience. Three to five judges is a reasonable number, and they should be given ratings cards to use, scored 1–10.[e]
- Finally, a poetry slam should provide small prizes for the performers with the top three scores at the end of the competition. Gift cards to a coffee shop, books of poetry, and the opportunity to publish their poems in a local magazine or newspaper are all great gifts.
- Poetry Slam offers a wealth of materials for poetry fans, poets, and people who want to hold slams in their community. For more information, see http://www.poetryslam.com/.

Notes:

a. Susan B. A. Somers-Willett, *The Cultural Politics of Slam Poetry: Race, Identity, and the Performance of Popular Verse in America* (Ann Arbor: University of Michigan, 2009), 3–4.
b. Scott Woods, "Poetry Slams: The Ultimate Democracy of Art," *World Literature Today* (January–February 2008): 18–19.
c. Ella W. Jones, *Start to Finish YA Programs: Hip-Hop Symposiums, Summer Reading Programs, Virtual Tours, Poetry Slams, Teen Advisory Boards, Term Paper Clinics, and More!* (New York: Neal-Schuman, 2009), 132.
d. Jones, *Start to Finish YA Programs*, 132.
e. Jones, *Start to Finish YA Programs*, 132.

Sponsoring poetry or music writing workshops is another great way to get young adults involved in trying their hand at creative writing—and this may have the added benefit of getting young people who thought that they did not like poetry interested in such arcane concepts as meter, rhyme schemes, and figurative language. Workshops can be conducted by visiting or local poets or musicians, and attendees can produce individual works, collaborative works, or both. Digital poetry/lyric writing can allow authors to add audio clips, images, and video to their compositions. Writing poetry or lyrics enhances writing skills for sure but also reading skills and technology skills.

National Poetry Writing Month (NaPoWriMo) is an annual event held every April, during which participants attempt to write a poem each day of the month. Participants who post their poems on a website can choose to have their site listed on the NaPoWriMo site, but posting online is not a requirement. Individuals can participate however they like, writing poems only for themselves or to share with select family and friends. Libraries and schools can organize local NaPoWriMo groups, as there are no licensing or processing fees. More information can be found on the NaPoWriMo website, http://www.napowrimo.net/.

SPOTLIGHT!

Writing Workshops

Writing workshops are structured activities that give young adults an opportunity to engage in creative writing. Paulette Rothbauer identifies three kinds of recreational writing activities that teens engage in: personal writing in the form of diaries or journals, writing intended for an audience, and writing inspired by the writing of other teens.[a] Workshops can help young adults hone their writing skills, find their voices, express their thoughts and feelings, and explore various genres and forms. Workshops also provide an immediate audience in that teens can easily share their work with one another and get feedback on it. Workshops can further provide teens with guidance from a writing expert, such as a published author, although workshops can also be facilitated by librarians and teachers. Any sort of creative writing can be the focus of a workshop, including fiction, nonfiction, poetry, songs, personal websites, blogs, and comics.

Tips:

- Schedule workshops on a regular basis, say, once a month, at a time when teens are likely to be available.
- Decide who will facilitate the workshop. A workshop might be held in conjunction with an author visit, or it could be led by a librarian, local writer, creative writing instructor, lyricist, or poet.
- Use collaborative writing as a way of helping teens get comfortable with creative writing. With collaborative writing, each teen contributes to part of the story, poem, or song. This can be an especially effective way of introducing teens to poetry writing.[b]
- Devote workshops to genres and forms popular among young adults. Horror and fan fiction are possibilities,[c] as are dystopian fiction and song lyrics.

- Provide a way for teens to publish their work. Some options include the young adult section of the library's website, local magazines and newspapers, and creative writing journals. An entire workshop could be devoted to tips on getting published.
- Consider holding a poetry slam as a way of concluding a series of workshops on writing poetry.[d]
- Maintain a group of creative writing resources in the library's print collection and links to online resources on the young adult section of the library's website.[e]

Notes:

a. Paulette M. Rothbauer, "Chapter 3: Young Adults and Reading," in *Reading Matters: What the Research Reveals about Reading, Libraries, and Community*, ed. Catherine Sheldrick Ross, Lynne (E.F.) McKechnie, and Paulette M. Rothbauer (Westport, CT: Libraries Unlimited, 2006), 101-131: 124-125.
b. Carl M. Tomlinson and Carol Lynch-Brown, *Essentials of Young Adult Literature*, 2nd ed. (Boston: Pearson, 2010), 134.
c. Michele Gorman and Tricia Suellentrop, *Connecting Young Adults and Libraries*, 4th ed. (New York: Neah-Schuman, 2009), 242.
d. Ella W. Jones, *Start to Finish YA Programs: Hip-Hop Symposiums, Summer Reading Programs, Virtual Tours, Poetry Slams, Teen Advisory Boards, Term Paper Clinics, and More!* (New York: Neal-Schuman, 2009), 36.
e. Rothbauer, 2006, 126.

Professionals who work with young adults and who are interested in learning more about poetry writing activities have a number of resources at their disposal. Kim Addonizio and Dorianne Laux's *The Poet's Companion: A Guide to the Pleasures of Writing Poetry*[75] offers advice in four areas: "subjects for writing," "the poet's craft," "the writing life," and "twenty-minute writing exercises." Geoff Hewitt's *Today You Are My Favorite Poet: Writing Poems with Teenagers*[76] demonstrates how poetry writing can help unlock the creative potential of young adults, even those who do not like to write. And Mark Dressman's *Let's Poem: The Essential Guide to Teaching Poetry in a High-Stakes, Multimodal World*[77] contains chapters on choral poetry, blues poetry, hip-hop, and digital remixes. Additional poetry activities can be found on the International Reading Association's "readwritethink" page, under "Lesson Plans" (http://www.readwritethink.org/classroom-resources/lesson-plans/), keyword: poetry. All these resources remind us that promoting poetry and music through reading, listening, and writing offers an excellent opportunity for librarians and teachers to collaborate on collection development, exhibits, lesson plans, and assignments.

SUMMARY

While many young adults may be resistant to poetry, few claim to not like music. Helping them see the similarities between poetry and lyrics and the fact that both are (usually) intended for performance can help them to appreciate both more fully. Poetry, lyrics, and music can help meet young adults' developmental, recreational, and informational needs and, in particular, can be outlets for self- expression and thus means for identity development. Librarians can work with teachers and other professionals to promote poetry, lyrics, and music among young adults through reading, listening, writing, and performing.

IMPLICATIONS FOR PRACTICE

- Professionals who work with young adults should examine their own attitudes toward poetry and should work to increase their own comfort level in reading and talking about poetry.
- Recognize that many young adults will be resistant to poetry, at least initially.
- In working with young adults, look for opportunities to connect music and poetry.
- Encourage young adults to write poetry, lyrics, and music.
- Encourage young adults to perform poetry, lyrics, and music.
- Provide ways that young adults can enhance poetry and lyrics with images, audio, and video.

QUESTIONS TO THINK ABOUT AND DISCUSS

1. If you were stranded on a desert island and could have only one album of songs on your listening device, what would it be? If you could have only one book of poems with you, what would it be?
2. If your library decided to sponsor an open-mic night for poetry readings and music performance, how could you ensure the presentation of age-appropriate material—that is, not too risqué for a young adult audience—while not engaging in censorship or stifling creativity?
3. If you were tasked with developing a young adult poetry award, how would you go about it? How would you define eligibility? How would you handle the selection process? Would you give the award every year or less frequently?

NOTES

1. Kathy H. Latrobe and Judy Drury, *Critical Approaches to Young Adult Literature* (New York: Neal-Schuman, 2009).

2. Janette Hughes and Sue Dymoke, "'Wiki-Ed Poetry': Transforming Preservice Teachers' Preconceptions about Poetry and Poetry Teaching," *Journal of Adolescent and Adult Literacy* 55, no. 1 (2011): 46–56.

3. Chris Baldick, "Poetry," In *The Concise Oxford Dictionary of Literary Terms* (New York: Oxford University Press, 2004), 198.

4. Latrobe and Drury, *Critical Approaches*, 94.

5. Carl M. Tomlinson and Carol Lynch-Brown, *Essentials of Young Adult Literature*, 2nd ed. (Boston: Pearson Education, 2010), 121.

6. Baldick, "Blank Verse," 28.

7. Baldick, "Free Verse," 102.

8. Baldick, "Poetry," 198.

9. Baldick, "Romance," 221.

10. The definitions of the more common kinds of lyric poetry are based on the corresponding entries in Baldick: "Sonnet," 239–40; "Ode," 177; "Elegy," 76–77; "Haiku," 109; "Limerick," 139–40; "Concrete Poetry," 48.

11. Liz Rosenberg, ed., *The Invisible Ladder: An Anthology of Contemporary American Poems for Young Readers* (New York: Holt, 1996).

12. Lori M. Carlson, ed., *Cool Salsa: Bilingual Poems on Growing Up Latino in the United States* (New York: Holt, 1994).

13. Lori M. Carlson, ed., *Red Hot Salsa: Bilingual Poems on Life, Love, and Victory* (New York: Holt, 2005).

14. Paul B. Janeczko, ed., *Blushing: Expressions of Love in Poems and Letters* (New York: Orchard Books, 2004).

15. J. D. McClatchey, ed. *Loves Speaks Its Name: Gay and Lesbian Love Poems* (New York: Knopf, 2001).

16. Naomi Shihab Nye, ed. *Time You Let Me In: 25 Poets under 25* (New York: Greenwillow, 2010).

17. Jan Greenberg, ed., *Heart to Heart: New Poems Inspired by Twentieth-Century American Art* (New York: Abrams, 2001).

18. Lillian Morrison, ed., *Way to Go! Sports Poems* (Honesdale, PA: Boyds Mills, 2001).

19. Paul B. Janeczko, ed., *A Poke in the I: A Collection of Concrete Poems*, illus. Chris Raschka (Cambridge, MA: Candlewick, 2001).

20. Siyu Liu and Orel Protopopescu, eds., *A Thousand Peaks: Poems from China* (Berkeley, CA: Pacific View, 2001).

21. Catherine Clinton, ed., *I, Too, Sing America: Three Centuries of African American Poetry*, illus. Stephen Alcorn (New York: Houghton Mifflin, 1998).

22. Catherine Clinton, ed., *A Poem of Her Own: Voices of American Women Yesterday and Today*, illus. Stephen Alcorn (New York: Abrams, 2003).

23. Naomi Shihab Nye and Paul B. Janeczko, eds., *I Feel a Little Jumpy around You: A Book of Her Poems and His Poems Collected in Pairs* (New York: Simon & Schuster, 1996).

24. Kathi Appelt, *Poems from Homeroom: A Writer's Place to Start* (New York: Holt, 2002).

25. Nikki Grimes, *A Dime a Dozen* (New York: Penguin Putnam, 1998).

26. Naomi Shihab Nye, *A Maze Me: Poems for Girls*, illus. Terre Maher (New York: Greenwillow, 2005).

27. Sara Holbrook and Allan Wolf, *More Than Friends: Poems from Him and Her* (Honesdale, PA: Boyds Mills, 2008).

28. Angela Johnson, *The Other Side: Shorter Poems* (New York: Orchard, 1998).

29. Walter Dean Myers, *Here in Harlem: Poems in Many Voices* (New York: Holiday House, 2004).

30. Curtis L. Crisler, *Tough Boy Sonatas* (Honesdale, PA: Boyds Mills, 2007).

31. Eve Merriam, *The Inner City Mother Goose*, 3rd ed., illus. David Diaz (New York: Simon & Schuster, 1996).

32. Gary Soto, *Neighborhood Odes* (New York: Harcourt, 1992).

33. Linda Sue Park, *Tap Dancing on the Roof: Sijo* (New York: Clarion, 2007).

34. John Grandits, *Blue Lipstick: Concrete Poems* (New York: Clarion, 2007).

35. Mel Glenn, *Jump Ball: A Basketball Season in Poems* (New York: Dutton, 1997).

36. Walter Dean Myers, *Street Love* (New York: HarperCollins, 2006).

37. Karen Hesse, *Out of the Dust* (New York: Scholastic, 1997).

38. Patricia McCormick, *Sold* (New York: Hyperion, 2006).

39. Thalia Chaltas, *Because I Am Furniture* (New York: Penguin, 2009).

40. Juan Felipe Herrera, *CrashBoomLove: A Novel in Verse* (Alburquerque: University of New Mexico Press, 1999).

41. Helen Frost, *Keesha's House* (New York: Frances Foster, 2003).

42. Stephanie Hemphill, *Your Own Sylvia: A Verse Portrait of Sylvia Plath* (New York: Random House, 2007).

43. Hemphill, *Wicked Girls: A Novel of the Salem Witch Trials* (New York: HarperCollins, 2010).

44. Paul B. Janeczko, *World's Afire* (Cambridge, MA: Candlewick, 2004).

45. Edgar Allan Poe, *The Raven*, illus. Ryan Price (Tonawanda, NY: Kids Can Press, 2006).

46. Ernest L. Thayer, *Casey at the Bat*, illus. Joe Morse (Tonawanda, NY: Kids Can Press, 2006).

47. Walter Dean Myers, *Harlem*, illus. Christopher Myers (New York: Scholastic, 1997).

48. Marilyn Nelson, *A Wreath for Emmett Till*, illus. Philippe Lardy (New York: Houghton Mifflin, 2005).

49. Bob Dylan, *Lyrics 1961–2001* (New York: Simon & Schuster, 2004).

50. Adam Bradley and Andrew DuBois, eds., *The Anthology of Rap* (New Haven, CT: Yale University Press, 2010).

51. Alan Sitomer and Michael Cirelli, *Hip-Hop Poetry and the Classics* (Beverly Hills, CA: Milk Mug, 2004).

52. *The Beatles Best: More Than 120 Great Hits*, 2nd ed. (Milwaukee, WI: Leonard, 1987).

53. Howard Shore, *The Lord of the Rings Trilogy: Music from the Motion Pictures Arranged for Solo Piano* (Van Nuys, CA: Alfred Music, 2009).

54. Walter Dean Myers, *Blues Journey*, illus. Christopher Myers (New York: Holiday House, 2003).

55. Walter Dean Myers, *Jazz*, illus. Christopher Myers (New York: Holiday House, 2006).

56. Alexs D. Pate, *In the Heart of the Beat: The Poetry of Rap* (Lanham, MD: Scarecrow, 2010).

57. Mark Flowers, "Books with Beat: Women Make Music but Men Keep Writing the Books," *Young Adult Library Services* 8, no. 4 (2010): 19–21.

58. Elsworth Rockefeller and Rollie Welch, "Man Up! Sex, Drugs, and Hip-Hop! Guys and Music," *Voice of Youth Advocates* 33, no. 4 (2010): 332–33.

59. Elizabeth Partridge, *John Lennon: All I Want Is the Truth* (New York: Viking, 2005).

60. Ann Angel, *Janis Joplin: Rise Up Singing* (New York: Abrams, 2010).

61. Betsy Franco, ed., *Things I Have to Tell You: Poems and Writing by Teenage Girls*, photo. Nina Nickles (Cambridge, MA: Candlewick, 2001).

62. Betsy Franco, ed., and Nina Nickles, photo., *You Hear Me? Poems and Writing by Teenage Boys* (Cambridge, MA: Candlewick, 2000).

63. Bill Aguado and Richard Newirth, eds., *Paint Me Like I Am: Teen Poems from WritersCorp* (New York: HarperTeen, 2003).

64. Dave Johnson, *Movin': Teen Poets Take Voice*, illus. Chris Raschka (New York: Orchard Books, 2000).

65. Korina M. Jocson, *Youth Poets: Empowering Literacies in and out of Schools* (New York: Lang, 2008).

66. Jen Scott Curwood and Lora Lee H. Cowell, "iPoetry: Creating Space for New Literacies in the English Curriculum," *Journal of Adolescent and Adult Literacy* 55, no. 2 (2011): 110–20.

67. Angela Kinney, "Loops, Lyrics, and Literacy: Songwriting as a Site of Resilience for an Urban Adolescent," *Journal of Adolescent and Adult Literacy* 55, no. 5 (2012): 395–404.

68. Wendy R. Williams, "'Untold Stories to Tell': Making Space for the Voices of Youth Songwriters," *Journal of Adolescent and Adult Literacy* 56, no. 5 (2013): 369–79.

69. Guadalupe Garcia McCall, *Under the Mesquite* (New York: Lee & Low Books, 2011).

70. Joyce Sidman, *Dark Emperor and Other Poems of the Night*, illus. Rick Allen (New York: Houghton Mifflin Harcourt Books for Young Readers, 2010).

71. Paul Fleischman, *Joyful Noise: Poems for Two Voices*, illus. Eric Beddows (New York: HarperCollins, 1988).

72. Paul Fleischman, *Big Talk: Poems for Four Voices*, illus. Beppe Giacobbe (Cambridge, MA: Candlewick, 2000).

73. Laura Amy Schlitz, *Good Masters! Sweet Ladies! Voices from a Medieval Village*, illus. Robert Byrd (Cambridge, MA: Candlewick, 2007).

74. Lynn R. Rudd, "Just *Slammin!* Adolescents' Construction of Identity through Performance Poetry," *Journal of Adolescent and Adult Literacy* 55, no. 8 (2012): 682–91.

75. Kim Addonizio and Dorianne Laux, *The Poet's Companion: A Guide to the Pleasures of Writing Poetry* (New York: Norton, 1997).

76. Geoff Hewitt, *Today You Are My Favorite Poet: Writing Poems with Teenagers* (Portsmouth, NH: Heinemann, 1998).

77. Mark Dressman, *Let's Poem: The Essential Guide to Teaching Poetry in a High-Stakes, Multimodal World* (New York: Teachers College Press, 2010).

Chapter Eight

Special Forms and Formats

This chapter discusses resources for young adults in special forms and formats:

- Graphic novels
- Picture books for young adults
- Movies
- Magazines and zines
- Evaluating and promoting special forms and formats
- Spotlight! Comics workshops
- Spotlight! Author visits
- Implications for practice
- Questions to think about and discuss

Many of the resources that young adults enjoy are in special forms and formats, and many of them make ample use of visuals as well as text or, in the case of movies, audio. At one time, these formats were not considered "proper" reading materials, in the sense of materials that facilitated thoughtful, analytical reading. Fortunately, that misconception has begun to change with the recognition that these formats can, in fact, foster "traditional" literacy skills, visual literacy skills, and critical thinking skills. Now, many libraries collect these kinds of materials, and they are even finding a place in school classrooms. In examining these kinds of resources, it is important to consider the key aspects and unique characteristics of each format.

GRAPHIC NOVELS

The term *graphic novel* is generally attributed to Will Eisner, who used it in 1978 to describe his collection of graphic narratives *A Contract with God, and Other Tenement Stories*.[1] Although there is evidence that the term did not originate with Eisner, his book is generally credited with making the term widely known. In the time since then, graphic novels have become quite popular among readers of all ages, including young adults, and all genres are represented in the format—fiction, nonfiction, poetry, and drama.

Before turning to a discussion of exemplary titles in the various genres, it is important that we establish a basic vocabulary for discussing and evaluating graphic resources. An excellent guide to how graphic resources work is Scott McCloud's *Understanding Comics: The Invisible Art*,[2] a detailed analysis cleverly and entertainingly presented as a graphic novel. Our discussion of comics terminology is drawn largely from McCloud's book.

First, it is important to understand the (sometimes fuzzy) distinction between a comic book and a graphic novel, but let us begin with a definition of "comic." As McCloud points out, Eisner defines comic as sequential art. A comic strip, then, is either a single panel or a short series of panels that present a scene or tell a brief story. A comic book is much longer series of panels that tell a story, although usually a single comic book issue tells only part of a story, the idea being that the story will be continued in the next issue. It may take several or even many issues for a "story arc" to be completed. Usually, comic strips and comic books focus on a particular character or characters.

Comic strips and comic books are relatively easy to define; graphic novels, however, are a bit more problematic. For one thing, the term *novel* can be misleading. Strictly speaking, a novel is a work of fiction. However, the term *graphic novel* has gained such parlance that it is now used to describe resources in graphic format that are not fiction—memoirs, for example, other kinds of nonfiction, and even poems. In terms of material production quality, graphic novels are generally superior to comic books. While comic books are usually printed on the same paper and bound in the same way as magazines, graphic novels are printed on heavier-weight paper and bound with sturdier covers. In terms of content, though, the boundaries are more blurred. Some graphic novels stand alone as single volumes, telling a particular story or, in the case of nonfiction, presenting information on a particular subject. But other graphic novels are part of a series, telling a series of stories over several volumes. Neil Gaiman's multivolume *Sandman* series is a notable example, as are most manga (Japanese graphic novels) series, which can run into scores of volumes. Further complicating matters in trying to distinguish between comic books and graphic novels is the fact that it is not unusual for a particular story arc that has been told over several issues of a comic book to be collected into a single-volume, high-quality edition and marketed as a graphic novel.

The United States has played an important role in the development of comic books and graphic novels, but other countries and cultures have made significant contributions to the graphic format as well. As previously mentioned, Japanese graphic novels are called *manga*, and they are distinguished from U.S. graphic novels in that each page is read from right to left and each book from back to front—or, to a Western reader, what appears to be back to front. In addition, characters in manga are drawn with exaggerated features and expressions, and there is a rather elaborate visual vocabulary for conveying different emotions.

Manga is popular among all age groups in Japan, and there are many types of manga, each designed for a particular niche audience based on age group, gender, and personal interests. Shonen manga, for example, consists of action and adventure stories and is usually intended for teenage boys. Shojo manga covers a variety of genres but tends to focus on relationships and is intended for teenage girls. Manhua are comics produced in China, Hong Kong, or Taiwan, and manhwa are comics produced in Korea. Manhwa, like Western comics, are read from left to right.

France and Belgium also have a rich tradition of comic art, called *bandes dessinées*, or "drawn strips." A history of comics and graphic novels is beyond the scope of this book, but readers interested in learning more can consult McCloud's book, referenced earlier, as well as Stephen Weiner's *Faster Than a Speeding Bullet: The Rise of the Graphic Novel*[3] and Fred Van Lente and Ryan Dunlavey's *The Comic Book History of Comics*.[4]

It is also helpful to understand some key terms related to the basic parts of comics and how they work:

Panel—essentially a single picture in a comic, usually with a border around it. Comic books and graphic novels are made up of many panels.

Gutter—the space between panels.

Bleed—a panel without a border, which appears to "bleed" to the edge of the page or to the edges of other panels.

Speech balloon—the space where a character's spoken words are printed. There is usually a funnel or line leading from the character's mouth to her or his speech balloon.

Thought balloon—the space where a character's thoughts are printed. There are usually "bubbles" or an ellipsis leading from the character's head to her or his thought balloon.

Caption—the space where narration is presented; it is usually a rectangular bar placed at the top or bottom of a panel. Not every panel has a caption.

Implied action—conveyed in at least a couple of ways. The most common is through the changes depicted as we move from one panel to another. These changes imply that some time has passed, even if only a few seconds, and something has occurred. It has been said that the "meaning" of comics lies in the gutter; in other words, readers make assumptions about what has happened as they move from one panel to the next—they fill in the blanks so to speak. The other means for depicting action is through action lines, which, while obviously stylized, are meant to convey a sense of movement.

Works in graphic format include all genres. We consider some of the more common ones and some of the more popular ones among young adults. The superhero genre, while often maligned as silly or sexist, nevertheless remains a strong favorite among readers and publishers. Superman, Batman, and Spider-Man continue to have a large fan base, along with Wonder Woman, the X-Men, and the Fantastic Four, to name just a few. While more recent superhero comics have reflected greater diversity, it is still the case that most superheroes are white straight men. In fact, there is a website vividly named "Women in Refrigerators" (http://lby3.com/wir/) devoted to documenting how women in many superhero comics, even female superheroes, are often injured, killed, or otherwise disenfranchised for the purpose of "enhancing" the male heroes' stories. For example, in *Batman: The Killing Joke,*[5] Batgirl (aka Barbara Gordon) is shot by the Joker, rendering her paralyzed while motivating Batman's heroic attempt to, once again, track down the villain.

There are hundreds of superhero titles, and an in-depth discussion of the genre is obviously beyond the scope of this chapter. However, two graphic novel titles should be mentioned as highly regarded works that elevated the status of the genre to a serious art form. One is Alan Moore and Dave Gibbons's *Watchmen,*[6] a tale of a world, not only in which superheroes have been outlawed, but that is approaching the brink of nuclear disaster. The main characters are superheroes who come out of "exile" to try to save civilization. The other work, published around the same time, is *The Dark Knight Returns*, by Frank Miller, Klaus Janson, and Lynn Varley.[7] This book tells the story of an aging Batman who comes out of retirement to battle Two-Face and the Joker. Both books contain intense violence and mature themes and are more appropriate for older teens and adults. Both books also interrogate the notion of what it means to be a superhero, and they implicitly suggest that in some respects the superheroes and the villains are motivated by the same dark forces.

Not all graphic novels, of course, are superhero titles; in fact, some of the most interesting work in the last 20 or so years has been in other genres. Fantasy is a popular genre, and two highly successful and well-regarded fantasy series are Neil Gaiman's *Sandman* and Jeff Smith's *Bone*. *Sandman*[8] is a series of dark fantasy books focusing on Morpheus and his siblings, known as the Endless. Each volume tells a different story of the dream realm and is illustrated by a different artist. In contrast, *Bone*[9] contains much humor and is more of an epic fantasy that tells the story of the three Bone cousins and their adventures battling the Hooded One and the Rat Creatures.

More realistic graphic novels are popular among teens as well, especially those that focus on coming-of-age stories of teens or twentysomethings. In *Drama*,[10] Raina Telgemeier relates the fun, trials, and, well, drama of middle schoolers who are working to put on a musical. *Anya's Ghost*,[11] by Vera Brosgol, uses magical realism in the form of a malicious ghost to portray that otherwise realistic story of an immigrant adolescent as she tries to make her way in a new school. Similar themes, minus the ghost, are grappled with in Gene Luen Yang's Michael L. Printz Award–winning *American Born Chinese*.[12] In this book of three interwoven stories, a Chinese American boy desperately wants to fit into the white culture of his school. Mariko and Jillian Tamaki's *Skim*[13] relates a more disturbing story of adolescent alienation, suicide, and illicit love. And Daniel Clowes's *Ghost World*[14] explores how the relationship changes between two eighteen-year-old girls as one of them prepares to go off to college.

A number of graphic novels focus on twentysomethings and their delayed coming-of-age experiences. Not surprising, teenagers often find characters of this age group to be even more fascinating than characters of their own age group. The *Scott Pilgrim*[15] series, by Bryan Lee O'Malley, presents the adventures of a 23-year-old slacker who is concerned less with getting a job than being in a band and pursuing romance. And Derek Kirk Kim's *Same Difference*[16] relates the stories of a group of young people in California who, long after graduating from high school, cannot quite seem to jump-start their adult lives.

Some of the most compelling coming-of-age stories can be found in graphic nonfiction, specifically biography and memoir. A classic of the graphic biography genre is Art Spiegelman's *Maus: A Survivor's Tale*.[17] This two-part masterwork tells the story of Spiegelman's father, a survivor of the Nazi concentration camps. In the books, the Jews are portrayed as mice, the Germans as cats, the French as frogs, the Poles as pigs, and the Americans as dogs. The books won numerous awards, including a Pulitzer Prize, the first for a work in graphic format. Marjane Satrapi's two-volume work *Persepolis*[18] tells of her childhood experiences coming of age in Iran during the Islamic Revolution. Volume 1 tells of her adolescence in Iran after the revolution, while volume 2 focuses on her experiences in Vienna, where she was sent to attend school at the age of 14, and her eventual return to Iran.

Closer to home is Alison Bechdel's *Fun Home: A Family Tragicomic*,[19] in which Bechdel describes coming to terms with her sexuality while growing up with a closeted gay father who was a high school English teacher, part-time funeral director (hence, the name "fun" home), and avid collector of antiques. Similarly, Craig Thompson's *Blankets*[20] recounts the difficulties of growing up in a strict fundamentalist Christian household. And, as a title already mentioned in chapter 5 as an example of urban fiction, *Yummy: The Last Days of a Southside Shorty*,[21] though a work of fiction, is nevertheless based on the true and tragic story of a boy who became a fugitive after accidentally killing a neighbor.

Another type of graphic novel that many young adults find appealing is the adaptation—specifically, graphic versions of the "classic" works often assigned in school. There are, for example, numerous graphic adaptations of Shakespeare's plays. Classical Comics (http://www.classicalcomics.com/index.html) has three graphic versions available for Shakespeare's more frequently taught plays: the "original text" version contains the unabridged text of the play; the "plain text" version translates the original text into modern English line for line; and the "quick text" version is a shortened version of the original text but retains all the characters and plot elements. Other texts frequently read in high school that are also available in graphic format include Herman Melville's *Moby Dick* (adapted by Lance Stahlberg)[22] and Jane Austen's *Pride and Prejudice* (adapted by Nancy Butler).[23] Classic works assigned in school are not the only kinds of adaptations available in graphic format. Hope Larson's graphic version of Madeleine L'Engle's *A Wrinkle in Time*[24] is a faithful adaptation of the beloved children's book, while Dean, Shannon, and Nathan Hale's *Rapunzel's Revenge*,[25] while not exactly an adaptation, offers a clever take inspired by the original fairy tale.

Manga is a popular format among young adults, and there are numerous series representing various genres, designed to appeal to a variety of tastes. As noted earlier, shonen manga is manga marketed to boys 10 to 18 years old, although it has fans among girls and readers of other ages as well. A classic is Keiji Nakazawa's *Barefoot Gen*,[26] an account of a Hiroshima boy and his family and their struggles to survive in the aftermath of the atomic bomb. *Dragon Ball*,[27] by Akira Toriyama, tells of the adventures of a forest-dwelling boy with a monkey tail who teams up with a girl to collect the seven Dragon Balls to be able to summon a dragon and be granted a wish. *Dragon Ball Z*,[28] the sequel, continues the adventures of the boy except that he is now grown up and his task is to protect Earth from alien invaders. In *Fullmetal Alchemist*,[29] by Hiromu Arakawa, two brothers use alchemy to transform things around them, but they find that their power causes them great harm that is difficult to undo. A similarly sinister power is possessed by the boy in Tsugumi Ohba and Takeshi Obata's *Death Note*[30] when he discovers a book in which he can write a person's name and specify how that person will die.

Shojo manga is marketed primarily to girls 10 to 18 years old, although, like shonen manga, it is read and enjoyed by boys and by people of all ages. One popular series is Naoko Takeuchi's *Sailor Moon*,[31] about a high school girl who discovers a magical brooch that allows her to transform herself into a crusader fighting against the forces of evil. Natsumi Ando's *Zodiac PI*[32] relates the crime-solving adventures of a teenage girl who, through a magic ring, can transform herself into a detective. Akimi Yoshida's *Banana Fish*,[33] a more realistic story, focuses on a young gang leader in New York who is investigating the connections among a series of suicides. *Fruits Basket*,[34] by Natsuki Takaya, is also a more realistic story, about a street orphan who finds both a home and romance. *Gravitation*,[35] by Maki Murakami, is an example of yaoi, a subgenre that focuses on male-male romantic relationships but is read primarily by women. In this series, a wannabe rock star becomes involved with another man who has criticized his songwriting ability.

There are far fewer manhwa (Korean comics) titles available in English, but there are some notable examples. Kim Dong Hwa's *The Color Trilogy*— *The Color of Earth, The Color of Water,* and *The Color of Heaven*[36] — explores the coming of age and sexual awakening of a young Korean girl from adolescence through marriage. There are even fewer manhua (Chinese comics) titles available, but one series that Western readers might be familiar with, or at least interested in, because of the live-action film is Wang Du Lu and Andy Seto's *Crouching Tiger, Hidden Dragon*,[37] about two martial arts masters, a woman and a man, and their developing relationship as they travel through China. The manga, manhwa, and manhua titles discussed provide only a thumbnail sketch of what is available. Many more titles, as well as a discussion of key characteristics of the three formats, can be found in Elizabeth F. S. Kalen's excellent resource *Mostly Manga: A Genre Guide to Popular Manga, Manhwa, Manhua, and Anime.*[38]

PICTURE BOOKS FOR YOUNG ADULTS

Picture books, like graphic novels, consist of both text and pictures (although there are some wordless picture books), but they differ from graphic novels in a couple of important respects. Whereas graphic novels are made up of a series of panels, with several panels on each page, picture books typically feature no more than one picture per page and may occasionally present a single picture over a two-page spread. Picture books are also shorter than most graphic novels; the standard format for picture books is 32 pages, although some are longer. Most picture books are intended for younger readers, usually preschool to third grade, but an increasing number of picture books are being published for older readers, including young adults. Picture books should not be confused with illustrated books. With the former, the words and pictures are both integral in conveying the content; with the latter, the pictures serve to illustrate key scenes or perhaps provide decoration, but they are not crucial to the content of the book.

What then distinguishes young adult picture books from the ones designed for younger children? Sunya Osborn[39] identifies six key characteristics:

- Mature themes
- More complex illustrations than those that would be easily appreciated or
  understood by younger readers
- More difficult text than what would be appropriate for the short attention
  span of younger readers
- Subtle meanings beyond the understanding of younger readers
- Two levels of meaning—one for younger readers and one for older readers
- Fiction or nonfiction

In relation to this last point, as Osborn notes, picture books for younger
readers can also be fiction or nonfiction, but it probably is fair to say that the
majority of picture books for younger readers are fiction, whereas more
nonfiction titles can be found among picture books for young adults.

Although many young adults might initially be reluctant to read a picture
book because they associate them with "little kids," they can soon learn to
enjoy the pleasures offered by the format. As Patricia Murphy[40] points out,
picture books are quick reads, offer interesting illustrations, provide concise
text, and overall are reader friendly. In addition, they can be especially appealing to English-language learners and to reluctant readers.

As noted in chapter 7, a number of individual poems are available in
illustrated versions, and most of these might be properly called picture
books. But other genres are also represented among picture books for young
adults. History is on view in Tom Feelings's *The Middle Passage: White
Ships / Black Cargo*,[41] a vivid pictorial account of the horrors that enslaved
Africans experienced during the trans-Atlantic passage to America. Ntozake
Shange and Rod Brown's *We Troubled the Waters*[42] relates the triumphs and
tragedies endured by activists during the civil rights era. Some historical
picture books take a more personal focus. Ed Young presents an account of
his early life in *The House Baba Built: An Artist's Childhood in China*,[43]
while Peter Sís portrays his childhood in the former Czechoslovakia in *The
Wall: Growing Up behind the Iron Curtain.*[44]

Math and science, with a humorous twist, are the topics in Jon Scieszka
and Lane Smith's *Math Curse*[45] and *Science Verse*,[46] respectively. In *The
Stinky Cheese Man and Other Fairly Stupid Tales*,[47] Scieszka and Smith turn
their satirical eye to the fairy tale, and their inventive and humorous approach
to well-known tales offers a lot of appeal to young adults who remember
these stories from their childhood. Readers who enjoy innovative narrative
strategies will enjoy David Macaulay's *Black and White*,[48] which tells four
different stories that may or may not be related. Admittedly, in books like

Black and White, the distinctions between picture books and graphic novels become blurred. This is even more the case with Shaun Tan's *The Arrival*,[49] a wordless book that portrays the immigration experience through sometimes surreal images. Tan himself has written of how he thought that he had produced a picture book, only to find it being received and reviewed as a graphic novel.[50] His *Lost and Found*,[51] a collection of three stories on the titular theme, is more clearly a picture book, albeit a sophisticated one. The narratives depend on both text and pictures to convey their meanings.

MOVIES

Most young adults enjoy movies, and the movie industry knows that young adults account for a sizable portion of the moviegoing public. Comedies, romances, and adventure stories; fantasy and realism; and live-action and animated films are all popular genres and formats. In developing a movie collection for young adults and promoting particular movies to young adults, it is important to be familiar with the ratings code established by the Motion Picture Association of America (http://www.mpaa.org/ratings/what-each-rating-means). A G rating means that a movie is deemed suitable for a general audience and does not contain objectionable language, nudity, sex, or violence. A PG rating means that "parental guidance" is suggested and that a movie does contain language, nudity, sex, or violence that some people might find objectionable. PG-13 indicates that parental guidance is strongly suggested, as the language and content are probably not suitable for anyone under the age of 13. An R rating means that anyone under 17 must be accompanied by a parent or adult guardian, while an NC-17 rating means that no one under 17 will be admitted.[52]

Many movies intended for, or at least popular among, young adults are based on books, either prose fiction or graphic novels. The *Harry Potter* movies[53] are a prime example, as are the movies based on the *Lord of the Rings* trilogy.[54] Other examples include the movies based on the horror/romance *Twilight* series[55] and those based on the dystopian *Hunger Games* trilogy.[56] Successful series books are especially attractive to Hollywood producers because they offer a ready-made audience and the opportunity for several sequels. Young adult fans of the books are likely to be interested in seeing the movies. Those who have not read the books but are fans of the movies may very well decide to read the original works. Of course, sometimes a single book will gain popular and critical attention and may catch the eye of a movie producer.

Two examples of stand-alone books that have been made into successful films include *Nick and Norah's Infinite Playlist*[57] and *The Perks of Being a Wallflower*.[58] *Nick and Norah's Infinite Playlist*, based on the book by Rachel Cohn and David Levithan, depicts the burgeoning romance of a boy and girl who travel around New York City one night trying to find a "secret" show that their favorite band is supposedly playing. *The Perks of Being a Wallflower*, based on the book by Stephen Chbosky, recounts a shy, troubled boy's first year in high school.

Graphic novels, including manga, are particularly attractive candidates for movie adaptations. Already part of a visual format, in many ways they resemble the storyboards used by filmmakers in the early stages of production. Superhero comics have large fan bases, so it is not surprising that a number of movies have been made based on superhero characters, if not always on specific stories. Superman, Batman, Spider-Man, and the X-Men have made frequent appearances in live-action films. But other graphic genres have also been adapted for the silver screen, some as live-action films and some as animation. *Ghost World*,[59] for example, was made into a live-action film starring Thora Birch and Scarlett Johansson. The movie version of the *Scott Pilgrim* books, *Scott Pilgrim vs. the World*,[60] features Michael Cera and Mary Elizabeth Winstead.

Manga has proven to be a fruitful source, and manga works are typically adapted as animated films, or "anime" as it is called in Japan. These are often multiple-episode offerings designed for the television and DVD/Blu-ray markets. Two popular shonen manga series, *Bleach* and *Death Note,* have been made into animated films, as have two popular shojo manga series, *Gravitation* and *Fruits Basket*. Not all anime is based on manga. *Howl's Moving Castle*,[61] about a girl who is turned into an old woman and her efforts to get help from the wizard Howl, is a highly regarded and successful film based on the book by Diana Wynne Jones. *Spirited Away*[62] is an original-screenplay anime written and directed by Hayao Miyazaki, about a girl's surreal adventure in an abandoned theme park.

Live-action films not based on books are also popular with young adults. *Juno*,[63] for example, is an award-winning comedy-drama about a teenage girl's unplanned pregnancy. *The Way, Way Back*,[64] also a comedy-drama, tells the coming-of-age story of a 14-year-old loner who accompanies his mother and her jerk of a boyfriend to a seaside resort for a summer vacation.

MAGAZINES AND ZINES

Many young adults enjoy reading magazines, especially those related to their hobbies and special interests. Though print magazines, like newspapers, are fighting to survive in the multimedia-saturated world in which we live today, there are still a variety of magazines available on a variety of topics—and most of them now have their own websites and even apps. One young adult magazine that we have already mentioned (in chapter 5) is *Teen Ink*, the magazine of creative writing for and by teens. Two perennially popular teen-focused magazines for adolescent girls is *Seventeen* and *Teen Vogue*, and there are a number of other titles aimed at this market.

But many teens also read magazines aimed at a general adult audience. Usually, these focus on a particular hobby, activity, or other interest. Computers and computer gaming are popular topics among many young adults, and they read such magazines as *PC Gaming, Official Xbox Magazine*, and *MacWorld.* Teens interested in technology may pick up *Popular Mechanics*, while those interested in cars may peruse *Car and Driver*. Most young adults have a favorite kind of music and favorite bands, and they may regularly read *Rolling Stone* or similar magazines. Those interested in sports may opt for *Sports Illustrated* or *ESPN the Magazine*, while those fascinated with celebrities in general will probably gravitate to *People*, one of the most popular magazines in the United States. Humor, especially transgressive humor, appeals to a lot of young adults, and *Mad Magazine* continues to have die-hard fans. And comic books, whether featuring superheroes or zombies, continue to have avid readers as well. Admittedly, in a time of tight budgets, libraries must make careful decisions about collecting and archiving print periodicals. Still, libraries should be cognizant of which magazines their young adult patrons regularly read and, to the extent possible, make the most popular ones available.

Young adults not only read magazines but also write and produce their own magazines, or zines. The word *zine* is a shortened version of *fanzine*. Zines were originally produced cheaply (usually on mimeograph machines or photocopiers) and distributed through local stores and via the postal service. Nowadays, zines are increasingly distributed online, through websites or e-mail. Zines may serve as outlets for fan fiction (discussed in chapter 5), but they may contain other kinds of material—from essays and reviews to stories and poems, from photographs and drawings to full-blown comics. In that sense, a publication such as *Teen Ink* can be seen as an adult-sanctioned zine. Most zines, however, are populist efforts, produced by an "amateur" for a niche audience. While it might be difficult for libraries to include zines as part of their collection development policies, they can serve as distribution points for the zines in their community, assuming, of course, that the content is appropriate for the users served.

EVALUATING AND PROMOTING SPECIAL FORMS AND FORMATS

All the special forms and formats discussed in this chapter are highly visual media, with the possible exception of some zines, which may be primarily text based. As such, it is important to consider words (whether printed, spoken, or implied) and images in evaluating these resources. Specifically, the following criteria should be considered:

- Engaging visuals that help to convey the story or, in the case of nonfiction works, the information. In the case of wordless graphic novels and picture books, the visuals bear sole responsibility for conveying meaning.
- Engaging text that helps to convey the story or, in the case of nonfiction works, the information. Of course, movies contain spoken rather than written text, but still the spoken dialogue and voice-over narration (if present) should be compelling enough to maintain the viewer's interest.
- In the case of nonfiction works, accuracy of content must also be considered carefully.
- Like other resources, works in special forms and formats should be evaluated on the basis of their age appropriateness for the intended audience. Many graphic novels and movies are intended for adult audiences and might not be considered appropriate for younger teens. The particular standards of the community being served should always be taken into consideration.

There are several resources available for discovering graphic novel titles for young adults, including YALSA's "Great Graphic Novels for Teens" lists (http://www.ala.org/yalsa/great-graphic-novels), No Flying No Tights website (http://noflyingnotights.com/), and *The Librarian's Guide to Anime and Manga* (http://www.koyagi.com/Libguide.html). A useful resource for locating picture book titles for young adults is the Cooperative Children's Book Center's "Never Too Old: Picture Books to Share with Older Children and Teens" (http://www.education.wisc.edu/ccbc/books/detailListBooks.asp?id BookLists=259). Though most of the books tend to skew toward older children rather than teens, it is nonetheless a useful list, and it is conveniently organized into eight topical categories.

In addition, graphic novels and picture books are regularly reviewed in journals such as *Voice of Youth Advocates*, *School Library Journal*, and *The Horn Book* and on websites such as Teenreads (http://www.teenreads.com/). YALSA provides a list of "Fabulous Films for Young Adults" each year, available at http://www.ala.org/yalsa/fabulous-films. Since 2009, the films have been selected according to a predetermined theme. The films for 2013, for example, are focused on the theme of "Survival," while the films for 2014 are on the theme "School's Out Forever!" Films for all ages are regularly reviewed in the popular press and online. Two popular websites that provide a wealth of information about movies are IMDb (Internet Movie Database) (http://www.imdb.com/) and Rotten Tomatoes (http://www.rotten-tomatoes.com/).

Librarians and other professionals can promote materials in special forms and formats using many of the same strategies used to promote other kinds of resources. Exhibits, booktalks, and book discussions, for example, can include graphic novels and picture books for older readers. Movies based on books can be used to promote the books themselves, and vice versa. Screenings of teen-friendly films can be held in the library, although a word of caution is in order here: while private viewings of a DVD or Blue-ray is fine, public showings within an institution (for nonclassroom use) require a public performance license. More information about this requirement and how to obtain such a license is available on the Motion Picture Association of America website (http://www.mpaa.org/contentprotection/public-performance-law).

SPOTLIGHT!

Comics Workshops

With the popularity of comics and graphic novels, many teens are interested in creating their own graphic stories. Libraries can sponsor comics workshops offering instruction in how to create graphic materials, access to technology, and opportunities to work with other teens and get constructive feedback. Published comics artists or local art instructors can be invited to demonstrate drawing techniques and provide instruction in the various kinds of technology now used to produce graphic works.[a] Comics workshops are also a great opportunity for teens to work together. Some may wish to focus on writing the story, while others concentrate on the doing the drawings. They can also display their finished work in the library or on the library's website and get feedback from viewers face-to-face or via short written surveys.

Fortunately, it's not a requirement that participants be gifted with freehand drawing skills. Software such as Manga Studio, SketchBook Pro, Comic Creator, Pixton, and Comic Life make creating comics on the computer relatively easy and are accessible for people with different skill levels. Comic Life, for instance, allows users to import photographs and transform them to make them look like comics, complete with panels, word balloons, and captions.[b] A variety of print materials are available that offer instruction in creating comics. Two especially noteworthy titles are Scott McCloud's *Making Comics: Storytelling Secrets of Comics, Manga, and Graphic Novels*[c] and Christopher Hart's

Manga for the Beginner: Everything You Need to Start Drawing Right Away![d] Comics workshops, aside from being fun and providing a creative outlet for teens, can help promote textual, visual, and technology literacies.

Tips:

- Consider investing in a comics creation software that can be installed on some of the library's computers. A quick web search on the terms "comics software" or "comics creation software" will yield a number of sites with reviews of specific software, prices, and open-access applications.
- Teens can develop comics versions of their own stories, but they can also borrow well-known fairy tales or folk tales.
- Teens interested in fan fiction might want to turn some of their fan fiction stories into graphic stories.
- Don't forget about nonfiction topics. You might, for example, ask teens to develop a graphic guide to using your library or some part of your library's collection, similar to *Library of the Living Dead: Your Guide to Miller Library at McPherson College.*[e]
- Have a friendly contest with an exhibit featuring graphic works produced by teens, opportunities for viewers to vote, and prizes for the top three entries.

Notes:

a. Michele Gorman and Tricia Suellentrop, *Connecting Young Adults and Libraries*, 4th ed. (New York: Neal-Schuman, 2009), 239.
b. Plasq, *Comic Life 3: Make It Your Story*, 2013, http://plasq.com/products/comiclife3/mac.
c. Scott McCloud, *Making Comics: Storytelling Secrets of Comics, Manga and Graphic Novels* (New York: Morrow, 2006).
d. Christopher Hart, *Manga for the Beginner: Everything You Need to Start Drawing Right Away!* (New York: Watson-Guptill, 2008).
e. Michael Hall and Matt Upson, *Library of the Living Dead: Your Guide to Miller Library at McPherson College*, 2011, http://blogs.mcpherson.edu/library/wp-content/uploads/2011/03/Library-of-the-Living-Dead-Online-Edition.pdf.

Special forms and formats can also be promoted by inviting graphic novelists, illustrators, and filmmakers to give talks or make presentations to young adults. These artists can offer readings or viewings and talk about their work, but they might also be willing to present workshops that provide instruction in how young adults can write and illustrate their own comics or make their own movies, individually or collaboratively. Such activities help promote multimodal literacies—that is, the skills involved in multiple modes of communication.

SPOTLIGHT!

Author Visits

Visits by authors are a good way to promote reading and writing as worthwhile activities. As tween author Dan Gutman says, "when kids get the chance to meet the author of a book they've read, a special connection is made. They are energized, inspired, touched with a new appreciation for reading."[a] Authors enjoy meeting young people, and, of course, they're particularly interested in promoting their own books. They will often read excerpts from their books, including works in progress, and talk about the process of writing and getting published. Some authors are also happy to do a writing workshop for a group of young people, but this is something that should be arranged well in advance and not sprung on an author the day of the presentation. Authors who visit can be fiction writers, nonfiction writers, poets, graphic novel authors and illustrators, and even musicians.

Author visits can be expensive, as there are typically travel costs and an honorarium involved. One way to deal with the cost is for several libraries and schools to jointly sponsor an author visit.[b] As a rule, the way to arrange an author visit is to contact the author's publisher, and a good place to start is with the author's or publisher's website.[c] Another option is to feature local or up-and-coming authors, as these folks may have little or no travel costs and considerably lower fees. Many state libraries, state library associations, and state reading associations maintain lists of local writers along with their contact information.[d]

Tips:

- Author Dan Gutman has some excellent tips for hosting an author visit, and these are available on his website.[e] Much of what follows here is based on his advice.

- Well in advance of the visit, make sure that you understand what the author is prepared to do, and make sure the author understands what you would like for her or him to do.
- Promote the visit well in advance. Ideally, young people in the audience would have read one or more of the author's books before the visit.
- Make sure that you have copies of the author's books available for checkout. Depending on the venue, it may be appropriate to have someone from a local bookstore bring copies of the author's books to sell. Again, this is something that should be worked out with the author, publisher, and bookstore well in advance.
- Don't forget, the author will probably need to have lunch or dinner at some point and might enjoy having a meal with a small group of young adults.
- If the author is visiting more than one location in town, it's important to have transportation available and to schedule the sessions with ample time in between.

Notes:

a. Dan Gutman, "The Perfect Author Visit," 2013, http://www.dangutman.com/pages/planvisits.html.
b. Carl M. Tomlinson and Carol Lynch-Brown, *Essentials of Young Adult Literature*, 2nd ed. (Boston: Pearson, 2010), 228.
c. Tomlinson and Lynch-Brown, *Essentials of Young Adult Literature*, 228.
d. Tomlinson and Lynch-Brown, *Essentials of Young Adult Literature*, 228.
e. Gutman, "The Perfect Author Visit."

SUMMARY

In today's highly visual culture, many young adults are attracted to resources in special forms and formats precisely because they use images to tell stories or present information. Avid, moderate, and reluctant readers are attracted to graphic novels, picture books, movies, magazines, and zines. Materials that were once considered by adults not to count as "real" reading are now seen as resources that can promote a constellation of literacies, including textual, visual, information, and digital literacy, as well as critical thinking and multimodal communication skills.

IMPLICATIONS FOR PRACTICE

- Make sure that resources in special forms and formats are included in the young adult collection.
- Promote resources in special forms and formats along with those in more "traditional" forms and formats.
- Recognize that reluctant readers, English-language learners, and struggling readers may find highly visual resources especially appealing and useful.
- Encourage young adults to write and draw their own graphic novels and picture books, make their own movies, and produce their own zines.
- Collaborate with teachers to facilitate the use of resources in special forms and formats in the classroom.

QUESTIONS TO THINK ABOUT AND DISCUSS

1. Are there particular special forms and formats that you enjoy reading? What are they?
2. How might you work with a teacher to develop a lesson plan incorporating resources in special forms and formats into a particular educational unit (something to coincide with Women's History Month, for instance)? What sort of activities would you develop?
3. What kind of program might you develop to encourage young adults to write and draw their own comics or picture books using local history as a source of inspiration?
4. Should information professionals promote the reading of graphic novels that are adapted from "classic" works of literature? Why or why not?

NOTES

1. Will Eisner, *A Contract with God* (New York: Baronet Books, 1978).
2. Scott McCloud, *Understanding Comics: The Invisible Art* (New York: Morrow, 1994).
3. Stephen Weiner, *Faster Than a Speeding Bullet: The Rise of the Graphic Novel*, 2nd ed. (New York: NBM, 2012).
4. Fred Van Lente and Ryan Dunlavey, *The Comic Book History of Comics* (San Diego, CA: IDW, 2012).
5. Alan Moore, *Batman: The Killing Joke*, illus. Brian Bolland (New York: DC Comics, 1988).
6. Alan Moore, *Watchmen*, illus. Dave Gibbons (New York: DC Comics, 1987).
7. Frank Miller, *The Dark Knight Returns*, illus. Klaus Jason, color. Lynn Varley (New York: DC Comics, 1986).
8. Neil Gaiman, *The Sandman*, 10 vols. (New York: Vertigo/DC Comics, 1991–1999).
9. Jeff Smith, *Bone: The Complete Cartoon Epic in One Volume* (Columbus, OH: Cartoon Books, 2004).
10. Raina Telgemeier, *Drama* (New York: Graphix, 2012).

11. Vera Brosgol, *Anya's Ghost* (New York: First Second, 2011).

12. Gene Luen Yang, *American Born Chinese* (New York: First Second, 2007).

13. Mariko Tamaki, *Skim*, illus. Jillian Tamaki (Toronto: Groundwood Books, 2008).

14. Daniel Clowes, *Ghost World* (Seattle, WA: Fantagraphics Books, 2001).

15. Bryan Lee O'Malley, *Scott Pilgrim* (Portland, OR: Oni Press, 2004–2010).

16. Derek Kirk Kim, *Same Difference* (New York: First Second, 2011).

17. Art Spiegelman, *Maus I: A Survivor's Tale—My Father Bleeds History* (New York: Random House, 1986); *Maus II: A Survivor's Tale—And Here My Troubles Began* (New York: Random House, 1991).

18. Marjane Satrapi, *Persepolis*, vol. 1, *The Story of a Childhood* (New York: Random House, 2003); vol. 2, *The Story of a Return* (New York: Random House, 2004).

19. Alison Bechdel, *Fun Home: A Family Tragicomic* (New York: Houghton Mifflin Harcourt, 2006).

20. Craig Thompson, *Blankets* (Portland, OR: Top Shelf Productions, 2002).

21. G. Neri, *Yummy: The Last Days of a Southside Shorty*, illus. Randy Duburke (New York: Lee and Low Books, 2010).

22. Herman Melville, *Moby Dick: The Graphic Novel*, adapt. Lance Stahlberg, illus. Lalit Kumar (Delhi, India: Campfire, 2010).

23. Jane Austen, *Pride and Prejudice*, adapt. Nancy Butler, illus. Hugo Petrus (New York: Marvel, 2009).

24. Madeleine L'Engle, *A Wrinkle in Time*, adapt. and illus. Hope Larson (New York: Farrar, Straus and Giroux, 2012).

25. Shannon Hale and Dean Hale, *Rapunzel's Revenge*, illus. Nathan Hale (New York: Bloomsbury USA Children's, 2008).

26. Keiji Nakazawa, *Barefoot Gen*, 10 vols. (San Francisco: Last Gasp, 2004–2010).

27. Akira Toriyama, *Dragon Ball*, 16 vols. (San Francisco: VIZ Media, 2000–2009).

28. Akira Toriyama, *Dragon Ball Z*, 26 vols. (San Francisco: VIZ Media, 2000–2010).

29. Hiromu Arakawa, *Fullmetal Alchemist*, 27 vols. (San Francisco: VIZ Media, 2005–).

30. Tsugumi Ohba, *Death Note*, 12 vols., illus. Takeshi Obata (San Francisco: VIZ Media, 2005–2007).

31. Naoko Takeuchi, *Sailor Moon*, 18 vols. (Los Angeles: Tokyopop, 1998–2001).

32. Natsumi Ando, *Zodiac PI*, 4 vols. (Los Angeles: Tokyopop, 2003).

33. Akimi Yoshida, *Banana Fish*, 19 vols. (San Francisco: VIZ Media, 1998–2009).

34. Natsuki Takaya, *Fruits Basket*, 23 vols. (Los Angeles: Tokyopop, 2004–2007).

35. Maki Murakami, *Gravitation*, 12 vols. (Los Angeles: Tokyopop, 2003–2005).

36. Kim Dong Hwa, *The Color of Earth* (New York: First Second, 2009); *The Color of Water* (New York: First Second, 2009); *The Color of Heaven* (New York: First Second, 2009).

37. Wang Du Lu, *Crouching Tiger, Hidden Dragon*, 13 vols., illus. Andy Seto (San Francisco: ComicsOne, 2005–2006).

38. Elizabeth F. S. Kalen, *Mostly Manga: A Genre Guide to Popular Manga, Manhwa, Manhua, and Anime* (Santa Barbara, CA: Libraries Unlimited, 2012).

39. Sunya Osborn, "Picture Books for Young Adult Readers," *ALAN Review* 28, no. 3 (2001): 24, http://scholar.lib.vt.edu/ejournals/ALAN/v28n3/osborn.html.

40. Patricia Murphy, "Using Picture Books to Engage Middle School Students," *Middle School Journal* 40, no. 4 (2009): 20–24.

41. Tom Feelings, *The Middle Passage: White Ships / Black Cargo* (New York: Penguin, 1995).

42. Ntozake Shange, *We Troubled the Waters*, illus. Rod Brown (New York: HarperCollins, 2009).

43. Ed Young, *The House Baba Built: An Artist's Childhood in China* (New York: Little, Brown, 2011).

44. Peter Sís, *The Wall: Growing Up behind the Iron Curtain* (New York: Farrar, Straus and Giroux, 2007).

45. Jon Scieszka, *Math Curse*, illus. Lane Smith (New York: Viking, 1995).

46. Jon Scieszka, *Science Verse*, illus. Lane Smith (New York: Viking, 2004).

47. Jon Scieszka, *The Stinky Cheese Man and Other Fairly Stupid Tales*, illus. Lane Smith (New York: Viking, 1992).

48. David Macaulay, *Black and White* (New York: Houghton Mifflin, 1990).

49. Shaun Tan, *The Arrival* (New York: Scholastic, 2007).

50. Shaun Tan, "The Accidental Graphic Novelist," *Bookbird: A Journal of International Children's Literature* 49, no. 4 (2011): 1–9.

51. Shaun Tan, *Lost and Found* (New York: Scholastic, 2011).

52. Motion Picture Association of America, "What Each Rating Means," http://www.mpaa.org/ratings/what-each-rating-means.

53. Chris Columbus, Alfonso Cuaron, Mike Newell, and David Yates, dirs., *Harry Potter: The Complete 8-Film Collection* (Burbank, CA: Warner Brothers, 2011), DVD.

54. Peter Jackson, dir., *The Lord of the Rings: The Fellowship of the Ring* (Los Angeles: New Line, 2002), DVD; *The Lord of the Rings: The Two Towers* (Los Angeles: New Line, 2003), DVD; *The Lord of the Rings: The Return of the King* (Los Angeles: New Line, 2004), DVD.

55. Catherine Hardwicke, Chris Weitz, David Slade, and Bill Condon, dirs., *The Twilight Saga: The Complete Collection* (Universal City, CA: Summit Entertainment, 2012), Blu-ray.

56. Gary Ross, dir., *The Hunger Games* (Santa Monica, CA: Lionsgate Entertainment, 2012), DVD. At the time of writing, this was the only movie in the series that had been released. The next installment, *The Hunger Games: Catching Fire*, was due in theaters in November 2013, with *Mockingjay—Part 1* due in 2014 and *Mockingjay—Part 2* due in 2015.

57. Peter Sollett, dir., *Nick and Norah's Infinite Playlist* (Culver City, CA: Sony Pictures Home Entertainment, 2008), DVD.

58. Stephen Chbosky, dir., *The Perks of Being a Wallflower* (Santa Monica, CA: Lionsgate Entertainment, 2013), DVD.

59. Terry Zwigoff, dir., *Ghost World* (Beverly Hills, CA: MGM, 2002), DVD.

60. Edgar Wright, dir., *Scott Pilgrim vs. the World* (Universal City, CA: Universal Studios, 2010), DVD.

61. Hayao Miyazaki, dir., *Howl's Moving Castle* (Burbank, CA: Walt Disney Home Entertainment, 2006), DVD.

62. Hayao Miyazaki, dir., *Spirited Away* (Burbank, CA: Walt Disney Home Entertainment, 2003), DVD.

63. Jason Reitman, dir., *Juno* (Century City, CA: Fox Searchlight Studios, 2008), DVD.

64. Nat Faxon and Jim Rash, dir., *The Way, Way Back* (Century City, CA: 20th Century Fox, 2013), DVD.

Chapter Nine

Bringing It All Together

This chapter discusses structures to support young adults' positive develop-ment, information-seeking behaviors, and recreational reading:

- Environments for learning
- Information access, access to technology, and intellectual freedom
- Planning and evaluating information programs and services for young adults
- Spotlight! Conducting a needs assessment
- Collaborating with other information providers: Outreach
- Implications for practice
- Questions to think about and discuss

The most recent research agenda published by YALSA focuses on four prior-ity areas that support the association's mission "to expand and strengthen library services for teens and young adults."[1] These priority areas are "im-pact of library services, reading and resources, information seeking behaviors and needs, and formal and informal learning environments and young adults."[2] Information related to all of these priority areas are embedded throughout this book. In this final chapter, the topic of environments for learning and ways to ensure quality programs and services for young adult take center stage.

ENVIRONMENTS FOR LEARNING

For a long time, it has been typical to think about and discuss learning in terms of where learning takes place, separating what happens in the context of the classroom from learning that takes place at work, at home, or in "third places." The concept of third place was developed by Oldenburg,[3] who believes that to have a balanced life, people need access to three different types of spaces: "One is domestic, a second is gainful or productive, and the third is inclusively sociable, offering both the basis of community and the celebration of it."[4] Home and work are generally spaces that are well defined for people, but third places are a little more elusive, and Oldenburg worries that they may be in decline in modern society. He describes the characteristics of third places as neutral ground for those who meet there and visit voluntarily, as informal in nature, and as often populated by "regulars," people who hang out in these places often.

The library as place has become a topic of much conversation in the library and information science literature and has been conceptualized and discussed as a third place by many authors.[5] Some of the discussion is focused on reframing ideas about the library as physical space in terms of user needs and making it more inviting by incorporating food and beverage services and comfortable furniture and facilitating collaborative work by adapting marketing approaches and techniques used in business. In contrast, Elmborg offers a sophisticated discussion, in the face of threats to the library as physical space, calling on third place theory to help aid in a total reconceptualization of the role of the library in the context of the user's real-life needs.[6] Of course, the library is no longer just a bricks-and-mortar place. The library is now also a virtual place that offers access to information as well as an array of programs and services to which the third place concept can also be applied. The concept of third place is also being applied to electronic games and to the Internet, particularly Web 2.0 applications, as they offer spaces where people can meet and enjoy a type of informal public life. Steinkuehler and Williams[7] analyzed massively multiplayer online games against the characteristics of third places described by Oldenburg and concluded that such games, despite their status as virtual locations, can function as a type of third place.

Just as thoughts about spaces that people use for learning have been typified and discussed in isolation, a popular conception of learning contextualizes it as formal and informal. Some theorists use the formal/informal designation to define learning environments.[8] For example a formal learning environment might be a classroom (traditional or online) or computer lab, while an informal learning environment could be the home or a social media tool. Libraries can be contextualized as both formal and informal learning environments.

The concept of informal learning is often attributed to Malcom Knowles, who was concerned with adult education.[9] Many theorists have taken up the terms "formal" and "informal" to describe learning, defining them in different ways.[10] However, formal learning generally refers to learning that takes place in educational institutions, and informal learning, to learning that takes place outside of educational institutions. Colley, Hodkinson, and Malcom analyzed the literature on formal and informal learning and came up with four ways to assess the formality or informality of learning situations: process, location and setting, purposes, and content. [11]

Process refers to whether the learning is structured and controlled by a teacher or the learner. An analysis of process also considers who does the teaching. For example, a teacher in a classroom or an industrial trainer in a work situation reflects a formal learning environment, while learning directly from a friend or colleague is more informal. Another criterion to consider is how learning is assessed. In formal learning, assessment tends to be the domain of the teacher and to reflect a formalized standard and results in a summative evaluation of student progress. In informal learning, there may not be any assessment, or if there is, the assessment tends to be formative (i.e., looks at incremental progress) and may involve input from both the teacher and the learner.

Location and setting, as mentioned earlier, describe where the learning takes place, but it also considers whether there is a formal curriculum, time constraints on the learning, and whether the learning results in matriculation to a higher level of learning, a degree, or some kind of certification. Informal learning tends not to have these characteristics.

The concept of purposes examines whether learning itself is the core reason for the activity. In informal learning, skills, knowledge, understanding, and behaviors may be attained in an incidental or ancillary way. Another consideration is whether the learning is meant to help the student attain outcomes that are determined by the teacher or overseeing governmental or other external organizations or up to the learner?

Content reflects the substance of the learning. In formal learning, the goal is normally to acquire competence in an established field or a set of defined skills. Informal learning tends to be more concerned with issues of everyday practice.

While these four characteristics provide a framework for considering the relative formality of a learning context, examination of the literature reveals that formal learning often has aspects of informal learning and vice versa. [12] There is a growing sense among researchers in this area that it may be too simplistic to suggest that learning can be fully examined and understood when only certain contexts for or types of learning are considered. This has been particularly true concerning the development of technology skills. The integration of technology into schools and into classrooms has not kept pace in many cases with the integration of technology into homes and the acquisition of personal mobile devices.

These developments make it increasingly problematic to talk about young adults' use of technology and their reading habits as taking place within the confines of home, school, or third spaces. [13] Erstead has called for a "Learninglife" approach to studying young adults' access to technology and the integration of formal, informal, semiformal, and incidental learning that takes into account the fluidity of learning across contexts and as mediated by individual identities. Researchers are calling for an approach to understanding learning and information in the lives of youth that takes a holistic approach and focuses on the experiences and interpretations provided by young people themselves.[14]

The literature of education is beginning to reflect much of this sentiment in recognizing that although technology and information literacy skills vary among students in the same classroom, it is not uncommon for at least some of the students to have more advanced technology skills than the teacher. Furthermore, students' sense of themselves as readers, writers, and learners has a life outside the classroom, and it is important pedagogically to recognize the interplay among formal, informal, and incidental learning and connect these to the identities that students are forming.[15] If the goal is to understand learning in a holistic way, over the life span of individuals, a broader approach in both teaching and research is needed.

INFORMATION ACCESS, ACCESS TO TECHNOLOGY, AND INTELLECTUAL FREEDOM

As noted in chapter 4, ownership of mobile devices among young adults is becoming increasingly common, and the presence of computers in homes and schools has greatly reduced the gap referred to as the digital divide. Access to technology and information, however, is not a completely autonomous activity for many young adults. Access can be limited by parental and school rules as well as through the use of filters and other devices for monitoring and limiting access.

The American Library Association has a long-standing commitment to information access "regardless of age, education, ethnicity, language, income, physical limitations or geographic barriers," regardless of media type.[16] The right to access information is also known as intellectual freedom and is considered by many to be fundamental to democracy. Censorship is an opposite idea. Censorship is about preventing access to information and suppressing ideas. Censorship is possible at many levels of society. For example, a government, organization, organized group, and even an individual can attempt to suppress information that is thought to be threatening, dangerous, offensive, obscene, or objectionable.

A challenge is a situation where someone is complaining about the accessibility of information with the intent of making content unavailable.[17] A challenge is not voicing disapproval, complaining, or even questioning the value of an information source or creative expression. Everyone has the right to his or her opinion. These actions become a challenge only if the objective is to remove materials or limit access to them. If a challenge prevails and an item is removed or access to the item is restricted, the situation is then referred to as censorship.

Unfortunately, limitations on space and funds create a situation in real life where it is not possible to purchase all the books and various types of media that are produced that might be of interest to a library's users. This means that choices have to be made about what to purchase for the library. The selection of materials to be purchased by a library should be guided by a collection development policy that is informed by the library's strategic plan, based on an understanding of the needs of the community being served, and the collection policy document should include formal procedures for how to address complaints and challenges should they occur. A formal collection policy is necessary to guide collection management, but it may not be sufficient to ensure that library purchases reflect "selection" and not "censorship."

Censorship versus Selection

Lester Asheim in his classic 1953 article "Not Censorship but Selection" suggests that the main difference in approach between selection and censorship is attitude.[18] He describes selectors as having a positive rather than a negative approach. A selector wants to find a reason to purchase or keep the item, considers the item as a whole (not based on isolated passages or parts), and is concerned with the work and its contributions rather than external values such as the orientations (cultural, sexual, political, religious, etc.) of the author or publisher. Furthermore, the selector is mindful of his or her personal prejudices, background, and potential pressures from users that might inappropriately affect selection and lead to censorship. Of all of these criteria, understanding one's own prejudices and being mindful of them may be the most difficult part of this prescription.

In contrast to the selector, Asheim describes the censor as one who looks for reasons to reject a work. A person whose orientation is to find fault with a work often focuses on one part of a work—the part may be as small as a single word or phrase—that he or she finds objectionable without considering the part in terms of the context of the work as a whole. Another approach used by a censor is to focus on issues external to the work itself, such as the attributes of the author, publisher, or others associated with the work that the censor finds troublesome or with whom the censor disagrees.

Librarians, teachers, and other adults who work with young people should consider the difference between selection and censorship as they make decisions about what to purchase, what to teach, and what to put into the hands of young people. Remember that the main concern of those who work with youth should be that young people have access to a range of ideas related to their developmental needs that will assist them in becoming the independent, literate, and critical thinkers that teachers and employers (and parents) want them to be.[19] Freedman and Johnson point out that "teacher self-censorship of literature for early adolescents [deprives] these students of opportunities for conversation and discovery at a crucial stage of their development."[20]

Handling a Challenge

Challenges do happen. One of the best ways to be prepared for questions about materials is to be familiar with what is in the collection. As much as possible, have firsthand knowledge of the works in the collection. While it is impossible to read every book published every year, familiarity with materials is one of the competencies that supports excellence in library services.[21] Pay attention to what experts in the field have to say about specific books. Keep current by reading professional reviews, bibliographic essays, and paying attention to award lists.

The second important consideration in handling challenges is to have a procedure in place ahead of time and to be familiar with the steps that it prescribes and where to find the necessary forms to file a complaint if needed. The procedures for collection development, including purchasing and weeding as well as the handing of complaints, should be formalized in the collection development policy. Be prepared to discuss books, and be prepared to follow the procedures for handling a challenge, should one happen. It can also help to discuss this topic in the workplace to make sure that everyone is trained in how to handle material complaints.

In addition to guidance available at the workplace, other resources can help:

- The American Library Association has a wealth of materials on its website, offering training and resources related to intellectual freedom issues (http://www.ala.org/advocacy/intfreedom) as well as support for information professionals dealing with a challenge (http://www.ala.org/advocacy/banned).
- The anticensorship center of the National Council of Teachers of English (http://www.ncte.org/action/anti-censorship) offers advice and a variety of documents to assist teachers facing challenges to either texts or teaching methods used in the classroom.
- The Cooperative Children's Book Center primarily serves the state of Wisconsin, but its website contains much useful information on the topic of intellectual freedom as well as a Q&A forum meant for librarians, teachers, school administrators, and others who have questions about prac-

ticing intellectual freedom (http://www.education.wisc.edu/ccbc/freedom/
default.asp).

PLANNING AND EVALUATING INFORMATION PROGRAMS AND SERVICES FOR YOUNG ADULTS

Approaches to the evaluation of programs and services have evolved over time from an emphasis on measuring inputs (resources used to support organizational goals) to considering the activities or processes used to leverage inputs (e.g., timeliness of response) to outputs (products produced; e.g., number of books circulated) to outcome measures, which focus on the benefits or impacts on the user for participating in the program or service. [22]

While all these approaches continue to have value, funding agencies—such as the Institute of Museum and Library Services (the federal agency that supports library and museum services)—increasingly want to see outcome evaluation for projects they sponsor. The outcome-based planning and evaluation (OBPE) model was developed and tested with youth at the Saint Louis Public Library with the support of the Institute of Museum and Library Services. [23] One of the strengths of the OBPE approach to evaluation is that it integrates evaluation into the organization's planning process, it is data driven, and it results in program and service goals that are intentional. Furthermore, the OBPE process ensures that what is learned in the design, delivery, and evaluation of programs and services is used to inform the next planning cycle.

OBPE is a four-phase logic model. In phase 1, "gathering information," information about the library's strategic plan and policies, information about the library's users and service area, and input from the library's various stakeholders are gathered as a basis for determining what kinds of outcomes should be the goal of programs and services. Some ways that you can learn about your community and what it is like for young adults is to review demographic data from sources such as the U.S. census, local school districts, and other community resources, such as law enforcement and real estate agents. A lot can be learned from getting out into the local area, walking around, and talking to people, young and old. Tell them who you are and ask how things are going in the community. See where young adults are congregating and what kinds of information outlets there are for them in the community. What are they happy about, concerned about, and what kinds of programs and services might help? Don't forget that library staff will also have data and insights that will be helpful.

When you are thinking about whom to talk to, consider who has information about young adults (e.g., clergy, teachers, scout leaders), and don't forget to talk to young adults! In fact, it is a good idea to set up a young adult advisory board (see chapter 2) that can be involved in every step of the OBPE process. Young adults from the local service area can help you plan, collect data, determine outcomes, design programs, as well as help with evaluation. Their involvement will help the library build a positive relationship with young adults in general as well as ensure that library programs and services meet their needs.

In phase 2, "determining outcomes," the knowledge gained in phase 1 is analyzed to determine what outcomes should be the goal of the programs and services meant to benefit young adults. Desired outcomes are determined first to ensure that programs and services are intentionally designed and developed to benefit young adults in specific ways. Determining outcomes ahead of time also provides a basis for evaluation. Knowing what outcomes a program is meant to achieve will assist in determining indicators that will demonstrate the achievement of goals and the need to tweak programs to make them more effective.

A helpful categorization of outcomes defines them as changes in attitude, skill, behavior, knowledge, or status that result from participation in a program or service.[24] Attitude has to do with how participants think and feel. An example of an attitude change is beginning to think that reading can be fun. Skill is about a specific ability to do something. Both reading and the ability to use a computer can be thought of as skills. As an outcome, skill may relate to an individual developing a skill that he or she did not previously have or reaching a higher level of expertise, such as moving from a beginner level to a higher level of ability. Behavior is what people do. One example of a behavior outcome is spending more time reading for fun. Knowledge is what people know—their command of information related to a topic, such as particular facts, statistics, or relationships among ideas. A program on local history, for example, would focus on increasing participants' knowledge of significant events, artifacts, or people that are important to know about the local community. The last category, status, has to do with personal or professional standing. Examples of changes in status include becoming a reader, computer user, high school student, or driver.

While it is possible for a program or service to have more than one outcome, it is not necessary to plan for more than one. For those using the OBPE process for the first time, it may be a good idea to start with one relatively simple program and to aim for one outcome. It is also important to recognize that all programs and services have outcomes, whether planned for or not. The purpose of the OBPE model is to make the outcomes from library use intentional and to integrate desired outcomes into the planning and evaluation process. It is not good practice to "fish" for outcomes. It is good practice to identify outcomes based on data gathering and strategic planning so that programs and services remain responsive to the needs of the community and the vision and mission of the library.

Phase 3, "developing programs and services," is the part of the process that many young adult librarians find to be the most fun and what they are typically very good at! In terms of the OBPE process, the important thing to keep in mind during development is to make sure that the program or service being developed is designed to result in the outcome developed in phase 2.

To help make sure that the program or service is in sync with the desired outcome, it is a good idea to develop a one-sentence description of the outcome as well as to consider how it will be possible to tell if it is achieved or not. For example, if a skill is the targeted outcome, a one-sentence description of this might be "young adults will learn basic skills in video production." This description provides a good basis for program design. Likewise, in terms of how to tell if the outcome has been achieved, an indicator could be developed, such as "young adult participants will be able to produce a short video about a favorite book." Establishment of this indicator, which describes program success, will be the basis for program evaluation in the next phase.

Phase 4, "conducting evaluations," describes the process of making sure that programs and services are attaining the outcomes that they were developed to achieve. Because outcome goals are part of program planning in the OBPE process, evaluation is simplified.

Program and service evaluation is nothing more than measuring progress toward a goal. Evaluation reveals the extent to which goals are being met, where improvements can be made, and whether a program or service needs to be retired. Evaluation also becomes an input to the next planning cycle. Evaluation that takes place during planning is referred to as up-front evaluation.[25] This kind of evaluation refers to the collection of data from stakeholders and the collection of baseline data (when needed) to inform the determination of desired outcomes and program and service development.

Another form of evaluation to consider is instant evaluation.[26] Instant evaluation takes place while the program is being delivered and lets the program leader know how things are going as the program is underway. Using the example of a program designed to teach video production skills, the program leader would be able to determine the effectiveness of the workshop by observing the participants as they worked to produce their videos. Observation of participants could be used to determine the effectiveness of the program and identify what changes might be needed to make it better. Instant evaluation is not good for gauging long-term effects and is difficult to use with multifaceted outcomes, but it can be very useful for adjusting a program as it is being delivered and for improving future iterations of the same program.

Ongoing or formative evaluation is a process of evaluation that occurs as a program or service is being developed to improve it before it reaches its final form. Formative evaluation allows for improvements along the way and helps to ensure that the final product achieves the outcomes that it is meant to achieve.

At-the-end, or summative, evaluation occurs after a program or service has been fully developed and deployed for a period of time. Summative evaluation can take place at the end of a big project or periodically (e.g., every six months or annually) for ongoing programs to make sure that they continue to provide the benefits that they were designed to provide and to ensure that they are as efficient as possible in terms of cost.

All forms of evaluation are useful for telling the story of the extent to which programs and services are benefiting participants. Evaluation, particularly evaluation focused on outcomes, allows librarians, administrators, funding agencies, the community, and other stakeholders to understand the importance of the library in the life of the user. Evaluation activities support future planning, help justify budgets, document improvements in service, and demonstrate commitment to planning and to the community. Furthermore, they create a focus within the library on programs and services as a way of reaching specified goals that can be reviewed and modified as communities change.

Last but not least, be sure to use what is learned from program and service evaluation to communicate within and outside the library. Communicate results with all stakeholders (including, of course, young adults). Let others know about the good work the library is doing. Use what is learned in the evaluation process to improve programs and services, and learn from both mistakes and triumphs!

SPOTLIGHT!

Conducting a Needs Assessment

Needs assessment, also called community analysis, is about understanding your users and their context. Needs assessment is an ongoing activity because, especially in our fast-paced world, young adults, communities, and libraries in many parts of the country are changing rapidly. Conducting a needs assessment allows the library to better serve its users, raises library visibility and credibility, and helps establish partnerships that facilitate effective outreach.

Tips for gathering data:

* Consult demographic sources such as the U.S. census, local school district, and chamber of commerce data.[a]

- Develop a firsthand sense of what living in the library's service area is like. Get out and walk around. Wear your library ID so that people know who you are. Talk to people. If you don't live in the community you work in, shop there on your way home.
- Develop a sense of what it is like to be young adults in this community. What are the problems they face? What sources and services are available outside of the library? Where do young adults like to congregate? How do they like to spend their free time?
- Surveys and focus groups with young adults will help you understand their informational and recreational needs as well as how they go about finding what they need in their community.[b]
- Develop relationships with key informants such as youth, teachers, coaches, and other adults who work with young people in your community.
- Involve your teen advisory board in planning and conducting the needs analysis.
- Remember to share what you learn with other librarians and staff at your library. They know things about the community too and are another data source that the library can use.

Needs Assessment Data:

- Help you assess the current effectiveness of the library in meeting the needs of young adults.
- Help determine the best role for the library in the lives of young adults by understanding what information resources are available in the community and what gaps exist that the library can fill.
- Inform collection development and program planning.
- Provide a basis for determining what kinds of program outcomes will best serve young adults.
- Open up possibilities for outreach to other organizations and agencies in the community who are interested in positive youth development.

Notes :

a. Tips taken from Virginia Walter and Melissa Gross's "Adding Value to Library Services with Outcome-Based Planning and Evaluation (OBPE)," a one-day workshop designed for the California State Library and funded by an Library Services and Technology Act grant, conducted at three locations (southern, central, and northern California), July and August 2013.

b. Sample survey and focus group questions for use with young adults can be found in Michele Gorman and Tricia Suellentrop's *Connecting Young Adults and Libraries: A How-to-Do-It Manual for Librarians*, 4th ed. (Chicago: Neal-Schuman, 2009).

COLLABORATING WITH OTHER INFORMATION PROVIDERS: OUTREACH

The concept that it takes a village to raise a child was popularized by Hillary Clinton in 1996.[27] Information professionals should keep in mind that there are many people and organizations in the community that can be useful partners in fostering positive youth development and in furthering youth access to information and skills that will help them transition into adulthood. In fact, YALSA's "Competencies for Librarians Serving Young Adults" specifies communication, marketing, and outreach skills as competencies that information professionals who work with youth need to develop.[28]

Such partnerships should begin with the young adults themselves. Get to know the young adults in the community, those who frequent the library and those who don't. Talk to them. Ask them their opinions and for their help in making the library a welcoming place for young adults. Ask them about their interests and how they go about finding information they need or want. Work to understand the local area and subgroups of young adults that may have special needs, such as those for whom English is a second language, LGBTQ youth, youth with disabilities, and other groups in situations that put them at risk.

Set up an advisory board so that young adults have a formal voice in the development of strategic plans and the development of programs and services that target their demographic. Listen to what they have to say. Young adults can help you make connections to other young adults and to people in the community who can be a resource for the library. Young adults can also help market and advertise library programs in the community.

Consider including teachers, coaches, scout leaders, administrators, clergy, and other members of the community known to have an interest in youth outcomes in outreach plans. Meet these people in person if possible, and communicate with them regularly. Involve them in strategic planning, and disseminate information about library programs and services to them regularly. Use your program evaluation data to help you promote the library, to demonstrate the value that the library has for young adults, and to explain how the library is helping to build a stronger community. Let them know about the great work the library does with young adults!

It is also important to remember to communicate internally to library staff how the youth program is serving the library's vision and mission and the outcomes that programs and services are providing young adults. Coworkers, administrators, and staff at all levels can help spread the word and offer support for further program development. Toward this end, consider providing continuing education to library staff on normal young adult development, information seeking and needs, and how to work with young adults in a positive way. This kind of knowledge can help ensure equity of service and an experience of inclusiveness in the library.

SUMMARY

Learning takes place in many different contexts, and it is important to consider the interrelationship between contexts and types of learning that young adults are exposed to and participate in. Learning that takes place in school can further learning in other contexts, and informal learning can supplement formal learning scenarios. Learning is best supported by an array of materials that present a range of information, points of view, cultures, thoughts, and human experience. Information professionals who manage collections do best to choose materials with this in mind.

The development of information programs and services is most effective when it is embedded in strategic planning, when desired outcomes are informed by all stakeholders, and when desired outcomes are intentionally pursued. Establishing desired outcomes as part of planning expedites evaluation, feeds future planning, provides a solid basis for program improvement, and facilitates communicating the benefits of services for young adults.

Outreach to young adults and to other organizations and people with a stake in positive youth development will expand opportunities and help to strengthen the community. Involve young adults themselves in all phases of program development, and listen to what they have to say.

IMPLICATIONS FOR PRACTICE

1. Recognize that learning takes place in multiple contexts and in multiple ways.
2. Get to know your community. The more you know about your community and the young adults you work with, the better you will be able to serve them.
3. Remember that understanding young adults, the materials they use, and the services that bring the two together is the core skill set of those who specialize in youth services.
4. Be sure to involve young adults in as many aspects of library services as possible: strategic planning; program design, development, and de-

livery; collection development; marketing efforts; and program and service evaluation.

5. Remember to use the results of evaluation to let others know about the outcomes that young adults receive from library programs and services.

QUESTIONS TO THINK ABOUT AND DISCUSS

1. What else do you need to know about the young adults you work with, your local service area, and your organization to determine appropriate outcome goals for your programs and services?
2. Have you ever had such a strong reaction to an item in a library's collection that you felt like it should be removed? What did that feel like? How did you handle the situation? Would you do the same thing again?
3. How would you handle a situation where you discovered that books on sex and sexuality (or any other sensitive topic) were consistently disappearing from the collection?
4. What would it take to develop a culture of evaluation among information professionals and the youth they serve?
5. What roles do you see for young adults in the OBPE process?

NOTES

1. Young Adult Library Services Association, "National Research Agenda on Libraries, Teens, and Young Adults 2012–2016," http://www.ala.org/yalsa/guidelines/research/researchagenda.

2. Young Adult Library Services Association, "National Research Agenda," 5.

3. Roy Oldenburg, *The Great Good Place* (New York: Paragon House, 1989), 14.

4. Oldenburg, *The Great Good Place.*

5. James K. Elmborg, "Libraries as the Spaces between Us: Recognizing and Valuing the Third Space," *Reference and User Services Quarterly* 50, no. 4 (2011): 338–50; Cathryn Harris, "Libraries with Lattes: The New Third Place," *Aplis* 20, no. 4 (2007): 145–52; Wayne Wiegand, "To Reposition a Research Agenda: What American Studies Can Teach the LIS Community about the Library in the Life of the User," *Library Quarterly* 73, no. 4 (2003): 369–82.

6. Elmborg, "Libraries as the Spaces between Us."

7. Constance A. Steinkuehler and Dmitri Williams, "Where Everybody Knows Your (Screen) Name: Online Games as 'Third Places,'" *Journal of Computer-Mediated Communication* 11 (2006): 885–909.

8. Annie Downey, "Formal and Informal Learning Environments: YALSA Research Agenda Priority Area 4," Young Adult Library Services Association Research Forum, American Library Association Midwinter Meeting, Dallas, TX, 2012.

9. Malcolm Knowles, *Informal Adult Education: A Guide for Administrators, Leaders, and Teachers* (New York: Association Press, 1950).

10. Helen Colley, Phil Hodkinson, and Janice Malcom, *Non-formal Learning: Mapping the Conceptual Terrain. A Consultation Report* (Leeds, England: University of Leeds, Lifelong Learning Institute), 2002.

11. Phil Hodkinson, Helen Colley, and Janice Malcom, "Interrelationships between Formal and Informal Learning," *Journal of Workplace Learning* 15, no. 7/8 (2003): 313–18.

12. Hodkinson et al., "Interrelationships," 314.

13. Ola Erstad, "The Learning Lives of Digital Youth: Beyond the Formal and Informal," *Oxford Review of Education* 38, no. 1 (2012): 25–43; John Furlong and Chris Davies, "Young People, New Technologies and Learning at Home: Taking Context Seriously," *Oxford Review of Education* 38, no. 1 (2012): 45–62.

14. Ola Erstad, "The Learning Lives of Digital Youth: Beyond the Formal and Informal," *Oxford Review of Education* 38, no. 1 (2012): 25–43; John Furlong and Chris Davies, "Young People, New Technologies and Learning at Home: Taking Context Seriously," *Oxford Review of Education* 38, no. 1 (2012): 45–62.

15. Bronwyn T. Williams, "Leading Double Lives: Literacy and Technology in and out of School," *Journal of Adolescent and Adult Literacy* 48, no. 8 (2005): 702–6.

16. American Library Association, "Access," 2013, para. 1, http://www.ala.org/advocacy/access.

17. American Library Association, "Challenges to Library Materials," 2013, http://www.ala.org/bbooks/challengedmaterials.

18. Lester Asheim, "Not Censorship but Selection," *Wilson Library Bulletin* 28 (September 1953): 63–67, http://www.ala.org/Template.cfm?Section=basics&Template=/ContentManagement/ContentDisplay.cfm&ContentID=109668.

19. Mary K. Chelton, "Musing on Intellectual Freedom and YA Services," *VOYA* (June 2011): 121.

20. Lauren Freedman and Holly Johnson, "Who's Protecting Whom? Self-Censorship in the Choice of Young Adult Literature for Use in Middle Level Classrooms," *Journal of Adolescent and Adult Literacy* 44, no. 4 (2000/2001): 356–69.

21. Young Adult Library Services Association, "YALSA's Competencies for Librarians Serving Youth: Young Adults Deserve the Best," January 2012, http://www.ala.org/yalsa/guidelines/yacompetencies2010.

22. United Way of America, *Current United Way Approaches to Measuring Program Outcomes and Community Change* (Alexandria, VA: United Way of America, 1995).

23. Eliza T. Dresang, Melissa Gross, and Leslie Edmonds Holt, *Dynamic Youth Services* (Chicago: American Library Association, 2006).

24. United Way of America, *Measuring Program Outcomes: A Practical Approach* (Alexandria, VA: United Way of America, 1996), http://www.unitedwaycv.org/media/Measuring_Program_Outcomes-UW.pdf.

25. Dresang et al., *Dynamic Youth Services*, 118–19.

26. Dresang et al., *Dynamic Youth Services*, 115–17.

27. Hillary Clinton, *It Takes a Village* (New York: Simon & Schuster, 1996).

28. Young Adult Library Services Association. "YALSA's Competencies."

Appendix 1

Young Adult Book and Media Awards

AMERICAN LIBRARY ASSOCIATION AWARDS

The American Library Association administers a variety of book and media awards, as well as book lists, that are appropriate for a young adult audience. Listed here are the annual awards conferred by the Association of Library Services for Children, the Ethnic Materials Information Exchange Round Table, and the Young Adult Library Services Association, all of which are divisions of the American Library Association.

Association of Library Services for Children Awards

The Association of Library Services for Children administers a variety of awards, some of which consider works that have an intended audience as old as 14 years. A full list of its awards is available on its website (http://www.ala.org/alsc/awardsgrants/bookmedia). Listed here are those that may include works of interest to young adults:

John Newbery Medal—the Newbery medal is one of the most well-known awards for children's literature. It is awarded annually for the most distinguished work intended for a child audience.

Mildred L. Batchelder Award—the Batchelder award is an annual book award for outstanding books published in a foreign country, translated into English, and published in the United States.

Pura Belpré—this annual award honors the work of a Latino/Latina writer and illustrator who provides a positive portrayal of Latino culture in an outstanding literary work.

Robert F. Sibert Informational Book Medal—awarded annually for the most outstanding informational book published in the preceding year.

Ethnic Materials Information Exchange Round Table

The Ethnic Materials Information Exchange Round Table administers the Coretta Scott King Book Awards (http://www.ala.org/emiert/cskbooka-wards/slction).

Coretta Scott King Book Awards for Authors and Illustrators—given to an African American author or illustrator who, in an outstanding work, expresses the African American experience. Works considered may address an intended audience from preschool through grade 12.

Young Adult Library Services Association

The Young Adult Library Services Association administers a variety of young adult literary awards that cover a number of publication types. A full list of its awards is available on its website (http://www.ala.org/yalsa/book-listsawards/bookawards). In addition to the awards listed here, the association publishes several book and media lists on its website: Amazing Audiobooks for Young Adults, Best Fiction for Young Adults, Fabulous Films for Young adults, Great Graphic Novels for Teens, Outstanding Books for the College Bound, Poplar Paperbacks for Young Adults, Quick Picks for Reluctant Young Adult Readers, Reader's Choice lists, and a Teens Top Ten list.

Alex Awards—given annually to 10 books that are considered to have a high level of appeal to young adults. In addition to naming 10 winners, the Young Adult Library Services Association publishes a list of all the books nominated for the award. The Margaret A. Edwards Trust is the official sponsor of the Alex Awards.

Margaret A. Edwards Award—this annual award honors an author whose work has been an important contribution to young adult literature. It is sponsored by the *School Library Journal.*

Michael L. Printz Award—given annually for the most distinguished work published for young adults during the previous year. This award is sponsored by *Booklist* (an American Library Association publication).

Odyssey Award—honors audiobooks produced in English in the United States. This award is coadministered with the Association of Library Services for Children and therefore considers audiobooks intended for either children or young adults.

William C. Morris YA Debut Award—the Morris award was established in memory of William C. Morris and is funded by the William C.

Morris Endowment. This award honors a first book for young adults by a previously unpublished writer. The short list of nominees is published in December before the winner is announced.

Young Adult Library Services Association Award for Excellence in Nonfiction—every year, the Young Adult Library Services Association honors the best in nonfiction writing for young adults. As with some of the other awards, the annual list of nominations for the award is also made public.

OTHER YOUNG ADULT BOOK AWARDS AND LISTS

Boston Globe Horn Book Award—honors children's and young adult literature, including prizes for picture books, fiction and poetry, and nonfiction published in the United States. http://www.hbook.com/boston-globe-horn-book-awards/.

Canadian Library Association Young Adult Canadian Book Award—honors Canadian fiction for young adults, written in English. Fiction includes novels, short story collections, and graphic novels. The author must be a citizen of Canada or have permanent resident status. http://www.cla.ca/AM/Template.cfm?Section=Young_Adult _Canadian_Book_Award.

Children's and Young Adult Bloggers' Literary Awards—a variety of awards for books that offer both literacy quality and "kid appeal." The awards cover the spectrum from easy readers on, but include awards for fiction and non-fiction targeted to young adult readers. http://www.cybils.com/.

Cooperative Children's Book Center—provides a large number of bibliographies of young adult titles in a variety of topic areas as well as other content of interest to adults interested in materials for young people. http://ccbc.education.wisc.edu/books/default.asp.

Edgar Allen Poe Award for Best Young Adult Novel—also referred to as the Edgar Award, this honor is determined annually by the Mystery Writers of America, and it is interested in mystery, suspense, crime, and intrigue published as a book or short story or written for television. The category of Best Young Adult Mystery should appeal to young people (12–18 years old). http://mysterywriters.org/edgars/edgar-award-category-information/.

Eisner Awards Best Publication for Teens—the Eisner Awards honor comics and graphic novels in a variety of categories. The current and past winner lists for Best Publication for Teens Award are available on the Comic-Con International website. http://www.comic-con.org/awards/eisner-award-recipients-2010-present.

Goodreads Choice Award: Best Young Adult Fiction—this is an annual award based on votes received from users of the Goodreads website. http://www.goodreads.com/choiceawards/best-young-adult-fiction-books-2012#74594-Best-Young-Adult-Fiction.

International Reading Association Children's and Young Adults Books Awards—honor new authors of works of fiction and nonfiction at the primary, intermediate, and young adult levels. As of 2013, books published in English outside the United States are eligible for nomination. http://www.reading.org/Resources/AwardsandGrants/childrens _ira.aspx.

International Reading Association Lee Bennett Hopkins Promising Poet Award—given every three years to honor a new poet publishing for children and young adults. Collections and book-length single poems are eligible for nomination. http://www.reading.org/resources/AwardsandGrants/childrens_hopkins.aspx.

Los Angeles Times Book Prizes—include a category for young adult literature. Prizes are awarded annually. http://events.latimes.com/book-prizes/.

National Book Award for Young People's Literature—a prestigious American literary prize that includes a category for young adult books. The award is presented annually by the National Book Foundation. http://www.nationalbook.org/nba_process.html#.UkGUhlPzLAw.

National Council of Teachers of English Award for Excellence in Poetry for Children—honors the body of work of a living American poet who has published works of poetry for children 3 to 13 years old. Award is given every two years. http://www.ncte.org/awards/poetry.

National Council of Teachers of English Orbis Pictus Award for Outstanding Nonfiction for Children—although this award is designated for children, the award criteria accept works that target young people up to the eighth grade. http://www.ncte.org/awards/orbispictus.

Royal Society Young People's Book Prize—an award for science content presented in books for an intended audience of up to age 14. The Royal Society is the National Science Academy of the United Kingdom. http://royalsociety.org/awards/young-people/.

State Awards for Children's and Young Adult books—this website lists readers' choice and other state-level awards for young adult literature. http://www.cynthialeitichsmith.com/lit_resources/awards/stateawards.html.

Street Literature Book Awards—honor fiction and nonfiction titles that tell stories set in an urban or inner-city context and are interested in the lives of people of lower socioeconomic status in historical or contemporary times. http://www.streetliterature.com/p/slbam.html.

Voice of Youth Advocates Nonfiction Honor List—magazine publishes a list of good nonfiction annually in its August issue. http://www.voyamagazine.com/2012/02/22/nonfiction-honor-list/.

Appendix 2

Recommended Young Adult Books

This list of selected titles includes citation information for all the young adult books discussed in this book. It also contains many more books that we would like to share with you. These books are among our favorites, but the list does not include every book by every author listed. Readers are encouraged to seek out other works by these authors as well as works by other authors. Readers are also encouraged to consult the various young adult book and media award listed in appendix 1. There may be a new personal favorite waiting for you at the library!

The books listed here are organized by their major categorization. So, even though a book may represent a mixed-genre approach (i.e., romance and mystery), it is categorized by its main type. For works in which an illustrator makes a significant contribution, the illustrator's name is included after the title. Book citations can also be located using the author and title indexes at the back of the book.

FANTASTIC FICTION

The books in this section include various categories of imaginative work. These are categorized as fantasy, modern folktales and legends, horror, and science fiction. Books that are considered classics in these genres are indicated by (C).

Fantasy

Adams, Richard. *Watership Down.* London: Rex Collings, 1972. (C)

Alexander, Lloyd. *The Book of Three*. New York: Holt, Rinehart and Winston, 1964. (C)
———. *The Black Cauldron*, New York: Holt, Rinehart and Winston, 1965. (C)
———. *The Castle of Lyr*. New York: Holt, Rinehart and Winston, 1966. (C)
———. *The High King*. New York: Holt, Rinehart and Winston, 1968. (C)
———. *Taran Wanderer*. New York: Holt, Rinehart and Winston, 1967. (C)
Allende, Isabel. *City of the Beasts*. Translated by Margaret Sayers Peden. New York: Harper-Collins, 2002.
———. *Forest of the Pygmies*. Translated by Margaret Sayers Peden. New York: HarperCollins, 2005.
———. *Kingdom of the Golden Dragon*. Translated by Margaret Sayers Peden. New York: HarperCollins, 2004.
Almond, David. *Clay*. New York: Delacorte, 2006.
———. *Kit's Wilderness*. New York: Delacorte, 2000.
Block, Francesca Lia. *Baby Be-Bop*. New York: HarperCollins, 1995.
———. *Cherokee Bat and the Goat Guys*. New York: HarperCollins, 1992.
———. *Missing Angel Juan*. New York: HarperCollins, 1993.
———. *Weetzie Bat*. New York: HarperCollins, 1989.
———. *Witch Baby*. New York: HarperCollins, 1991.
Colfer, Eoin. *Artemis Fowl*. New York: HarperCollins, 2001.
Farmer, Nancy. *Sea of Trolls*. New York: Atheneum/Richard Jackson Books, 2004.
Funke, Cornelia. *Inkheart*. New York: Scholastic, 2003.
Howard, A. G. *Splintered*. New York: Abrams, 2013.
Kindl, Patrice. *Owl in Love*. Houghton Mifflin, 1993.
Le Guin, Ursula. *The Farthest Shore*. New York: Atheneum, 1972. (C)
———. *The Other Wind*. New York: Harcourt Brace, 2001.
———. *Tales from Earthsea*. New York: Harcourt Brace, 2001.
———. *Tehanu*. New York: Atheneum, 1990.
———. *The Tombs of Atuan*. New York: Atheneum, 1971. (C)
———. *A Wizard of Earthsea*. Berkeley, CA: Parnassus, 1968. (C)
McCaffrey, Anne. *Dragonflight*. New York: Ballantine, 1968. (C)
McKinley, Robin. *The Blue Sword*. New York: Greenwillow, 1982.
———. *The Hero and the Crown*. New York: Greenwillow, 1985.
Mosley, Walter. *47*. New York: Little, Brown, 2005.
Nix, Garth. *Abhorsen*. New York: HarperCollins, 2003.
———. *Lirael, Daughter of the Clayr*. New York: HarperCollins, 2001.
———. *Sabriel*. New York: HarperCollins, 1996.
Paolini, Christopher. *Brisingr*. New York: Knopf, 2008.
———. *Eldest*. New. York: Knopf, 2005.
———. *Eragon*. New. York: Knopf, 2002.
———. *Inheritance*. New York: Knopf, 2011.
Pierce, Meredith Ann. *The Darkangel*. New York: Little, Brown, 1982.
———. *A Gathering of Gargoyles*. New York: Little, Brown, 1984.
———. *The Pearl of the Soul of the World*. New York: Little, Brown, 1990.
Pratchett, Terry. *The Amazing Maurice and His Educated Rodents*. New York: Doubleday, 2001.
———. *A Hat Full of Sky*. New York: HarperCollins, 2004.
———. *I Shall Wear Midnight*. New York: Harper, 2010.
———. *The Wee Free Men*. New York: HarperCollins, 2003.
———. *Wintersmith*. New York: HarperTempest, 2006.
Pullman, Philip. *The Amber Spyglass*. London: Fickling, 2000.
———. *The Golden Compass*. London: Scholastic Point, 1995.
———. *The Subtle Knife*. London: Scholastic Point, 1997.
Riordan, Rick. *The Battle of the Labyrinth*. New York: Disney Hyperion, 2008.
———. *The Last Olympian*. New York: Disney Hyperion, 2009.
———. *The Lightning Thief*. New York: Disney Hyperion, 2005.
———. *The Sea of Monsters*. New York: Disney Hyperion, 2006.

————. *The Titan's Curse.* New York: Disney Hyperion, 2007.
Rowling, J. K. *Harry Potter and the Chamber of Secrets.* New York: Scholastic, 1998.
————. *Harry Potter and the Deathly Hallows.* New York: Scholastic, 2007.
————. *Harry Potter and the Goblet of Fire.* New York: Scholastic, 2000.
————. *Harry Potter and the Half-Blood Prince.* New York: Scholastic, 2005.
————. *Harry Potter and the Order of the Phoenix.* New York: Scholastic, 2003.
————. *Harry Potter and the Prisoner of Azkaban.* New York: Scholastic, 1999.
————. *Harry Potter and the Sorcerer's Stone.* New York: Scholastic, 1997.
Tolkien, J. R. R. *The Fellowship of the Ring.* London: Allen & Unwin, 1954. (C)
————. *The Return of the King.* London: Allen & Unwin, 1955. (C)
————. *The Two Towers.* London: Allen & Unwin, 1954. (C)
Uehashi, Nahoko. *Morbito: Guardian of the Spirit.* New York: Scholastic, 2008.
Walton, Jo. *Among Others.* New York: Tor, 2011.

Modern Folktales and Legends

Block, Francesca Lia. *The Rose and the Beast: Fairy Tales Retold.* New York: HarperCollins, 2000.
Bradley, Marion Zimmer *The Mists of Avalon.* New York: Ballantine, 1982.
Datlow, Ellen, and Terri Windling. *A Wolf at the Door and Other Retold Fairy Tales.* New York: Simon & Schuster, 2000.
Hale, Shannon. *The Goose Girl.* USA: Bloomsbury, 2003.
Hoover, H. M. *Dawn Palace: The Story of Medea.* New York: Dutton, 1988.
Jones, Diana Wynne. *The Merlin Conspiracy.* New York: Greenwillow, 2003.
Lanagan, Margo. *Tender Morsels.* New York: Knopf, 2008.
Lee, Tanith. *White as Snow.* New York: Tor, 2000.
Lo, Malinda. *Ash.* New York: Little, Brown Books for Young Readers, 2009.
Maguire, Gregory. *Confessions of an Ugly Stepsister.* New York: Regan, 1999.
McKinley, Robin. *Beauty: A Retelling of the Story of Beauty and the Beast.* New York: HarperCollins, 1978. (C)
————. *Outlaws of Sherwood.* New York: Greenwillow, 1988.
McNeal, Tom. *Far Far Away.* New York: Knopf Books for Young Readers, 2013.
Meyer, Marissa. *Cinder.* New York: Feiwel & Friends, 2012.
————. *Cress.* New York: Feiwel & Friends, 2013.
————. *Scarlett.* New York: Feiwel & Friends, 2013.
Mourlevat, Jean Claude. *The Pull of the Ocean.* Translated by Y. Maudet. New York: Delacorte, 2006.
Napoli, Donna Jo. *Breath.* New York: Simon & Schuster, 2003.
————. *Crazy Jack.* New York: Delacorte, 1999.
————. *The Magic Circle.* New York: Dutton, 1993.
————. *Zel.* New York: Dutton 1996.
Paterson, Katherine. *Parzival: The Quest of the Grail Knight.* New York: Lodestar, 1998.
Pattou, Edith. *East.* New York: Harcourt, 2003.
Sutcliff, Rosemary. *The Sword and the Circle: King Arthur and the Knights of the Round Table.* New York: Dutton, 1981.
Valente, Catherine M. *The Girl Who Circumnavigated Fairyland in a Ship of Her Own Making.* New York: Feiwel and Friends, 2011.
Velde, Vivian Vande. *Never Trust a Dead Man.* New York: Harcourt, 1999.
White, T. H. *The Once and Future King.* London: Collins, 1958. (C)
Yolen, Jane. *Briar Rose.* New York: Doherty, 1992.
————. *Sword of the Rightful King: A Novel of King Arthur.* San Diego, CA: Harcourt, 2003.

Horror

Anderson, M. T. *Thirsty.* Cambridge: MA: Candlewick, 1997.

Brewer, Heather. *Eighth Grade Bites*. New York: Dutton, 2007.
Cormier, Robert. *Fade*. New York: Delacorte, 1988.
Gaiman, Neil. *Coraline*. New York: HarperCollins, 2002.
———. *The Wolves in the Walls*. New York: HarperCollins, 2003.
Garcia, Kami, and Margaret Stohl. *Beautiful Creatures*. New York: Little, Brown, 2009.
———. *Beautiful Darkness*. New York: Little, Brown, 2010.
———. *Beautiful Redemption*. New York: Little, Brown, 2012.
Jenkins, A. M. *Repossessed: A Novel*. New York: HarperTeen, 2007.
Klause, Annette Curtis. *Blood and Chocolate*. New York: Delacorte Press, 1997.
———. *The Silver Kiss*. New York: Delacorte, 1990.
Meyer, Stephanie. *Breaking Dawn*. New York: Little, Brown, 2008.
———. *Eclipse*. New York: Little, Brown, 2007.
———. *New Moon*. New York: Little, Brown, 2006.
———. *Twilight*. New York: Little, Brown, 2005.
Ryan, Carrie. *The Forest of Hands and Teeth*. New York: Random House, 2009.
Velde, Vivian Vande. *Being Dead*. New York: Harcourt, 2001.
Walpole, Horace. *The Castle of Otranto*. New York: Oxford University Press, 2009.
Yancey, Rick. *The Monstrumologist*. New York: Simon & Schuster, 2009.

Science Fiction

Adams, Douglas. *The Hitchhiker's Guide to the Galaxy*. London: Pan, 1979. (C)
Anderson, M. T. *Feed*. Somerville, MA: Candelwick, 2002.
Asimov, Isaac. *I, Robot*. New York: Gnome, 1950. (C)
Card, Orson Scott. *Ender's Game*. New York: Tor, 1985.
Cline, Ernest. *Ready Player One*. New York: Random House, Crown, 2011.
Collins, Suzanne. *Catching Fire*. New York: Scholastic, 2009.
———. *The Hunger Games*. New York: Scholastic, 2008.
———. *Mockingjay*. New York: Scholastic, 2010.
Cormier, Robert. *Fade*. Delacorte, 1988.
Dick, Philip K. *Do Androids Dream of Electric Sheep?* New York: Doubleday, 1968. (C)
Dickinson, Peter. *Eva*. London: Victor Gollancz, 1988.
Doctorow, Cory. *Little Brother*. New York: Tor Teen, 2008. http://craphound.com/littlebrother/download/.
———. *Makers*. New York: Doherty, 2009.
Etchemendy, Nancy. *The Power of Un*. Honesdale, PA: Front Street/Cricket, 2000.
Farmer, Nancy. *The Ear, the Eye, and the Arm*. New York: Orchard Books, 1994.
———. *The House of the Scorpion*. New York: Atheneum, 2002.
Gibson, William. *Neuromancer*. New York: Ace, 1984.
Goodman, Alison. *Singing the Dogstar Blues*. New York: Viking, 1998.
Hoffman, Alice. *Green Angel*. New York: Scholastic Press, 2003.
Johnson, Alaya Dawn. *The Summer Prince*. New York: Levine Books, 2013.
L'Engle, Madeline. *An Acceptable Time*. New York: Farrar, Straus and Giroux, 1989.
———. *Many Waters*. New York: Farrar, Straus and Giroux, 1986.
———. *A Swiftly Tilting Planet*. New York: Farrar, Straus and Giroux, 1978. (C)
———. *A Wind in the Door*. New York: Farrar, Straus and Giroux, 1973. (C)
———. *A Wrinkle in Time*. New York: Farrar, Straus and Giroux, 1962. (C)
Lowry, Lois. *Gathering Blue*. New York: Houghton Mifflin, 2000.
———. *The Giver*. New York: Houghton Mifflin, 1993.
———. *Messenger*. New York: Houghton Mifflin, 2004.
———. *Son*. New York: Houghton Mifflin, 2012.
Marsden, John. *Tomorrow When the War Began*. Boston: Houghton Mifflin, 1995.
Niven, Larry, and Jerry Pournelle. *The Mote in God's Eye*. New York: Simon & Schuster, 1974. (C)
Nix, Garth. *Shade's Children*. New York: HarperCollins, 1997.
O'Brien, Robert C. *Z for Zachariah*. New York: Atheneum, 1974. (C)

Oppel, Kenneth. *Airborn.* New York: HarperCollins, 2004.
Pfeffer, Susan Beth. *Life As We Knew It.* New York: Harcourt, 2006.
Philbrick, Rodman. *Last Book in the Universe.* New York: Blue Sky Press, 2000.
Rosoff, Meg. *How I Live Now.* New York: Random House, 2004.
Schusterman, Neil. *The Dark Side of Nowhere.* New York: Little, Brown, 1996.
Sleator, William. *House of Stairs.* New York: Dutton, 1974. (C)
————. *Interstellar Pig.* New York: Bantam, 1984.
————. *Strange Attractors.* New York: Dutton, 1990.
Snead, Rebecca. *When You Reach Me.* New York: Random house, 2009.
Wells, H. G. *The Time Machine.* London: Heinemann, 1895. (C)
Westerfeld, Scott. *Extras.* New York: Simon & Schuster, 2007.
————. *Pretties.* New York: Simon & Schuster, 2005.
————. *Specials.* New York: Simon & Schuster, 2006.
————. *Uglies.* New York: Simon & Schuster, 2005.
Yancey, Rick. *The Fifth Wave.* New York: Putnam, 2013.

REALISTIC FICTION

Books in this category have settings and characters that reflect the "real world" as we know and experience it, but they are also stories invented by the authors. Categories presented in this section include contemporary issues (including urban fiction); romance; mystery, adventure, survival, and suspense; and historical fiction. Books that are considered classics in these genres are indicated by (C). Books that are identified as multicultural are indicated by (M). Books that represent urban fiction in these genres are indicated by (U).

Contemporary Issues

Alexie, Sherman. *The Absolutely True Story of a Part Time Indian.* New York: Little, Brown Young Readers, 2007. (M)
Anderson, Laurie Halse. *Speak.* New York: Farrar, Straus and Giroux, 1999.
————. *Wintergirls.* New York: Viking, 2009.
Anonymous. *Go Ask Alice.* Englewood Cliffs, NJ: Prentice Hall, 1971. (C)
Asher, Jay. *Thirteen Reasons Why.* New York: Razorbill, 2007.
Bloor, Edward. *Tangerine.* New York: Scholastic, 1997.
Blume, Judy. *Are You There God? It's Me, Margaret.* New York: Yearling, 1970. (C)
Booth, Coe. *Tyrell.* New York: Scholastic, 2007. (U)
Bray, Libba. *Going Bovine.* New York: Delacorte Press, 2009.
Chbosky, Stephen. *The Perks of Being a Wallflower.* New York: Simon & Schuster, 1999.
Childress, Alice. *A Hero Ain't Nothin' but a Sandwich.* New York: McCann, 1973. (C)
Cooner, Donna. *Skinny.* New York: Scholastic, 2012.
Cormier, Robert. *The Chocolate War.* New York: Pantheon, 1974. (C)
Crutcher, Chris. *Athletic Shorts: Six Short Stories.* New York: Greenwillow, 1991.
————. *Staying Fat for Sarah Byrnes.* New York: Greenwillow, 1993.
Flake, Sharon. *Bang!* New York: Jump at the Sun/Hyperion Books for Children, 2005. (U)
Green, John. *An Abundance of Katherines.* New York: Dutton, 2006.
Hautman, Pete. *Godless.* New York: Simon & Schuster, 2004.
Hinton, S. E. *The Outsiders.* New York: Viking, 1967. (C)
Holland, Isabelle. *The Man without a Face.* Philadelphia, PA: Lippincott, 1972. (C)
Hollman, Felice. *Slake's Limbo.* New York: Scribner, 1974. (C)
Horvath, Polly. *The Canning Season.* New York: Farrar, Straus and Giroux, 2003.

Hunt, Samantha. *The Seas*. San Francisco: McAdam/Cage, 2004.

Klass, David. *You Don't Know Me*. New York: Farrar, Straus and Giroux, 2003.

Klein, Norma. *Mom, the Wolfman, and Me*. New York: Knopf, 1972. (C)

Knowles, John. *A Separate Peace*. New York: Macmillan, 1960. (C)

Lipsyte, Robert. *The Contender*. New York: Harper & Row, 1967. (C)

Lockhart, E. *The Disreputable History of Frankie Landau-Banks*. New York: Hyperion Books, 2008.

Mazer, Norma Fox. *Out of Control*. New York: Morrow, 1993.

Myers, Walter Dean. *Autobiography of My Dead Brother*. Illustrated by Christopher Myers. New York: HarperTempest, 2005.

———. *Monster*. Illustrated by Christopher Myers. New York: HarperCollins, 1999.

Nolan, Han. *Born Blue*. New York: Harcourrt, 2001.

Perera, Anna. *The Glass Collector*. Chicago: Whitman, 2012.

———. *Guantanamo Boy*. Chicago: Whitman, 2011.

Peters, Julie Anne. *Luna*. New York: Little, Brown, 2004. (M)

Plath, Sylvia. *The Bell Jar*. New York: Harper, 1971. (C)

Rylant, Cynthia. *A Fine White Dust*. New York: Bradbury Press, 1986.

Sáenz, Benjamin Alire. *Aristotle and Dante Discover the Secrets of the Universe*. New York: Simon & Schuster, 2012. (M)

Salinger, J. D. *The Catcher in the Rye*. Boston: Little, Brown, 1951. (C)

Sapphire. *Push*. New York: Knopf, 1996.

Smith, Betty. *A Tree Grows in Brooklyn*. New York: Harper & Brothers, 1943. (C)

Souljah, Sister. *The Coldest Winter Ever*. New York: Pocket Books, 1999. (U)

Staples, Suzanne Fisher. *Shabanu: Daughter of the Wind*. New York: Knopf, 1989.

Stratton, Allan. *Chanda's Secrets*. Toronto: Annick Press, 2004.

Teller, Janne. *Nothing*. New York: Atheneum Books for Young Readers, 2010.

Thomas, Rob. *Rats Saw God*. New York: Simon & Schuster, 1996.

Tyree, Omar. *Flyy Girl*. New York: Simon & Schuster, 1993. (U)

Voight, Cynthia. *When She Hollers*. New York: Scholastic, 1994.

Williams-Garcia, Rita. *Jumped*. Harper Teen, 2009.

———. *Like Sisters on the Homefront*. Lodestar, 1995.

Woods, Teri. *True to the Game*. Special collector's ed. New York: Grand Central, 2007. (U)

Zindel, Paul. *The Pigman*. New York: Harper, 1968. (C)

Romance

Block, Francesca. *Violet & Claire*. New York: HarperCollins, 1999.

Blume, Judy. *Forever*. New York: Bradbury, 1975. (C)

Brooks, Bruce. *What Hearts*. New York: HarperCollins, 1992.

Burgess, Melvin. *Doing It*. New York: Holt, 2006.

Cart, Michael. *My Father's Scar*. New York: Simon & Schuster, 1996.

Christiansen, C. B. *I See the Moon*. New York: Simon & Schuster/Athenaeum, 1994.

Cohn, Rachel, and David Levithan. *Nick and Norah's Infinite Playlist*. New York: Knopf, 2006.

Cole, Sheila. *What Kind of Love? The Diary of a Pregnant Teenager*. New York: Lothrop Lee & Shepard, 1995.

Corbet, Robert. *Fifteen Love*. New York: Walker, 2003.

Daly, Maureen. *Seventeenth Summer*. New York: Dodd, Mead, 1942. (C)

Danforth, Emily M. *The Miseducation of Cameron Post: A Novel*. New York: HarperCollins, 2012.

DeWoskin, Rachel. *Big Girl Small*. New York: Farrar, Straus and Giroux, 2011.

Doherty, Berlie. *Dear Nobody*. New York: Beech Tree Books.

Donovan, John. *I'll Get There, It Better Be Worth the Trip*. New York: HarperCollins, 1969.

Garden, Nancy. *Annie on My Mind*. New York: Farrar, Straus and Giroux, 1982.

Green, John. *The Fault in Our Stars*. New York: Dutton, 2012.

———. *Looking for Alaska*. New York: Dutton Books, 2005.

Handler, Daniel. *Why We Broke Up.* Illustrated by Maira Kalman. New York: Little, Brown, 2011.

Hartinger, Brent. *Geography Club.* New York: HarperCollins, 2003.

Johnson, Angela. *The First Part Last.* New York: Simon & Schuster, 2003.

Kerr, M. E. *Deliver Us from Evie.* New York: HarperCollins, 1994. (M)

Klein, Norma. *No More Saturday Nights.* New York: Knopf, 1988.

Koertge, Ron. *The Arizona Kid.* New York: Little, Brown, 1988.

Konigsberg, Bill. *Openly Straight.* New York: Scholastic, 2013.

Larson, Rodger. *What I Know Now.* New York: Holt, 1997.

Le Guin, Ursula K. *Very Far Away from Anywhere Else.* New York: Atheneum, 1976. (C)

Lennon, Tom. *When Love Comes to Town.* Chicago: Whitman, 2013.

Levithan, David. *Boy Meets Boy.* New York: Knopf, 2003.

Myers, Walter Dean. *A Time to Love: Stories from the Old Testament.* New York: Scholastic, 2003.

Rennison, Louise. *Angus, Thongs, and Full Frontal Snogging: Confessions of Georgia Nicolson.* New York: HarperCollins, 2000.

Sanchez, Alex. *Rainbow Boys.* New York:, Simon & Schuster, 2001.

———. *Rainbow High.* New York: Simon & Schuster, 2003.

———. *Rainbow Road.* New York: Simon & Schuster, 2005.

Townsend, Sue. *The Adrian Mole Diaries.* New York: Grove Press, 1986.

Woodson, Jacqueline. *The House You Pass on the Way.* New York: Delacorte, 1997.

———. *If You Come Softly.* New York: Putnam, 1998.

———. *I Hadn't Meant to Tell You This.* New York: Delacorte, 1994.

Zindel, Paul. *My Darling, My Hamburger.* New York: Harper, 1969. (C)

Mystery, Adventure, Survival, and Suspense

Block, Francesca Lia. *Love in the Time of Global Warming.* New York : Holt, 2013.

Cormier, Robert. *Tenderness.* New York: Delacorte, 1997.

Donnelly, Jennifer. *A Northern Light.* New York: Harcourt, 2003.

Duncan, Lois. *Don't Look Behind You.* New York: Delacorte, 1989.

———. *I Know What You Did Last Summer.* New York: Little, Brown, 1973. (C)

———. *Killing Mr. Griffin.* New York: Little, Brown, 1978. (C)

Farmer, Nancy. *A Girl Named Disaster.* New York: Orchard, 1996.

Funke, Cornelia. *The Thief Lord.* New York: Scholastic, 2002.

Green, John. *Paper Towns.* New York: Dutton, 2008.

Haddon, Mark. *The Curious Incident of the Dog in the Night-Time.* New York: Doubleday, 2003.

Lake, Nick. *In Darkness.* New York: Bloomsbury Books, 2012.

McCaughrean, Geraldine. *The White Darkness: A Novel.* New York: HarperTempest, 2007.

Oliver, Lauren. *Before I Fall.* New York: Harper, 2010.

Paulsen, Gary. *Hatchet.* New York: Bradbury, 1987.

Plum-Ucci, Carol. *The Body of Christopher Creed.* New York: Houghton Mifflin Harcourt, 2000.

———. *Following Christopher Creed.* New York: Harcourt, 2011.

———. *What Happened to Lani Garver.* New York: Harcourt, 2002.

Riggs, Ransom. *Miss Peregrine's Home for Peculiar Children.* Philadelphia: Quirk Books, 2011.

Rosoff, Meg. *Picture Me Gone.* New York: Putnam, 2013.

Russell, Karen. *Swamplandia.* New York: Knopf Doubleday, 2011.

Stork, Francisco. *Marcelo in the Real World.* New York: Scholastic, 2009.

Historical Fiction

Anderson, Laurie Halse. *Chains.* New York: Atheneum, 2008.

Anderson, M. T. *The Astonishing Life of Octavian Nothing, Traitor to the Nation.* Vol. 1, *The Pox Party.* Cambridge, MA: Candlewick Press, 2006.

————. *The Astonishing Life of Octavian Nothing, Traitor to the Nation.* Vol. 2, *The Kingdom on the Waves.* Cambridge, MA: Candlewick Press, 2008.

Avi. *Crispin: The Cross of Lead.* New York: Hyperion, 2002.

Gantos, Jack. *Dead End in Norvelt.* New York: Farrar, Straus and Giroux, 2011.

Geras, Adele. *Troy.* New York: Harcourt, 2001.

Kadohata, Cynthia. *Kira-Kira.* New York: Atheneum, 2004.

Lee, Harper. *To Kill a Mockingbird.* Philadelphia: Lippincott, 1960. (C)

Lester, Julius. *Day of Tears: A Novel in Dialogue.* New York: Hyperion, 2005.

McCaughrean, Geraldine. *The Kite Rider: A Novel.* New York: HarperCollins, 2002.

McCormick, Patricia. *Never Fall Down.* New York: Balzer & Bray/Harper Teen, 2011.

Myers, Walter Dean. *The Glory Field.* New York: Scholastic, 1994. (M)

Ryan, Pam Muñoz. *Esperanza Rising.* New York: Scholastic, 2000. (M)

Wein, Elizabeth. *Code Name Verify.* New York: Hyperion, 2012.

————. *Rose under Fire.* New York: Hyperion, 2013.

Whaley, John Corey. *Where Things Come Back.* New York: Atheneum Books for Young Readers, 2011.

Zuzak, Markus. *The Book Thief.* New York: Random House. 2006.

NONFICTION

Included here are books of fact and information. Categories include art and architecture; biography, autobiography, and memoir; history; health and sexuality; science and technology; social science; and self-improvement.

Art and Architecture

Aronson, Marc. *Art Attack: A Short Cultural History of the Avant-Garde.* New York: Clarion, 1998.

Hill, Laban Carrick. *Harlem Stomp! A Cultural History of the Harlem Renaissance.* New York: Little, Brown, 2003.

Macaulay, David. *Castle.* Boston: Houghton Mifflin, 1977. (C)

————. *Cathedral.* Boston: Houghton Mifflin, 1973. (C)

————. *Mosque.* Boston: Houghton Mifflin, 2003.

Rubin, Susan Goldman. *Whaam! The Art and Life of Roy Lichtenstein.* New York: Abrams Books for Young Readers, 2008.

Biography, Autobiography, and Memoir

Angel, Ann. *Janis Joplin: Rise Up Singing.* New York: Abrams, 2010.

Angelou, Maya. *I Know Why the Caged Bird Sings.* New York: Random House, 1969. (C, M)

Crowe, Chris. *Getting Away with Murder: The True Story of the Emmett Till Case.* New York: Fogelman, 2003.

Fleming, Candace. *Our Eleanor: A Scrapbook Look at Eleanor Roosevelt's Remarkable Life.* New York: Atheneum, 2005.

Freedman, Russell. *Lincoln: A Photobiography.* New York: Clarion, 1987.

————. *The Wright Brothers: How They Invented the Airplane.* New York: Holiday House, 1991.

Gantos, Jack. *Hole in My Life.* New York: Farrar, Straus and Giroux, 2002.

Giblin, James Cross. *The Rise and Fall of Senator Joe McCarthy.* Boston: Clarion. 2009.

Greenberg, Jan, and Sandra Jordon. *Vincent van Gogh.* New York: Delacorte Press, 2001.

Heiligman, Deborah. *Charles and Emma: The Darwins' Leap of Faith.* New York: Holt, 2009.

Hoose, Phillip. *Claudette Colvin: Twice toward Justice.* New York: Melanie Kroupa Books/ Farrar, Straus and Giroux, 2009.

Myers, Walter Dean. *Bad Boy: A Memoir.* New York: HarperCollins, 2001.

Partridge, Elizabeth. *John Lennon: All I Want Is the Truth.* New York: Viking, 2005.

Runyon, Brent. *The Burn Journals.* New York: Knopf, 2004.

Sheinkin, Steve. *The Notorious Benedict Arnold: A True Story of Adventure, Heroism and Treachery.* New York: Roaring Brook, 2010.

Stone, Tanya Lee. *Almost Astronauts: 13 Women Who Dared to Dream.* Somerville, MA: Candlewick, 2009.

Warren, Andrea. *Surviving Hitler: A Boy in the Nazi Death Camps.* New York: HarperCollins, 2001.

History

Alsenas, Linas. *Gay America: Struggle for Equality.* New York: Amulet, 2008.

Anderson, Laurie Halse. *Fever 1793.* New York: Simon & Schuster., 2000.

Aronson, Marc. *Witch-Hunt: Mysteries of the Salem Witch Trials.* New York: Simon & Schuster, 2003.

Aronson, Marc, and Marina Budhos. *Sugar Changed the World: A Story of Magic, Spice, Slavery, Freedom, and Science.* New York: Clarion, 2010.

Bartoletti, Susan Campbell. *Black Potatoes: The Story of the Great Irish Famine, 1845–1850.* Boston: Houghton Mifflin, 2001.

———. *Hitler Youth: Growing Up in Hitler's Shadow.* New York: Scholastic, 2005.

———. *They Called Themselves the KKK: The Birth of an American Terrorist Group.* New York: Houghton Mifflin Harcourt, 2010.

Bausum, Ann. *Freedom Riders: John Lewis and Jim Zwerg on the Front Lines of the Civil Rights Movement.* Washington, DC: National Geographic, 2005.

Colman, Penny. *Corpses, Coffins, and Crypts: A History.* New York: Holt, 1997.

Freedman, Russell. *The Voice That Challenged a Nation: Marian Anderson and the Struggle for Equal Rights.* Boston: Clarion, 2004.

———. *The War to End All Wars: World War I.* Boston: Clarion, 2010.

Hoose, Phillip. *Moonbird: A Year on the Wind with the Great Survivor B95.* New York: Farrar, Straus and Giroux, 2012.

Hopkinson, Deborah. *Titanic: Voices from the Disaster.* New York: Scholastic, 2012.

Macy, Sue. *Wheels of Change: How Women Rode the Bicycle to Freedom (with a Few Flat Tires along the Way).* Washington, DC: National Geographic, 2011.

Meltzer, Milton. *Witches and Witch Hunts: A History of Persecution.* New York: Scholastic, 1999.

Murphy, Jim. *An American Plague: The True and Terrifying Story of the Yellow Fever Epidemic of 1793.* New York: Clarion, 2003.

Myers, Walter Dean. *Jazz.* Illustrated by Christopher Myers. New York: Holiday House, 2006.

Sheinkin, Steve. *Bomb: The Race to Build—and Steal—the World's Most Dangerous Weapon.* New York: Roaring Brook, 2012.

Stone, Tanya Lee. *Almost Astronauts: 13 Women Who Dared to Dream.* Somerville, MA: Candlewick, 2009.

———. *The Good, the Bad, and the Barbie: A Doll's History and Her Impact on Us.* New York: Viking, 2010.

Walker, Sally M. *Secrets of a Civil War Submarine: Solving the Mysteries of the H. L. Hunley.* Minneapolis, MN: Carolrhoda, 2005.

Health and Sexuality

Alsenas, Linas. *Gay America: Struggle for Equality.* New York: Amulet, 2008.

Brynie, Faith Hickman. *101 Questions about Sex and Sexuality . . . with Answers for the Curious and Confused.* Brookfield, CT: Twenty-First Century, 2003.

Harris, Robie H. *It's Perfectly Normal: A Book about Changing Bodies, Growing Up, Sex, and Sexual Health*. 3rd ed. Cambridge, MA: Candlewick, 2009.

Hinds, Maureen J. *Fighting the AIDS and HIV Epidemic: A Global Battle*. Berkeley Heights, NJ: Enslow, 2007.

Locricchio, Matthew. *Teen Cuisine*. Tarrytown, NY: Marshall Cavendish, 2010.

Macaulay, David, and Richard Walker. *The Way We Work: Getting to Know the Amazing Human Body*. Boston: Houghton Mifflin, 2008.

Madaras, Lynda, and Area Madaras. *What's Happening to My Body: Book for Boys*. New York: HarperCollins, 2007.

———. *What's Happening to My Body: Book for Girls*. New York: HarperCollins, 2007.

Savage, Dan, and Terry Miller, eds. *It Gets Better: Coming Out, Overcoming Bullying, and Creating a Life Worth Living*. New York: Dutton, 2011.

Schlosser, Eric, and Charles Wilson. *Chew on This: Everything You Didn't Want to Know about Fast Food*. Boston: Houghton Mifflin, 2006.

Science and Technology

Beres, D. B. *Dusted and Busted: The Science of Fingerprinting*. New York: Watts, 2007.

Bishop, Nic. *Butterflies and Moths*. New York: Scholastic, 2009.

———. *Frogs*. New York: Scholastic, 2008.

———. *Lizards*. New York: Scholastic, 2010.

———. *Marsupials*. New York: Scholastic, 2009.

———. *Snakes*. New York: Scholastic, 2012.

———. *Spiders*. New York: Scholastic, 2007.

Brain, Marshall. *How Stuff Works*. Edison, NJ: Chartwell, 2001.

Burns, Loree Griffin, and Ellen Harasimowicz. *The Hive Detectives: Chronicle of a Honey Bee Disaster*. Boston: Houghton Mifflin, 2010.

Deem, James M. *Bodies from the Bog*. Boston: Houghton Mifflin, 1998.

DK Publishing. *Ideas That Changed the World: Incredible Inventions and the Stories behind Them*. New York: DK, 2010.

Giblin, James. *The Mystery of the Mammoth Bones and How It Was Solved*. New York: HarperCollins, 1999.

Jackson, Donna M. *The Bone Detectives: How Forensic Anthropologists Solve Crimes and Uncover Mysteries of the Dead*. New York: Little, Brown, 1996.

Macaulay, David, and Neil Ardley. *The New Way Things Work*. Boston: Houghton Mifflin, 1998.

Macaulay, David, and Richard Walker. *The Way We Work: Getting to Know the Amazing Human Body*. Boston: Houghton Mifflin, 2008.

Menzel, Peter, and Faith D'Alusisio. *Man Eating Bugs: The Art and Science of Eating Insects*. Berkeley, CA: Ten Speed Press, 1998.

Montgomery, Sy, and Nic Bishop. *Kakapo Rescue: Saving the World's Strangest Parrot*. Boston: Houghton Mifflin, 2010.

———. *The Quest for the Tree Kangaroo: An Expedition to the Cloud Forest of New Guinea*. Boston: Houghton Mifflin, 2006.

———. *The Tarantula Scientist*. Boston: Houghton Mifflin, 2004.

Owen, David. *Hidden Evidence: The Story of Forensic Science and How It Helped to Solve 50 of the World's Toughest Crimes*. Revised 2nd ed. Buffalo, NY: Firefly Books, 2009.

Platt, Richard. *Forensics*. Boston: Kingfisher, 2005.

Prokos, Anna. *Guilty by a Hair! Real-Life DNA Matches!* New York: Watts, 2007.

Roach, Mary. *Stiff: The Curious Lives of Human Cadavers*. New York: Norton, 2003.

Rubalcaba, Jill, and Peter Robertshaw. *Every Bone Tells a Story: Hominin Discoveries, Deductions, and Debates*. Watertown, MA: Charlesbridge, 2010.

Walker, Sally M. *Written in Bone: Buried Lives of Jamestown and Colonial Maryland*. Minneapolis: Carolrhoda Books, 2009.

Social Science

Cohen, Daniel. *Cults*. Minneapolis, MN: Millbrook Press, 1994.

Duncan, Lois. *Who Killed My Daughter?* New York: Delacorte, 1992.

Holt, David, and Bill Mooney. *Spiders in the Hairdo: Modern Urban Legends*. Chicago: August House, 1999.

Montgomery, Sy, and Nic Bishop. *Kakapo Rescue: Saving the World's Strangest Parrot*. Boston: Houghton Mifflin, 2010.

Self-Development

Appelt, Kathi. *Poems from Homeroom: A Writer's Place to Start*. New York: Holt, 2002.

Canfield, Jack, Mark Victor Hansen, and Kimberly Kirberger. *Chicken Soup for the Teenage Soul: 101 Stories of Life, Love, and Learning*. Deerfield Beach, FL: Health Communications, 1997.

Covey, Sean. *The 7 Habits of Highly Effective Teens: The Ultimate Teenage Success Guide*. New York: Simon & Schuster, 1998.

Fletcher, Ralph. *Guy-Write: What Every Guy Writer Needs to Know*. New York: Holt, 2012.

Fogarty, Mignon. *Grammar Girl Presents: The Ultimate Writing Guide for Students*. New York: Holt, 2011.

Singh, Simon. *The Code Book: How to Make It, Break It, Hack It, Crack It*. New York: Delacorte, 2001.

Wallace, David Foster. *This Is Water: Some Thoughts, Delivered on a Significant Occasion about Living a Compassionate Life*. New York: Little, Brown, 2009.

POETRY

This section contains work of poetry by single poets as well as edited collections of works by multiple poets. It also includes separate categories for novels written in verse and for works that focus on lyrics and music notation.

Works by a Single Poet

Adoff, Arnold. *Slow Dance Heart Break Blues*. New York: Lothrop, Lee & Shepard Books, 1995.

Crisler, Curtis L. *Tough Boy Sonatas*. Honesdale, PA: Boyds Mills, 2007.

Fleischman, Paul. *Big Talk: Poems for Four Voices*. Illustrated by Beppe Giacobbe. Cambridge, MA: Candlewick, 2000.

———. *Joyful Noise: Poems for Two Voices*. Illustrated by Eric Beddows. New York: HarperCollins, 1988.

Glenn, Mel. *Jump Ball: A Basketball Season in Poems*. New York: Dutton, 1997.

Grandits, John. *Blue Lipstick: Concrete Poems*. New York: Clarion, 2007.

Grimes, Nikki. *A Dime a Dozen*. New York: Penguin Putnam, 1998.

Holbrook, Sara, and Allan Wolf. *More Than Friends: Poems from Him and Her*. Honesdale, PA: Boyds Mills, 2008.

Johnson, Angela. *The Other Side: Shorter Poems*. New York: Orchard, 1998.

Merriam, Eve. *The Inner City Mother Goose*. 3rd ed. Illustrated by David Diaz. New York: Simon & Schuster, 1996.

Myers, Walter Dean. *Blues Journey*. Illustrated by Christopher Myers. New York: Holiday House, 2003.

———. *Harlem*. Illustrated by Christopher Myers. New York: Scholastic, 1997.

———. *Here in Harlem: Poems in Many Voices*. New York: Holiday House, 2004.

———. *Street Love*. New York: HarperCollins, 2006.

Nelson, Marilyn. *A Wreath for Emmett Till.* Illustrated by Philippe Lardy. New York: Houghton Mifflin, 2005.

Nye, Naomi Shihab. *A Maze Me: Poems for Girls.* Illustrated by Terre Maher. New York: Greenwillow, 2005.

Park, Linda Sue. *Tap Dancing on the Roof: Sijo.* New York: Clarion, 2007.

Poe, Edgar Allan. *The Raven.* Illustrated by Ryan Price. Tonawanda, NY: Kids Can Press, 2006.

Schlitz, Laura Amy. *Good Masters! Sweet Ladies! Voices from a Medieval Village.* Illustrated by Robert Byrd. Cambridge, MA: Candlewick, 2007.

Sidman, Joyce. *Dark Emperor and Other Poems of the Night.* Illustrated by Rick Allen. New York: Houghton Mifflin Harcourt Books for Young Readers, 2010.

Soto, Gary. *Neighborhood Odes.* Illustrated by David Diaz. New York: Harcourt, 1992.

Thayer, Ernest L. *Casey at the Bat.* Illustrated by Joe Morse. Tonawanda, NY: Kids Can Press, 2006.

Edited Poetry Collections

Aguado, Bill, and Richard Newirth, eds. *Paint Me Like I Am: Teen Poems from WritersCorp.* New York: HarperTeen, 2003.

Carlson, Lori M., ed. *Cool Salsa: Bilingual Poems on Growing Up Latino in the United States.* New York: Holt, 1994.

———, ed. *Red Hot Salsa: Bilingual Poems on Life, Love, and Victory.* New York: Holt, 2005.

Clinton, Catherine, ed. *I, Too, Sing American: Three Centuries of African American Poetry.* Illustrated by Stephen Alcorn. New York: Houghton Mifflin, 1998.

———, ed. *A Poem of Her Own: Voices of American Women Yesterday and Today.* Illustrated by Stephen Alcorn. New York: Abrams, 2003.

Franco, Betsy, ed. *Things I Have to Tell You: Poems and Writing by Teenage Girls.* Photographs by Nina Nickles. Cambridge, MA: Candlewick, 2001.

———, ed. *You Hear Me? Poems and Writing by Teenage Boys.* Photographs by Nina Nickles. Cambridge, MA: Candlewick, 2000.

Greenberg, Jan, ed. *Heart to Heart: New Poems Inspired by Twentieth-Century American Art.* New York: Abrams, 2001.

Janeczko, Paul B., ed. *Blushing: Expressions of Love in Poems and Letters.* New York: Orchard Books, 2004.

———, ed. *A Poke in the I: A Collection of Concrete Poems.* Illustrated by Chris Raschka. Cambridge, MA: Candlewick, 2001.

Johnson, Dave, ed. *Movin': Teen Poets Take Voice.* Illustrated by Chris Raschka. New York: Orchard Books, 2000.

Liu, Siyu, and Orel Protopopescu, eds. *A Thousand Peaks: Poems from China.* Berkeley, CA: Pacific View, 2001.

McClatchey, J. D., ed. *Loves Speaks Its Name: Gay and Lesbian Love Poems.* New York: Knopf, 2001.

Morrison, Lillian, ed. *Way to Go! Sports Poems.* Honesdale, PA: Boyds Mills, 2001.

Nye, Naomi Shihab, ed. *Time You Let Me In: 25 Poets under 25.* New York: Greenwillow, 2010.

Nye, Naomi Shihab, and Paul B. Janeczko, eds. *I Feel a Little Jumpy around You: A Book of Her Poems and His Poems Collected in Pairs.* New York: Simon & Schuster, 1996.

Rosenberg, Liz, ed. *The Invisible Ladder: An Anthology of Contemporary American Poems for Young Readers.* New York: Holt, 1996.

Novels in Verse

Chaltas, Thalia. *Because I Am Furniture.* New York: Penguin, 2009.

Frost, Helen. *Keesha's House.* New York: Frances Foster, 2003.

Glenn, Mel. *The Taking of Room 114: A Hostage Drama in Poems.* New York: Dutton, 1997.

————. *Who Killed Mr. Chippendale? A Mystery in Poems*. New York: Penguin, 1996.
Hemphill, Stephanie. *Wicked Girls: A Novel of the Salem Witch Trials*. New York: HarperCollins, 2010.
————. *Your Own Sylvia: A Verse Portrait of Sylvia Plath*. New York: Random House, 2007.
Herrera, Juan Felipe. *CrashBoomLove: A Novel in Verse*. Alburquerque: University of New Mexico Press, 1999.
Hesse, Karen. *Out of the Dust*. New York: Scholastic, 1997.
Janeczko, Paul B. *World's Afire*. Cambridge, MA: Candlewick, 2004.
Koertge, Ron. *Shakespeare Bats Cleanup*. Cambridge, MA: Candlewick Press, 2003.
Lai, Thanhha. *Inside Out and Back Again*. New York: HarperCollins, 2011.
McCall, Guadalupe Garcia. *Under the Mesquite*. New York: Lee & Low Books, 2011.
McCormick, Patricia. *Sold*. New York: Hyperion, 2006.
Wolff, Virginia E. *Make Lemonade*. New York: Holt, 1993.
————. *This Full House*. New York: Bowen Press, 2009.
————. *True Believer*. New York: Atheneum Books for Young Readers, 2001.

Music Lyrics and/or Notation

Beatles. *The Beatles Best: More than 120 Great Hits*. 2nd ed. Milwaukee, WI: Hal Leonard, 1987.
Bradley, Adam, and Andrew DuBois, eds. *The Anthology of Rap*. New Haven, CT: Yale University Press, 2010.
Dylan, Bob. *Lyrics 1961–2001*. New York: Simon & Schuster, 2004.
Pate, Alexs D. *In the Heart of the Beat: The Poetry of Rap*. Lanham, MD: Scarecrow, 2010.
Shore, Howard. *The Lord of the Rings Trilogy: Music from the Motion Pictures Arranged for Solo Piano*. Van Nuys, CA: Alfred Music, 2009.
Sitomer, Alan, and Michael Cirelli. *Hip-Hop Poetry and the Classics*. Beverly Hills, CA: Milk Mug, 2004.

SPECIAL FORMS AND FORMATS

This section presents lists of graphic novels, picture books for young adults, and movies. The topics covered in these works include both fiction and nonfiction and also rely heavily on visual content. Under graphic novels, the *Sandman* citation and the manga titles all point to a series, rather than individual works.

Citations for movies are all arranged by the director of the work, and whenever possible, the complete boxed set is cited, rather than individual titles, when movies are presented as a sequential work. The DVD version of the movie is cited unless the work is only available in Blu-ray. Only published movies are listed. For example, at the time of this writing, several installations in the *Hunger Games* series are planned but have not yet been released and so are not included in this bibliography.

Graphic Novels

Ando, Natsumi. *Zodiac P.I.* 4 vols. Los Angeles: Tokyopop, 2003.
Arakawa, Hiromu. *Fullmetal Alchemist*. 27 vols. San Francisco: VIZ Media, 2005–.
Austen, Jane. *Pride and Prejudice*. Adapted by Nancy Butler. Illustrated by Hugo Petrus. New York: Marvel, 2009.

Avi. *City of Light, City of Dark: A Comic Book Novel.* Illustrated by Brian Floca. New York: Orchard Books, 1993.

Barry, Lynda. *The Good Times Are Killing Me* . Seattle, WA: Sasquatch Books, 1998.

―――. *One Hundred Demons.* Seattle, WA: Sasquatch Books, 2002.

Bechdel, Alison. *Fun Home: A Family Tragicomic.* New York: Houghton Mifflin Harcourt, 2006.

Brosgol, Vera. *Anya's Ghost.* New York: First Second, 2011.

Clowes, Daniel. *Ghost World.* Seattle, WA: Fantagraphics Books, 2001.

Eisner, Will. *A Contract with God.* New York: Baronet Books, 1978. (C)

Gaiman, Neil. *The Sandman.* 10 vols. New York: Vertigo/DC Comics, 1991–1999.

Hale, Shannon, and Dean Hale. *Rapunzel's Revenge.* Illustrated by Nathan Hale. New York: Bloomsbury USA Children's, 2008.

Hosler, Jay. *Clan Apis.* Columbus, OH: Active Synapse, 2000.

Hwa, Kim Dong. *The Color of Earth.* New York: First Second, 2009.

―――. *The Color of Heaven.* New York: First Second, 2009.

―――. *The Color of Water.* New York: First Second, 2009.

Kashyap, Keshni. *Tina's Mouth: An Existential Comic Diary.* New York: Houghton Mifflin Harcourt, 2012.

Kim, Derek Kirk. *Same Difference.* New York: First Second, 2011.

L'Engle, Madeleine. *A Wrinkle in Time.* Adapted and illustrated by Hope Larson. New York: Farrar, Straus and Giroux, 2012.

Lewis, John, and Andrew Aydin. *March: Book 1.* Illustrated by Nate Powell. Marietta, GA: Top Shelf Productions, 2013.

Long, Mark, and Jim Demonakos. *The Silence of Our Friends.* Illustrated by Nate Powell. New York: First Second, 2012.

Lu, Wang Du. *Crouching Tiger, Hidden Dragon.* 13 vols. Illustrated by Andy Seto. San Francisco: ComicsOne, 2005–2006.

Melville, Herman. *Moby Dick: The Graphic Novel.* Adapted by Lance Stahlberg. Illustrated by Lalit Kumar. Delhi, India: Campfire, 2010.

Miller, Frank. *The Dark Knight Returns.* Illustrated by Klaus Jason. Color by Lynn Varley. New York: DC Comics, 1986.

Moore, Alan. *Batman: The Killing Joke.* Illustrated by Brian Bolland. New York: DC Comics, 1988.

―――. *Watchmen.* Illustrated by Dave Gibbons. New York: DC Comics, 1987.

Murakami, Maki. *Gravitation.* 12 vols. Los Angeles: Tokyopop, 2003–2005.

Nakazawa, Keiji. *Barefoot Gen.* 10 vols. San Francisco: Last Gasp, 2004–2010.

Neri, G. *Yummy: The Last Days of a Southside Shorty.* Illustrated by Randy DuBurke. New York: Lee and Low, 2010. (U)

Ohba, Tsugumi. *Death Note.* 12 vols. Illustrated by Takeshi Obata. San Francisco: VIZ Media, 2005–2007.

O'Malley, Bryan Lee. *Scott Pilgrim.* Portland, OR: Oni Press, 2004–2010.

Satrapi, Marjane. *Persepolis.* Vol. 1, *The Story of a Childhood.* New York: Random House, 2003.

―――. *Persepolis.* Vol. 2, *The Story of a Return.* New York: Random House, 2004.

Say, Allen. *Drawing from Memory.* New York: Scholastic, 2011.

Siegel, Siena Cherson. *To Dance: A Ballerina's Graphic Novel.* Illustrated by Mark Siegel. New York: Atheneum Books for Young Readers, 2006.

Smith, Jeff. *Bone: The Complete Cartoon Epic in One Volume.* Columbus, OH: Cartoon Books, 2004.

Spiegelman, Art. *Maus I: A Survivor's Tale: My Father Bleeds History.* New York: Random House, 1986.

―――. *Maus II: A Survivor's Tale: And Here My Troubles Began.* New York: Random House, 1991.

Takaya, Natsuki. *Fruits Basket.* 23 vols. Los Angeles: Tokyopop, 2004–2007.

Takeuchi, Naoko. *Sailor Moon.* 18 vols. Los Angeles: Tokyopop, 1998–2001.

Tamaki, Mariko. *Skim.* Illustrated by Jillian Tamaki. Toronto: Groundwood Books, 2008.

Telgemeier, Raina. *Drama.* New York: Graphix, 2012.

Thompson, Craig. *Blankets.* Portland, OR: Top Shelf Productions, 2002.

Toriyama, Akira. *Dragon Ball.* 16 vols. San Francisco: VIZ Media, 2000–2009.

———. *Dragon Ball Z.* 26 vols. San Francisco: VIZ Media, 2000–2010.

Van Lente, Fred, and Ryan Dunlavey. *The Comic Book History of Comics.* San Diego, CA: IDW, 2012.

Weiner, Stephen. *Faster Than a Speeding Bullet: The Rise of the Graphic Novel.* 2nd ed. New York: NBM, 2012.

Yang, Gene Luen. *American Born Chinese.* New York: First Second, 2007.

Yoshida, Akimi. *Banana Fish.* 19 vols. San Francisco: VIZ Media, 1998–2009.

Picture Books for Young Adults

Feelings, Tom. *The Middle Passage: White Ships / Black Cargo.* New York: Penguin, 1995.

Gallaz, Christophe. *Rose Blanche.* Illustrated by Roberto Innocenti. Mankato, MN: Creative Editions, 1985.

Macaulay, David. *Black and White.* New York: Houghton Mifflin, 1990.

Nelson, Kadir. *We Are the Ship.* New York: Jump at the Sun / Hyperion Books for Children, 2008.

Scieszka, Jon. *Math Curse.* Illustrated by Lane Smith. New York: Viking, 1995.

———. *Science Verse.* Illustrated by Lane Smith. New York: Viking, 2004.

———. *The Stinky Cheese Man and Other Fairly Stupid Tale.* Illustrated by Lane Smith. New York: Viking, 1992.

Shange, Ntozake. *We Troubled the Waters.* Illustrated by Rod Brown. New York: HarperCollins, 2009.

Sís, Peter. *The Wall: Growing Up behind the Iron Curtain.* New York: Farrar, Straus and Giroux, 2007.

Tan, Shaun. *The Arrival.* New York: Scholastic, 2007.

———. *Lost and Found.* New York: Scholastic, 2011.

Young, Ed. *The House Baba Built: An Artist's Childhood in China.* New York: Little, Brown, 2011.

Movies

Chbosky, Stephen, dir. *The Perks of Being a Wallflower.* DVD. Santa Monica, CA: Lionsgate Entertainment, 2013.

Columbus, Chris, Alfonso Cuaron, Mike Newell, and David Yates, dirs. *Harry Potter: The Complete 8-Film Collection.* DVD. Burbank, CA: Warner Brothers, 2011.

Faxon, Nat, and Jim Rash, dirs. *The Way, Way Back.* DVD. Century City, CA: 20th Century Fox, 2013.

Hardwicke, Catherine, Chris Weitz, David Slade, and Bill Condon, dirs. *The Twilight Saga: The Complete Collection.* Blu-ray. Universal City, CA: Summit Entertainment, 2012.

Jackson, Peter, dir. *The Lord of the Rings: The Fellowship of the Ring.* DVD. Los Angeles: New Line, 2002.

———, dir. *The Lord of the Rings: The Return of the King.* DVD. Los Angeles: New Line, 2004.

———, dir. *The Lord of the Rings: The Two Towers.* DVD. Los Angeles: New Line, 2003.

Miyazaki, Hayao, dir. *Howl's Moving Castle.* DVD. Burbank, CA: Walt Disney Home Entertainment, 2006.

———, dir. *Spirited Away.* DVD. Burbank, CA: Walt Disney Home Entertainment, 2003.

Reitman, Jason, dir. *Juno.* DVD. Century City, CA: Fox Searchlight Studios, 2008.

Ross, Gary, dir. *The Hunger Games.* DVD. Santa Monica, CA: Lionsgate Entertainment, 2012.

Sollett, Peter, dir. *Nick and Norah's Infinite Playlist.* DVD. Culver City, CA: Sony Pictures Home Entertainment, 2008.

Wright, Edgar, dir. *Scott Pilgrim vs. the World.* DVD. Universal City, CA: Universal Studios, 2010.
Zwigoff, Terry, dir., *Ghost World.* DVD. Beverly Hills, CA: MGM, 2002.

Appendix 3

Professional Resources

The following bibliography contains books discussed in the individual chapters as well as additional titles that we have found useful for thinking, writing, and teaching in the areas of young adult information behaviors, young adult services, and young adult resources. Due to limitations of space, this bibliography contains only books, organized by the headings Young Adults, Young Adult Literature, Writing and Reading, and Library Services.

YOUNG ADULTS

American Psychological Association. *Developing Adolescents: A Reference for Professionals.* Washington, DC: American Psychological Association, 2002. http://www.apa.org/pi/cyf/develop.pdf.

Chelton, Mary K., and Colleen Cool, eds. *Youth Information Seeking Behavior: Theories, Models, and Issues.* Lanham, MD: Scarecrow Press, 2004.

———, eds. *Youth Information Seeking Behavior II: Context, Theories, Models, and Issues.* Lanham, MD: Scarecrow Press, 2007.

Dweck, Carol S. *Self-Theories: Their Role in Motivation, Personality, and Development.* New York: Psychology Press, 2000.

Gross, Melissa. *Studying Children's Questions: Imposed and Self-Generated Information Seeking at School.* Lanham, MD: Scarecrow Press, 2006.

Ito, Mizuko, et al. *Hanging Out, Messing Around, and Geeking Out: Kids Living and Learning with New Media.* Cambridge, MA: MIT Press, 2009.

Kuhlthau, Carol C. *Seeking Meaning: A Process Approach to Library and Information Services.* 2nd ed. Westport, CT: Libraries Unlimited, 2004.

YOUNG ADULT LITERATURE

Bodart, Joni Richards. *They Suck, They Bite, They Eat, They Kill: The Psychological Meaning of Supernatural Monsters in Young Adults Fiction.* Lanham, MD: Scarecrow Press, 2011.

Cart, Michael. *Cart's Top 200 Adult Books for Young Adults: Two Decades in Review.* Chicago: American Library Association, 2013.

———. *From Romance to Realism.* New York: HarperCollins, 1996.

Cart, Michael, and Christine A Jenkins. *The Heart Has Its Reasons: Young Adult Literature with Gay/Lesbian/Queer Content, 1969–2004.* Landham, MD: Scarecrow Press, 2006.

Cole, Pam B. *Young Adult Literature in the 21st Century.* New York: McGraw-Hill, 2009.

Donelson, Kenneth L., and Alleen Pace Nilsen. *Literature for Today's Young Adults.* 7th ed. Boston: Pearson, 2005.

Dresang, Eliza T. *Radical Change: Books for Youth in a Digital Age.* New York: Wilson, 1999.

Gross, Melissa, Annette Y. Goldsmith, and Debi Carruth. *HIV/AIDS in Young Adult Novels: An Annotated Bibliography.* Lanham, MD: Scarecrow Press, 2010.

Herald, Diana Tixier. *Teen Genreflecting: A Guide to Reading Interests.* 3rd ed. Westport, CT: Libraries Unlimited, 2010.

Kalen, Elizabeth F. S. *Mostly Manga: A Genre Guide to Popular Manga, Manhwa, Manhua, and Anime.* Santa Barbara, CA: Libraries Unlimited, 2012.

Latrobe, Kathy H., and Judy Drury. *Critical Approaches to Young Adult Literature.* New York: Neal-Schuman, 2009.

Lukenbill, W. Bernard. *Biography in the Lives of Youth: Culture, Society, and Information.* Westport, CT: Libraries Unlimited, 2006.

Lukenbill, W. Bernard, and Barbara Froling Immroth. *Health Information for Youth: The Public Library and School Library Media Center Role.* Westport, CT: Libraries Unlimited, 2007.

Lundin, Anne, and Wayne A Wiegand, eds. *Defining Print Culture for Youth: The Cultural Work of Children's Literature.* Westport, CT: Libraries Unlimited, 2003.

Morris, Vanessa Irvin. *The Readers' Advisory Guide to Street Literature.* Chicago: American Library Association, 2011.

Tomlinson, Carl, and Carol Lynch-Brown. *Essentials of Young Adult Literature.* 2nd ed. Boston: Pearson, 2010.

Trites, Roberta Seelinger. *Disturbing the Universe: Power and Repression in Adolescent Literature.* Iowa City: University of Iowa Press, 2000.

WRITING AND READING

Addonizio, Kim, and Dorianne Laux. *The Poet's Companion: A Guide to the Pleasures of Writing Poetry.* New York: Norton, 1997.

Aronson, Marc. *Exploding the Myths: The Truth about Teenagers and Reading.* Lanham, MD: Scarecrow Press, 2001.

Dressman, Mark. *Let's Poem: The Essential Guide to Teaching Poetry in a High-Stakes, Multimodal World.* New York: Teachers College Press, 2010.

Hart, Christopher. *Manga for the Beginner: Everything You Need to Start Drawing Right Away!* New York: Watson-Guptill, 2008.

Hewitt, Geoff. *Today You Are My Favorite Poet: Writing Poems with Teenagers.* Portsmouth, NH: Heinemann, 1998.

Jocson, Korina M. *Youth Poets: Empowering Literacies in and out of Schools.* New York: Lang, 2008.

McCloud, Scott. *Making Comics: Storytelling Secrets of Comics, Manga and Graphic Novels.* New York: Morrow, 2006.

———. *Understanding Comics: The Invisible Art.* New York: Morrow, 1994.

Rosenblatt, Louise M. *Literature as Exploration.* New York: Modern Language Association of America, 1995.

Ross, Catherine Sheldrick, Lynne McKechnie, and Paulette M. Rothbauer, eds. *Reading Matters: What the Research Reveals about Reading, Libraries, and Community.* Westport, CT: Libraries Unlimited, 2006.

LIBRARY SERVICES

Anderson, Sheila B. *Extreme Teens: Library Services to Nontraditional Young Adults.* Westport, CT: Libraries Unlimited, 2005.

Agosto, Denise E., and June Abbas, eds. *Teens, Libraries, and Social Networking: What Librarians Need to Know.* Santa Barbara, CA: Libraries Unlimited, 2011.

Agosto, Denise E., and Sandra Huhes-Hassell, eds. *Urban Teens in the Library: Research and Practice.* Chicago: American Library Association, 2010.

Auguste, Margaret. *VOYA's Guide to Intellectual Freedom for Teens.* Bowie, MA: VOYA Press, 2012.

Booth, Heather. *Serving Teens through Readers' Advisory.* Chicago: American Library Association, 2007.

Dresang, Eliza T., Melissa Gross, and Leslie Edmonds Holt. *Dynamic Youth Services through Outcome-Based Planning and Evaluation.* Chicago: American Library Association, 2006.

Edwards, Margaret A. *The Fair Garden and the Swarm of Beasts: The Library and the Young Adult.* Centennial ed. Chicago: American Library Association, 2002.

Gorman, Michele, and Tricia Suellentrop. *Connecting Young Adults and Libraries: A How-to-Do-It Manual for Librarians.* 4th ed. Chicago: Neal-Schuman, 2009.

Harper, Meghan. *Reference Services and Sources for Youth.* New York: Neal-Schuman, 2011.

Jones, Ella W. *Start to Finish YA Programs: Hip-Hop Symposiums, Summer Reading Programs, Virtual Tours, Poetry Slams, Teen Advisory Boards, Term Paper Clinics, and More!* New York: Neal-Schuman, 2009.

Littlejohn, Carol. *Booktalks to Promote Reading.* Vol. 1, *Talk That Book!* Worthington, OH: Linworth, 1999.

———. *Booktalks to Promote Reading.* Vol. 2, *Keep Talking That Book!* Worthington, OH: Linworth, 2000.

Martin, Hillias J., and James R. Murdock. *Serving Lesbian, Gay, Bisexual, Transgender, and Questioning Teens: A How-to-Do-It Manual for Librarians.* New York: Neal-Schuman, 2007.

Nicholson, Scott. *Everyone Plays at the Library: Creating Great Gaming Programs for All Ages.* Medford Township, NJ: Information Today, 2010.

Pierce, Jennifer Burek. *Sex, Brains, and Video Games: A Librarian's Guide to Teens in the Twenty-First Century.* Chicago: American Library Association, 2008.

Tuccillo, Diane P. *Library Teen Advisory Groups.* Lanham, MD: VOYA Books, 2005.

Vaillancourt, Renee J. *Managing Young Adult Services: A Self-Help Manual.* New York: Neal-Schuman, 2002.

Walter, Virginia A., and Elaine Meyers. *Teens and Libraries: Getting It Right.* Chicago: American Library Association, 2003.

Name Index

Title Index

Subject Index

About the Authors

Don Latham is associate professor of library and information studies at Florida State University, where he teaches Information Needs of Young Adults, Graphic Novels in Libraries, and International Literature for Youth. His research focuses on information behavior and digital literacies of young adults and literature for young adults, and he has published extensively in the areas of information literacy among college undergraduates and literacy, identity, and gender in young adult literature.

Melissa Gross is a professor in the School of Library and Information Studies at Florida State University and past president of the Association for Library and Information Science Education. She received her PhD in library and information science from the University of California, Los Angeles, in 1998, received the prestigious American Association of University Women Recognition Award for Emerging Scholars in 2001, and has published extensively in the areas of information-seeking behavior, information literacy, library program and service evaluation, and information resources for youth. Current projects include investigations into the information literacy needs of undergraduates and improving collaboration between librarians and instructors in educational settings. Her most recent books are *HIV/AIDS in Young Adult Novels: An Annotated Bibliography*, coauthored with Annette Goldsmith and Debi Carruth; *Studying Children's Questions: Information Seeking Behavior in School*; and *Dynamic Youth Services through Outcome-Based Planning and Evaluation,* coauthored with Eliza Dresang and Leslie Holt.

Made in the USA
Middletown, DE
28 August 2017